TAKING CHARGE OF **ADHD**

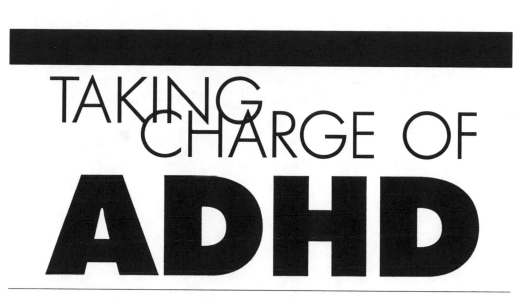

TAKING CHARGE OF ADHD

The Complete, Authoritative Guide for Parents

RUSSELL A. BARKLEY, Ph.D.

The Guilford Press   New York / London

©1995 The Guilford Press
A Division of Guilford Publications, Inc.
72 Spring Street, New York, NY 10012

Printed in the United States of America

This book is printed on acid-free paper.

Last digit is print number: 9 8 7 6 5 4 3

Library of Congress Cataloging-in-Publication Data

Barkley, Russell A., 1949–
    Taking charge of ADHD: the complete, authoritative guide for
parents / Russell A. Barkley.
        p.   cm.
    Includes bibliographical references and index.
    ISBN 0-89862-099-6 (pbk.)
    1. Attention-deficit hyperactivity disorder—Popular works.
I. Title.
RJ506.H9B373   1995
618.92′8589—dc20   95-37424
                                                          CIP

*To Sandra F. Thomas and Mary C. Fowler,
two extraordinary parents who started a national movement
and awakened a nation to the suffering of children
with attention-deficit/hyperactivity disorder*

Preface

I t is quite normal for children to be more active, more exuberant, less attentive, and more impulsive than adults. It is hardly surprising that children have
more problems than adults in following through on directions and consistently
finishing their work. So when parents complain that their child has difficulty
paying attention, controlling his or her activity, or resisting impulses, others may
be quick to dismiss these problems simply as normal behavior, and reassure parents that they are natural qualities of children, that there is no need for alarm.
If a child's behavior problems seem a little excessive, even for a child, it is probably the case that he or she is simply a little immature, and will likely outgrow
these problems.

Usually this is true—but there are times when it is not. In some cases a child's
attention span is so short, activity level so high, and impulse control so limited
that her behavior in these areas is clearly extreme for her age. Most people have
known such a child—one who is having trouble completing schoolwork and who
may not be getting along well with the neighborhood children, whose inability
to follow through and complete assigned chores without parental supervision is
causing conflict at home.

Behavior problems in these areas that have become so severe as to impair
a child's adjustment are not likely to be outgrown, and they can hardly be considered normal. If you have such a child, it is not only misguided but potentially
harmful to your child's psychological and social well-being to downplay the
problems or simply to give your child time to mature a little more. Doing so could
also cause future problems for you and other family members, who must deal with
this child every day.

Children whose problems with attention, overactivity, and lack of inhibition reach a certain level have a developmental disability known as *attention-
deficit/hyperactivity disorder,* or *ADHD.* This book is about ADHD. It is intended
for parents who are raising an ADHD child and for others who wish to know

more about the disorder and its management. The main goal is to empower parents to take charge of the care of these often demanding children in a way that ensures the health of the entire family, collectively and individually.

Numerous books on this subject directed to parents have already been published. Most are pretty good, and there are a few I recommend to the families we see at our clinic. Then why did I want to write another? The answer is that the books available just don't go far enough in educating parents about what is currently known about ADHD and, more important, about what can be done to help those with the disorder. Most books for parents successfully convey what has been gained from years of clinical experience in treating children with ADHD and their families, but they fail to integrate the most current scientific breakthroughs. And the conclusions derived only from clinical experience have often been wrong.

For instance, for several decades most clinical professionals operated according to the fallacious notions that ADHD was caused by brain injuries or poor parenting; that children would eventually outgrow it by adolescence; that stimulant medications would be effective only with children (not with adults and older adolescents) and only on school days; and that ADHD children would benefit from a diet free of certain food additives and sugar—all despite the absence of any set of findings in the scientific literature to support such claims. We now understand that many children with ADHD have an inherited or genetic form of the disorder, that many do not outgrow their problems by adolescence, that medication can be taken year-round by adolescents and adults as well as children, and that altering diets does little to benefit most people with ADHD. How far we have come in just 20 years of research! In fact exciting changes, some profound, now taking place in our scientific understanding of the nature of ADHD may radically change the way we look at this disorder.

Within the last few years scientific studies have shown, for example, that ADHD probably is not primarily a disorder of paying attention but one of *self-regulation:* how the self comes to manage itself within the larger realm of social behavior. Thus, even the name *ADHD* may now be incorrect. To label it a disorder of attention trivializes the disorder, since it grossly understates the substantial and dramatic problems these children face in trying to meet the challenges of their daily lives and the increasing demands of their families, schools, and society to regulate themselves as they mature. Attention deficit is also not able to account for the myriad ways that the disorder diminishes an individual's capacity to meet his or her responsibilities toward self and others.

In spite of how debilitating ADHD can be, it is not surprising that many remain skeptical about the seriousness of the disorder. All of us occasionally have trouble paying attention, and children do especially. Conquering impulsivity and restlessness is just a matter of buckling down. Or is it? Teachers, relatives, neighbors, and others may try to convince you that it is. They don't understand what you do: that there is something fundamentally and significantly wrong with your child's conduct.

The phenomenon we call ADHD is, I have come to believe, a disturbance in the child's ability to use self-control with regard to the future. That is, those with ADHD suffer from an inability to use a sense of time and of the past and future to guide their behavior. What is not developing properly in your child is the capacity to shift from focusing on the here and now to focusing on the future. That capacity is crucial to our ability to be organized, planful, and goal-directed, and it is directly dependent on how much control we have over our impulses. It frees us from being controlled by the moment and allows us to be influenced by the future. This view of ADHD dignifies the condition and its consequent problems significantly. It explains why those with ADHD are not always able to act as others act and provides us with the basis for respecting them, deepening our understanding of how ADHD impairs a person's daily life. This book has much more to say on this point and what it means for understanding ADHD. Indeed, the chief reason I wrote it was to develop this idea. I believe it comes much closer to conveying the scientific reality of ADHD than other viewpoints have done.

I also felt compelled to write this book because I saw a need to teach parents to be *scientific* in their attempts to get information or seek help from professionals. To be scientific is to be inquisitive, to challenge your sources of information for their rationale. So another goal of this book is to give you as a parent the tools you need to stay well informed and to question *everything* you hear and read—including the information in this book. Arming yourself with the facts, as they are uncovered, is the first step toward becoming an "executive parent," one who retains the ultimate decision-making authority over the child's care by others, whether physicians, psychologists, nurses, social workers, or educators. These professionals are merely your advisers in their areas of specialization. No one—and I mean *no one*—knows your child as well as you do. An underlying tenet of this book is that *you* are in charge of your child's professional and educational care. Each of the following chapters has been written with the goal of *empowering you* to take that responsibility, to relieve you of the distressing feeling that you are losing control of your child's care—and perhaps, in the process, your child. In short, this book will teach you *how* to make decisions and even *when* they should be made. But it cannot and should not make your decisions about your child for you. Neither should any other book or person.

The lessons offered in this volume have emerged from my clinical work and research with several thousand families of ADHD children over the last 17 years. They have also evolved from my own continuing journey of attempted self-improvement as a person, a father, a husband, a scientist, a teacher, a supervisor, and a clinical professional. It was no single case that resulted in the conclusions in this book, no one book shaped my ideas, no great flash of insight occurred. Instead, I had an ever-growing sense of the importance of certain principles as I worked with each new family, read each new book on the subject, and taught each new student. Unlike the techniques of management I have taught to parents, or the facts I have provided them about the disorder and the treatments currently available, these principles cut across a wide variety of situations, families, and problem areas. They can form a bedrock attitude for any actions you may take on behalf of your child with ADHD.

The information and advice contained in this book are similar to what I would say to a parent who came to the ADHD Clinic at the University of Massachusetts Medical Center. These recommendations have been drawn from extensive scientific research and represent the equivalent of approximately 20 to 25 sessions of counseling or therapy. Still, you will not find everything you need in this one book. It is impossible to encapsulate here the more than 6,000 scientific articles on the subject. And even though ADHD is probably the most well studied of all childhood psychological disorders, as clinical scientists there is much that my colleagues and I still do not know. ADHD remains misunderstood and controversial in the minds of the general public as well as the educational establishment.

This volume attempts to cut through myths and misinformation about ADHD by relying on what is currently understood to be accurate and scientifically verifiable. For particular issues about which no information is available or about which the information is not certain, I have said so. Our research continues. Also, every case of ADHD is unique. I must leave it to you to tailor information and advice to the circumstances of your own child's case and your own family's unique context. Where you still have questions about how to handle certain problems with your child, I strongly suggest that you seek out the professionals in your community who are most informed about ADHD to see if they can be of help.

What you will find in this book is much of what you need to know about ADHD and the special changes you will have to make in your life and that of your child to raise your ADHD child to a well-adjusted adulthood. Throughout, this information is presented with the goal of teaching you executive parenthood, scientific inquiry, and principle-centered action.

There are many people to be thanked for their assistance with this book. During its preparation, I was supported by the Department of Psychiatry of the University of Massachusetts Medical Center and by two grants from the National Institute of Mental Health. For that I am most grateful. I also wish to thank Bonnie Murphy and Pamela Lanava for their assistance in preparing parts of the manuscript and Barry Kaplan for his illuminating discussions on the manner in which this material might best be presented. Nevertheless, the opinions expressed here are strictly my own or those of my coauthors in the chapters they assisted me in writing.

I also, once more, wish to thank my wife, Pat, and our sons, Ken and Steve, for their patience with my writing in general and this project in particular. It regrettably stole time from our family life for which I will strive to make amends. As Milton says, "They also serve who only stand and wait," and this is surely true of the members of an author's family. I am grateful to my colleagues who have worked in the ADHD Clinic at the University of Massachusetts Medical Center—Arthur Anastopoulos, Ph.D., George DuPaul, Ph.D., Terri Shelton, Ph.D., Gwen Edwards, Ph.D., Kevin Murphy, Ph.D., and Ross Greene, Ph.D.—and to my friends working elsewhere—Charles Cunningham, Ph.D., Michael Gordon, Ph.D., and Eric Mash, Ph.D.—for their insights into ADHD and many of the matters discussed in this book.

Again, I wish to express much gratitude to Seymour Weingarten and Robert Matloff of The Guilford Press for their support of the idea for this book and their nurturance of the manuscript to its final, published stage. I must express my deep appreciation for their unwavering support of the book. Among the many members of the Guilford "family," substantial credit must go to Christine M. Benton for her tremendous investment in the editing and organization of the book and her constant encouragement of me to say what I wanted and needed to say in the most effective way. It reads and lives as it does mostly because of her.

Finally, I wish to thank all of those parents of children with ADHD who have shared their lives with me in seeking assistance for their children. Much of what you will learn from this book they have taught me. I can only hope that I have learned their lessons well enough to benefit you and your child.

RUSSELL A. BARKLEY, PH.D.
Worcester, Massachusetts

Contents

Part III
Managing Life with ADHD:
How to Cope at Home and at School

Part IV
Medications for ADHD

TAKING CHARGE OF **ADHD**

A Guiding Philosophy for Parents of ADHD Children

"Help me. I'm losing my child."

A few years ago I became part of the herculean effort by parents and professionals to gain access to special education services for ADHD children. In the midst of my preoccupation with a battle waged on federal and state levels, I received one of life's profound lessons, a lesson that shed much light on the monumental task this book encourages you to undertake on behalf of your child's academic success.

The best clinicians say that they learn as much from their clients as their clients do from them, if only they will listen and be guided and moved by what they hear. This particular lesson was taught to me one very busy morning in my practice at our ADHD clinic several years ago, and the wise mother that offered it probably has no idea how her family's dilemma affected me or how many subsequent families she may have helped through the change she inspired in my own professional practices. This was an experience that shook me mentally to the core, the wonderment of which lasted several days, and the lesson from which has stayed with me since.

The morning I was to meet this mother and her eight-year-old child, whom I'll call Steve, was hectic even before our scheduled 9:00 A.M. appointment. I

Portions of this chapter are adapted from the speech "Help Me, I'm Losing My Child" that I gave as keynote speaker at the national convention of Children with ADD (CHADD) in Chicago on October 15, 1992. The complete transcript is available on tape from CHADD, 305-587-3700.

am sure I must have entered the clinic with a flurry of activity, charts, and papers about me, probably apologizing for running late. As I quickly scanned the chart for the demographic form and its information that we obtain routinely by mail before the appointment, I was fully expecting the usual complaints from the mother about how terribly her ADD child and their family were doing. When I ask my typical first question—"What are you most concerned about with your son?" or "What brings you to our clinic today?"—it is a rare parent who does not immediately respond with a myriad of school-related problems; second to this is often an equally long list of all of the child's negative and unruly behaviors at home. So conditioned are we clinicians to hear this response that we virtually hallucinate hearing this litany before parents speak it. I had, in fact, already headed my paper with "School Problems" and "Home Problems" in such anticipation.

Steve's mother's response was so astonishing to me, so unpredictable, that I was stunned into silence. I am sure my mouth must have hung open in surprise. For she did not say what I knew to expect: My child is failing at school, my child is about to be suspended, or my child won't listen to anything I say. No, quite the contrary, what she said was "Help me. I'm losing my child."

In shock, I must have said, "Pardon me?" She simply said it again. "Help me. I'm losing my child." What on earth could she mean? I thought to myself. What new species of parent was this? "I see," I said, nodding with a knowing, sympathetic glance. "You are in the midst of a custody battle with your ex-husband."

A clinician being caught off guard once can be glossed over quickly by moving on with the interview, but to be stunned twice by unexpected responses left me off balance and utterly bewildered. My only response to her "No" while trying to regain my composure was "I'm sorry, I don't think I understand what you mean." Clearly this was true. There was no place on my notepad for such a response.

Tears came to her eyes then, further adding to my own clumsiness and discomfort, and she proceeded to explain. "It has been going on for some time," she said, "at least a few years. I can't pinpoint when it started, but I sense it is happening as surely as a mother can know her own child. I am losing him; he is drifting away from me, and I may never get him back. That would be the worst thing in the world for me."

I had no clinical hunches to guide me, so I softly asked to go on.

"He is my first child," she said, "and we were always very close until this all began to happen several years ago. Now I think he hates me. I know he doesn't want to spend time with me."

"Why do you say that?" I asked.

"Because when I come into a room he becomes cool toward me, very clipped when I speak with him, and sometimes even sarcastic," she replied. "If I suggest we do things together, which he used to love to do, he says 'no' and seems to find any excuse to avoid me. When I try to talk with him, he doesn't look at me the way he used to do, but looks away and tries to quickly end the conversation. He is also spending more time away from home, at friends' houses, and doesn't bring his friends around here the way he used to. He always seemed proud that

I was his Mom, until this began to happen. Now he doesn't even acknowledge that I exist unless he absolutely has to and certainly doesn't introduce his new friends to me the way he used to do."

"Go on," I said, still not fully comprehending the problem or the exact nature of her grief. She then explained in detail how her relationship with her son seemed lost, ruined, and possibly even irreparable. This is what she had lost or was in the process of losing: her bond with her first child, the natural reciprocal love between parent and offspring, the foundation on which all of the rest of successful and fulfilling parenting truly depends. Oh, you can certainly raise a child without this bond—in some technical, logistical, or pragmatic sense, but not in the real sense, not in that emotional or spiritual sense of having fully brought up a child.

I have never known a parent to cut so quickly to the root issue in her life, the very crux of her own—and probably her son's—unhappiness. The loss she was describing is so deeply embedded in family life that it is rarely articulated even when it is happening. It is a loss that may be exceeded only by the real loss of a child through death. The relationship she was losing is the dynamic that truly drives all parent–child interactions and all actions by parents on behalf of their families. It has been said about death that when we lose our parents we lose our past, but to lose one's child is to lose the future. How true for this woman who sensed the loss of her bond with her child. She could not see what meaningful future lay before her without the love and friendship of her child whom she had once known so deeply.

She spoke so clearly of this change in her relationship with her child that I could not help examining, in parallel, my own relationship to my two sons. Was I losing them, as she was? What a fool I seemed to myself in the presence of this woman's profound wisdom about her life—our lives. How blind I was not to have seen in countless cases before her, in the unhappiness I had encountered in families who had come to our clinic, that this had really been the significant issue in their lives all along?

You may be reading this book because you, too, feel you are losing your child. Your child has been diagnosed as having ADHD, and you have been doing your best to help the child and the rest of your family to adjust. But it just isn't working.

Or perhaps you have not reached this stage; you know something is wrong with your child and are beginning to seek professional help. So far, however, you have more questions than answers.

Wherever you and your family stand, you are not alone. Current figures put the number of people with ADHD at over 2 million school-age children, conservatively estimated. Talk to a parent of any one of them and you're likely to hear a familiar story:

Something is clearly wrong with your child's behavior. He is losing precious parts of his childhood, and you feel frustrated and confused about what is causing this to happen and what to do about it. Your child is not at peace within the dynamics of your family. There is much daily conflict over chores, homework, relations with siblings, and behavior at school or in the neighborhood.

Your child has few if any friends. The phone calls from classmates, the knocks at the door by neighborhood children, the adventures such playmates share in growing up together, and the invitations to birthday parties and sleep-overs that are daily events in most young lives are either missing or rare in your child's life. Success at school and excitement about learning—grades, certificates of achievement and citizenship, compliments from teachers—are not where they should be for your child's ability and talent, and you know it.

Valuable years and experiences of childhood are being tarnished by something you cannot see but know is there. Whatever this problem may be, it handicaps the very fabric of your child's daily interaction with others. And more painful than all of this is that you sense—as only a parent can—that your child is not at peace with himself. He is gradually becoming aware that he is not what he wants to be, cannot control as well as others what he knows he should do, cannot make himself into the child he somehow knows you wish he could be. He discourages you, dissatisfies others, and disappoints himself, and at some primitive level of awareness, he has come to know it. Perhaps you see a familiar sequence played out almost daily. The low self-esteem, the dragging through the door after school with a downcast look, the efforts to escape discussions about schoolwork, the lies to himself and others about how bad things really are, the promises to try harder next time that never quite materialize, and, for some children, the wish that he were dead. You hurt; your child hurts.

What is wrong? Your child looks physically normal. Nothing outward suggests a problem. Your child is not mentally delayed. Most likely she walks, talks, hears, and sees normally and has at least normal intellect or better. Yet with each passing year, she seems increasingly less able than other children to inhibit her behavior, manage herself, and meet the challenges the future is throwing at her. You know that if you do not do something to help soon, she is destined to lead a troubled life of underachievement as surely as today rises out of the past and the future out of today. Your desire for a normal, peaceful, loving family life with this child, your hopes for her educational and occupational success, your striving to give her a life perhaps better than you had yourself, to have her stand on your shoulders to reach further ahead in life now all seem in jeopardy because of something you cannot quite see or understand. You are at times perplexed, puzzled, angry, sad, anxious, fearful, guilty, and helpless in the face of what afflicts your child. You seek answers and guidance.

Instinctively, you may have sensed that what you face with this child is in some way a disability of self-control or will. What constitutes our will? What makes us do what we know we should do, behave toward others as we know we ought, and complete the work that we know how to do and that must be done? More generally, what makes us self-disciplined and persistent so we can turn away from immediate gratification and meet the challenges of today to prepare for the future like others of our age? Whatever it is within us that permits us to act with self-control, to adhere to our morals and values, to "walk our talk," and to act with a sense of the future is not developing so well in your child. Perhaps that is what has brought you to this book. Perhaps your child has ADHD. This book can help you find out. It can also advise you on how to cope effectively if your child has the disorder.

The Challenge of Raising a Child with ADHD

Raising a child with ADHD can be incredibly challenging for any parent. These children are very inattentive, impulsive or uninhibited, overactive, and demanding. Their problems can place a burden on your role as a parent that you never thought possible when you first considered having a child. These problems may even have caused you to rethink the wisdom of that decision.

In areas where any reasonable and competent parent *wishes* to be involved in child rearing, parents of children with ADHD *must* become involved—doubly involved. They must search out schools, teachers, professionals, and other community resources. They will find themselves having to supervise, monitor, teach, organize, plan, structure, reward, punish, guide, buffer, protect, and nurture their ADHD child far more than is demanded of a typical parent. They also will have to meet more often with other adults involved in the child's daily life—school staff, pediatricians, and mental health professionals. Then there is all the intervention with neighbors, scout masters, coaches, and others in the community necessitated by the greater behavior problems the child is likely to have when dealing with these outsiders.

To make matters more difficult, the increased need of an ADHD child for parental guidance, protection, advocacy, love, and nurturance can be hidden behind the facade of his excessive, demanding, and at times obnoxious behavior. Margaret Flacy from Dallas, mother of two boys, now young adults, with ADHD put it beautifully when she wrote to me recently: " . . . early in my career as a teacher [when] I was bemoaning my inability to cope with a particularly difficult child . . . who in hindsight was probably as ADHD as they come . . . a wonderful and wise retired teacher took my hand and said, 'Margaret, the children who need love the most will always ask for it in the most unloving ways.' "

Many parents with whom I have had the privilege to work find that the challenge of raising a child with ADHD elevates parenting to a new, higher plane. Bringing up a child with ADHD may be the hardest thing you ever have to do. Some parents succumb to the stress an ADHD child can place on them, winding up with a child or a family in constant crisis or, worse, a family that breaks apart over time. But if you rise to the challenge, raising a child with ADHD can provide a tremendous opportunity for self-improvement and fulfillment as a parent. You can watch your direct investment of time and energy pay off in the happiness and well-being of your child—not always, but often enough to make it richly fulfilling to many parents. To know that you are needed by such a child can bring a deeper purpose to your life than few other things afford.

The words of Margaret Flacy's mentor became the keystones for the rearing of Flacy's own sons and all the children she taught over 30 years. They also illustrate the importance of centering your child-rearing philosophy on certain proven principles. If you view your parental responsibility as resting on a tripod, the first leg is the principle-centered approach. Add executive parenthood and scientific thinking, and your strategy for raising a well-adjusted child will have a firm and balanced base.

Becoming a Principle-Centered Parent

For almost two decades I have counseled hundreds of parents on the methods that seem most effective in managing children with ADHD. For the first five years of developing my clinical practice that is all I did. Then, from both my practice and research, a feeling began to emerge that some larger, deeper principles were at work. As these became clearer, I wrote them down. They became some of the first things taught in my parent training classes on child management, and I passed them on to my junior colleagues and to others through my many workshops for professionals. The list eventually grew to the 10 principles presented in Chapter 9. They are useful because, simply, when you see the why, you are more likely to do the how. That is, you are more likely to use the special management aids your ADHD child needs—and to adopt them creatively—when you know why you're using them and why they work.

Being principle-centered also keeps you on a straight course through a labyrinthine journey. It establishes a pattern whereby you act not on impulses but on rules, from a sense of the future and what is right, not from the transitory feelings of the moment. It frees your behavior from control by the immediate actions of your child and the negative emotions these actions may elicit and directs your behavior according to your ideals. Being principle-centered allows you to disengage from the downward spiraling of hostilities with your child (or others) and to act from a plan and sense of what is right. In short, it enables you to hold yourself to higher standards of parenting than others may follow.

Being principle-centered in your interactions with your child is both liberating and encumbering. It means you have far more control over the outcome of the interaction than does your child, because you have the freedom to act to change what happens. It means you cannot blame your child entirely for the conflicts or hostilities between you, that you cannot blame professionals or others who counsel you if things go wrong between you and your child, and that you cannot divert the responsibility for your actions with your child to your past or to others who raised and taught you. Principle-centered parenting means owning the responsibility of your self-determined actions. It makes you both immensely free and awesomely accountable.

As I continued my study of ADHD and my own journey of self-improvement, I came to realize that another set of principles, which I now think of as first-order principles, applies to *all* parents. Dr. Stephen R. Covey has spelled them out far more clearly and forcefully than I could in *The Seven Habits of Highly*

Effective People, a book I highly recommend, but here I have rewritten them to apply to raising a child with ADHD:

1. *"Be proactive."* Far too often we *react* to our children's behavior, often on impulse, without regard to the consequences and with no plan for what we are trying to achieve. In those instances we are being acted on and not consciously choosing to act. Seeing a situation from a reactive frame of mind can sometimes make it seem hopeless—your destiny with your child is being controlled by the child or other outside agents. Negative interactions with your child simply wash over you unpredictably, knocking you off balance like waves when you stand backward (and unprepared) in the surf. You feel helpless, and your relationship with your ADHD child can become hostile, negative, discouraging, stressful, or dysfunctional. But it is not *what your child does* or does to you that creates these problems for you but *your responses.* Take responsibility for your own behavior as a parent and for the interactions and relationship with your ADHD child. Take the initiative to change what you do not like in the way you act toward your child and accept the responsibility to make this relationship happen the way you would like it to be. You have the ability to subordinate your impulses to your values, Dr. Covey says. You have the freedom to choose your actions with your child. Develop that sense of choice, practice it, exercise it.

2. *"Begin with the end in mind."* When faced with a problem, try to envision how you want it to turn out. You can apply this principle on a small scale, such as envisioning how you wish the evening's homework session to turn out before you begin, or on a larger scale, such as how you would like your child to reflect on your having helped him complete an important goal, like graduating from high school. Even more broadly, you can try an exercise Dr. Covey recommends. Picture your own funeral service. Your ADHD child has been asked to say a few words about you during the service. What would you want him to say you were like as a parent? Beginning with the end in mind helps us focus more clearly on what matters most and see what we must do to make situations turn out the way we would like. You cannot have a plan without a goal, a map without a destination, or a set of strategies to use with your ADHD child without knowing what outcome you desire. Your relationship with your child and the manner in which smaller interactions turn out by design or by default are entirely up to you. I find that this principle is most needed in situations of potential conflict. Before acting, see the end in your mind and clarify the goal; the steps toward your goal will emerge from this process.

3. *"Put first things first."* What is important in your relationship with your ADHD child? What matters most in your role as a parent to this child? What are the major hurdles and responsibilities you must assist your child in overcoming or fulfilling? I have often counseled parents of ADHD children to distinguish the battles from the wars, the trivial and unimportant things they must get done with their children (e.g., making a bed before school) from the far more important goals to be accomplished (being prepared for school and leaving home in a peaceful, loved atmosphere). Too often parents of ADHD children find them-

selves caught in struggles over the trivial. Children with ADHD can do so many things wrong that parents could confront them on their transgressions throughout much of the day. But is this the kind of relationship you want with your handicapped child? Parents must develop a sense of priorities with their ADHD children.

Learn to distinguish among the four categories of work and responsibilities with your ADHD child: (a) urgent and important, (b) urgent and not important, (c) important but not urgent, and (d) not important and not urgent. As parents we are likely to accomplish category a and unlikely to waste much time on d. The hard part is distinguishing b from c. Racing around and arguing with your child to meet deadlines for less important activities (sports, clubs, music lessons, etc.) can often take precedence over more important but nonurgent things. For instance, you may well get your child to a piano lesson on time but destroy your relationship with that child in the process. On Sunday evening as you contemplate the busy week ahead, think about what is important for you and your ADHD child and concentrate on doing these things first. Insert them into your calendar first so they don't get swept away by the onrush of the seemingly urgent but relatively unimportant things that you will have to attend to that week (such as returning calls to others, doing housework, preparing meals on time, getting children to bed on time, etc.). And it is not just your activities with your ADHD child that require sorting out by this method. Think about your own work and obligations apart from this child. Have you overcommitted yourself to committee work, volunteer activities, babysitting for others' children, etc.? Do you need to learn to say "no" to others who call and ask you to help with things about which you do not feel strongly?

4. *"Think win/win."* Throughout your daily life with your ADHD child, especially as the teenage years approach, you will have to ask your child to do schoolwork and chores, keep social commitments, and adhere to household rules. Each of these requests constitutes a negotiation. As Dr. Covey says, when you enter into a negotiation with anyone, think win/win. That is, approach the interaction with the idea that whenever possible you want both you and your child to get what you want. Don't concentrate only on what you want the child to do; you must try to understand how difficult it may be for her to do as you ask. Do you ever find yourself simply spewing forth commands for obedience all day long? It's certainly easy to do, but is it the kind of relationship you want with your children? Begin with the end in mind and think of how you wish to be remembered: as a tyrant or a respectful negotiator?

5. *"Seek first to understand, then to be understood."* Dr. Covey uses the metaphor of an emotional bank account to convince us of the importance of this principle. It refers to the amount of trust that has been built up in a relationship with someone, in this case your ADHD child. By being honest, kind, and courteous and keeping your promises, you make deposits into this account. Avoiding discourtesy, disrespect, dishonesty, overreaction, threats, insults or putdowns, and betrayals of trust increases your balance with your ADHD child. Then, when it is most important that your child seek you out and follow your advice, he is likely to

do so; when you most need him to understand and help you, he will be there for you.

Remember that your love for your ADHD child is a bedrock of emotional support that he can count on because he is your child and belongs to your family. Be sure he knows it has no strings attached, that your love is not dependent on how well he behaved that day, how well he did in school, how many friends he has, or how terrific he is at sports or other recreational pursuits.

Dr. Covey describes six types of deposits you can make into this account, but the first is the most important: (a) Understand your child's point of view and make what is important to him important to you; be a good listener—reflect what you think he has said in your own words, and see the situation from his point of view. (b) Attend to the little things, the small kindnesses and courtesies. (c) Keep your commitments to your child. (d) Make your expectations clear and explicit at the beginning of any task or negotiation with your child. (e) Show personal integrity; do not be two-faced or dishonest; make your behavior conform to your words. (f) Apologize sincerely to your ADHD child when you make a withdrawal from that account; that is, admit when you are wrong, have been unkind or disrespectful, have embarrassed or humiliated your child, or have failed to make the other five deposits. Only when you have really tried to see things from your ADHD child's point of view should you seek to make yourself understood.

6. "*Synergize.*" Work with your child in creative cooperation and strive to combine all of the foregoing principles into your interactions with your child. The combination, as Dr. Covey says, unleashes the greatest power within people, freeing us to act imaginatively with others. This means being open to whatever outcomes this creative cooperation with your ADHD child may bring forth. If you truly strive not to have everything go your way but to incorporate the other five principles into your parenting of your ADHD child, the course and outcome of your relationship will not be entirely predictable. They will flow and change as your child grows, and you must be open to that change. Some parents will be frightened of this uncertainty, but if you come to relish the adventure, you will be prepared for whatever may come, secure in the strength of your relationship and your trust in each other. Value the differences between your ADHD child and others, be open to new ways of solving difficulties you may face together, and remember, there is no one right way to raise your ADHD child. There may, in fact, be several excellent ways to work together in facing the challenges life holds for you both.

7. "*Renewal.*" This principle supports all of the others. It recognizes that you are the most important resource that you and your ADHD child have and that you must care for yourself to renew that resource. As Dr. Covey says, just as machinery requires downtime, effective people need rejuvenation. Dr. Covey identifies four dimensions of our lives that require renewal: physical, mental, social/emotional, and spiritual. Renewing the physical dimension of your life may mean proper nutrition, exercise, and stress management. Mental maintenance may mean reading and broadening your knowledge, continuing education, en-

gaging in creative pursuits, visualizing and planning your goals, or writing. Socially and emotionally, you may want to be of service to others, show empathy, act synergistically with others, create a close relationship with your spouse, and draw on your inner security that comes from habits 1–6. Caring for the spiritual dimension might mean continuing to clarify your values and commitments, studying your relationship to your world, and thinking about your morals and your life's purposes.

Too often parents of ADHD children dedicate so much of their time and energy exclusively to their children that they exhaust themselves. Such martyrdom may seem heroic and altruistic at first glance but is actually foolish and destructive in the long run. Failing to take time to renew yourself leaves you increasingly less to give your children. Industrial machinery that is never shut down may be tremendously productive in the short run but will have a brief life, says Dr. Covey. The best gift you can give your ADHD child is your gift of self-renewal.

If you find that you are not using many of these seven effective habits, you are hardly alone—nor are you a bad parent or a horrible person. All of us get tired, stressed, angry, and shortsighted at times, and this interferes with our ability to keep these principles in mind and to act accordingly. It is the striving toward self-improvement that matters most, and all of us can succeed at committing ourselves to that course even though we fall short of it occasionally.

Becoming an Executive Parent

Many parents have told me of the shame and humiliation they have experienced at the hands of educators and professionals involved with their ADHD child. Some have described feeling lost or misunderstood or being treated like a child during school planning meetings, their views and opinions dismissed as biased or naive. Their overall impression was that those involved simply wanted to reach some quick conclusion—to do what was cheap and expedient for the school system or the professional and not what was best for the child. The outcome of such meetings is often disillusionment, dissatisfaction, and distrust in the parent–school relationship as well as a sense of loss of control over the child's fate. In encounters with physicians and mental health specialists, these parents have been dismissed as hysterical, easily stressed, or naive, especially if the ADHD child was well behaved during the appointment. Or the professionals have launched the child on a treatment program without asking about the parents' concerns and without explaining the program's rationale, goals, or side effects.

"The last time we had a school meeting there were six people there—
his teacher, a psychologist, a social worker, someone called
an LD specialist, his counselor, and the principal.

I couldn't understand most of what they said.
What can I do next time to avoid feeling intimidated
and make sure my son gets the help he needs?"

Meetings with *your* advisers—which is how you should view the educators and professionals involved with your child—do not have to go that way. Maintaining an attitude of executive parenting gives you the self-confidence of knowing that *you* are ultimately in charge of this meeting and of what happens to your ADHD child.

You are the *case manager* of your child's life, and you must be a proactive executive prepared to take charge—and to keep it longer than most parents must. As you watch other parents increasingly relinquish responsibility and control to their maturing children, your child's deficits in self-control and willpower guarantee that you will have to retain much of the management and control of her behavior. You are the child's advocate with others in the community who control the resources you will need. You are the child's buffer from excessive criticism and rejection.

No doubt you already know this, but your encounters with those who are supposed to work for you and your child may have left you feeling disenfranchised and disenchanted. Being an executive parent is the way to take back that power. No matter how much help they offer, you cannot rely on professionals to take on this role for you. There are, of course, many competent and compassionate professionals available for consulting. But professionals come and go, and even when they stay put, they have other things on their agenda.

Only you are in a position to make your child a top priority. Others can provide medication, special education, counseling, tutoring, and coaching in sports, among other special services. But you are always the pivotal person who coordinates these activities and determines, ultimately, when and how much of these services your child requires and can stand at one time. You can change or terminate your child's involvement whenever you believe it is not in your child's best interests to continue with those services. Yes, you should listen and actively evaluate information given to you, but any professional who bullies or browbeats you into submitting your child to activities or services just because of more professional degrees or higher education than you have should be replaced.

This theme of being an executive parent to your ADHD child echoes throughout this book. Explicitly reminding yourself of your role as decision maker will encourage you to act more like the executive: to solicit advice and information, to ask questions of others when they are unclear, to make your feelings about your child's care in that system known, to help flesh out the variety of options before you, to select among them, and to give your consent to the best of these choices. Use the information in this book to empower yourself as an executive parent who takes every step with your child's best interest in mind.

The benefits can be extraordinary. Just thinking in the executive mode provides you with an inner sense of control over your fate and that of your ADHD child. It removes the sense of helplessness or second-class status that can come from allowing others to usurp your role. All of this makes you a far more effective decision maker as a parent of a child with ADHD. As a side benefit, it will also bring with it a deeper sense of respect from the professionals and specialists with whom you must deal and of pride and respect for yourself as you strengthen your role as a parent.

Becoming a Scientific Parent

Buttressing your work as an executive parent is an approach I call *scientific parenting.* Scientists admit their uncertainty about something and then seek as much information as they can on that subject. They question, remain open to new information, but also are generally skeptical toward claims not supported by facts. Finally, they experiment with new ways of doing things and revise their plans based on the results. These steps can be just as useful in being a parent of an ADHD child as they are in discovering a cure for cancer.

Admit Uncertainty

To be a scientific parent, therefore, means to start out admitting that you (and I as well as any other professional) do not know everything there is to know about raising your child with ADHD. When you face a new problem with your ADHD child, remember that it is when you are most certain about something that you are most likely to be wrong. Many parents become so wedded to an idea about the cause or treatment of their child's ADHD that they are blinded to other potentially useful information.

Seek Knowledge

Admitting that you don't know something naturally leads to the second thing that good scientists do—seek knowledge. So should you. Be voracious about it. You need to learn as much as you can about ADHD and the treatments that may help your child. You cannot be an executive or a scientific parent without the facts. Before scientists study a problem, they conduct a search of the available literature on the topic. Even if they don't find the answer to their questions, they can discover what mistakes others have made and thus avoid repeating them. But they are also likely to find information that points them in a better direction than they might have taken originally. You must do the same. Read! Listen! Seek! Question! Find out as much as you can, reasonably, about your child's disorder. You have started this process just by reading this book. Like a scientist, the more you know about ADHD as a parent, the less likely you are to fall prey to the past mistakes of others and the better prepared you will be to discover the right direction to take with your child.

A good scientist remains open to new ideas but challenges those ideas, subjecting them to experiments before accepting them as part of the body of scientific findings on the topic. So whatever you discover, be open-minded about it, entertain the value of the information to your research, but question everything. Be prepared to abandon any theory or hypothesis that does not stand up to critical scrutiny.

Be an especially critical consumer of new information on ADHD. Do not accept everything you hear or read. Be open to an idea, but challenge it, test it, criticize it. Ask others what they think about it. If the new information can stand up to this kind of logical inspection, maybe it is true and can be of help to you in understanding and raising your ADHD child. But always ask for the evidence that supports a new idea, especially if it disagrees with information you already have.

Call national parent support groups like Children and Adults with ADD (CHADD) or the Attention Deficit Disorders Association (ADDA)—addresses and phone numbers are at the back of this book—to see what they know about this new concept. Talk with local professionals about their opinions on the subject. Ask the people promoting a new treatment for any copies of published research articles that support their claims. This can keep you from leaping into an unproven treatment that may be a waste of your time and money or even detrimental to your child.

One point that will be made frequently throughout this book is that truth is an assembled entity. It comes from no single source, text, or person but emerges as we acquire more and more information about a subject.

Experiment and Revise

The logical next step is experimentation. Use the results of your experiments to revise your thinking about the problem and to chart the course for your next experiment on the problem. Indeed, experimenting and revising are never-ending processes for parents of an ADHD child.

When an experiment fails, do not be discouraged. Use what you have learned to try solving the problem a different way. This time what you do might just help your child. Above all, keep trying. Never conclude that the failure of a particular plan means you are a bad parent. As you go back to the drawing board, reassure yourself that you are doing the best you can as this child's executive parent to develop plans that may help.

The ultimate purpose of this volume is, therefore, to empower you—to help you become a scientific, principle-centered, executive parent who is as effective as possible in meeting the many challenges involved in raising any child with this disorder. In the following chapters you'll find the most up-to-date information available as well as guidelines for finding the ever-emerging new resources that can keep you informed as our knowledge of the subject evolves. You'll find advice for taking care of your child, preserving your family, and protecting your own health and welfare in the process. Throughout the book I'll remind you of those fundamental truths that thousands of parents have helped me to see—the principles that can keep you on a steady course in your daily effort to raise a happy, healthy child and keep you from veering off into a downward spiral of knee-jerk reactions, frustration, and resentment.

The book is divided into four major sections. Part I tells you what the latest research has revealed: what ADHD is, what causes it—and, just as important, what doesn't cause it—and what all of this tells us about how to treat it. Integral to this discussion is my recently formed theory that ADHD is more than just a deficiency in attention and impulse control; rather, I believe it is a fundamental deficiency in the ability to look toward the future and control one's behavior based on that foresight. You'll also learn in this section about the features and problems you can expect to encounter as a child with ADHD grows and how ADHD in children typically affects their families. With this knowledge in hand, you should be well equipped to pursue your responsibilities as a scientific parent.

Part II prepares you to become an effective executive parent, beginning with your child's evaluation for ADHD by a professional. Knowing what to expect and what resources may be at your disposal will help you take charge of your child's destiny from the start. Here you will also find my 10 principles for managing children with ADHD. Use these to supplement the more general habits of effective parenting discussed here, and you will have a solid framework for meeting a wealth of everyday challenges that ADHD in the family can present. Because all smart executives take care of themselves as well as their job responsibilities, Part II also attends to *your* needs, telling you how to cope with the natural emotional reactions to your child's diagnosis of ADHD and how to renew yourself throughout your years in this demanding role.

In Part III, you will find full descriptions of the most effective methods for managing ADHD symptoms and associated problems with your child, whether a preschooler or an adolescent. Here are dozens of proven techniques designed to acknowledge and work with your child's disabilities rather than to deny and struggle futilely against them. Maximally applied, these methods can restore harmony to your home, help your child fit in with peers, enhance achievement at school and the all-important self-esteem that goes with it, and generally improve behavior to set your child on the road to well-adjusted adulthood. I cannot and will not promise miracles, but you will undoubtedly be surprised by how much you and your child can accomplish together with perseverance—and understanding.

Finally, Part IV provides current information on the medications that are often recommended for helping to manage the symptoms of ADHD.

PART I

Understanding ADHD

CHAPTER 1

What Is Attention-Deficit/ Hyperactivity Disorder?

Attention-deficit/hyperactivity disorder, or ADHD, is a developmental disorder of self-control. It consists of problems with attention span, impulse control, and activity level. But, as you will discover here, it is much more. These problems are reflected in impairment in a child's will or capacity to control his or her own behavior relative to the passage of time—to keep future goals and consequences in mind. It is not, as other books will tell you, just a matter of being inattentive and overactive. It is not just a temporary state that will be outgrown, a trying but normal phase of childhood. It is not caused by parental failure to discipline or control the child, and it is not a sign of some sort of inherent "badness" in the child.

ADHD is real—a real disorder, a real problem, often a real obstacle. It can be heartbreaking and nerve-wracking.

"Why Don't They Do Something about That Kid?"

It's easy to see why many people find it hard to view ADHD as a disability like blindness, deafness, cerebral palsy, or other physical disabilities. ADHD children look normal. There is no outward sign that something is physically wrong within their central nervous system or brain. Yet I believe it is an imperfection in the brain that causes the constant motion and other behavior that people find so intolerable in a child who has ADHD.

By now you may be familiar with the way others react to ADHD behavior: At first many adults attempt to overlook the child's interruptions, blurted remarks, and violation of rules. With repeated encounters, however, they try to exert more control over the child. When the child still fails to respond, the vast majority decide that the child is willfully and intentionally disruptive. Ultimately most will come to one conclusion: The child's problems result from how the child is being raised. The ADHD child needs more discipline, more structure, more limit setting. The parents are ignorant, careless, permissive, amoral, antisocial, or, in contemporary parlance, "dysfunctional."

"So, Why Don't They Do Something about That Kid?"

Of course the parents often *are* doing something. But when they explain that the child has been diagnosed as having ADHD, judgmental outsiders typically react with skepticism. They see the label as simply an excuse by the parents to avoid the responsibility of child rearing and an attempt to make the child yet another type of helpless victim unaccountable for his actions. This hypocritical response—viewing the child's behavior so negatively while at the same time labeling the child as "just normal"—leaves outsiders free to continue blaming the parents.

Even the less censorious reaction of considering ADHD behavior as a stage to be outgrown is not so benign in the long run. Many adults, including professionals, counsel the parents not to worry. "Just hang in there," they advise, "and by adolescence the child will have outgrown it." This is certainly true in some milder forms of ADHD: In over 70% of these mild cases, the behaviors are likely to be within the normal range by adulthood. If your preschool child has more serious problems with ADHD symptoms, however, such advice is small comfort. Being advised to "hang in there" for 7 to 10 years is hardly consoling. Worse, it is often grossly mistaken, harmful advice. The life of a child whose ADHD is left unrecognized and untreated is likely to be filled with failure and underachievement. Up to 30–50% of these children may be retained in a grade at least once. As many as 35% may fail to complete high school altogether. For half of such children, social relationships are seriously impaired, and for more than 60%, seriously defiant behavior leads to misunderstanding and resentment by siblings, frequent scolding and punishment, and a greater potential for delinquency and substance abuse later on. Failure by the adults in a child's life to recognize and treat ADHD can leave that child with an unremitting sense of failure in all arenas of life.

"Isn't ADHD overdiagnosed? Aren't *most* children inattentive, active, and impulsive?"

Imagine the toll on society when, conservatively estimated, more than 2 million school-age children have ADHD. This means that at least one or even two children with ADHD are in every classroom throughout the United States. It also means that ADHD is one of the most common childhood disorders of which professionals are aware. Finally, it means that all of us know someone with the disorder, whether we could identify it by name or not.

The costs of ADHD to society are staggering, not only in lost productivity and underemployment but also in reeducation. And what of the costs to society in antisocial behavior, crime, and substance abuse? More than 20% of children with ADHD have set serious fires in their communities, more than 30% have engaged in theft, more than 40% drift into early tobacco and alcohol use, and more than 25% are expelled from high school because of serious misconduct. Recently the effects of ADHD on driving have also been studied. Within their first two years of independent driving, adolescents with a diagnosis of ADHD have nearly four times as many auto accidents, are more likely to cause bodily injury in such accidents, and have three times as many citations for speeding than young drivers without ADHD.

Recognition of these consequences has spawned a huge effort to understand ADHD. Besides the 6,000 scientific papers mentioned in the Preface, more than 50 textbooks have been devoted to the subject, with again as many books written for parents and teachers. Countless newspaper stories have addressed ADHD over the course of the nearly 100 years that clinical science has recognized the disorder as a serious problem. Many local parents' support associations have sprung up, most notably Children and Adults with ADD (CHADD), which has grown into a national organization of more than 40,000 members. One professional organization, the Professional Group for ADD and Related Disorders (PGARD), devotes its entire annual, three-day scientific meeting to advances in research on the disorder. At least five other professional organizations include a number of scientific presentations on the subject in their convention programs each year. (See Chapter 18's section on Parent Support Groups for more information on these resources.) Hardly what you would expect if the disorder were not "real" as some critics have claimed.

A Question of Perspective

Intense interest in demystifying ADHD has instigated voluminous research. As I will describe in detail in Chapter 2, the research to date has led me to a new view of ADHD. I now see ADHD as a developmental disorder of the ability to regulate one's behavior with an eye toward the future. I believe the disorder stems from underactivity in an area of the brain that, as it matures, provides us with ever-greater means of behavioral inhibition, self-organization, self-regulation, and foresight. Relatively hidden from view in the child's moment-to-moment behavior, the behavioral deformity this underactivity causes is pernicious, insidious, and disastrous in its impact on the person's ability to manage the critical day-to-day affairs through which we prepare for the future, both near and far.

The fact that its daily impact is subtle but its consequences for the child's adaptive functioning are severe has led to many changes in the labels and concepts applied to the disorder over the last century. It explains why clinical science, in its attempts to pin down the nature of the problem, has moved from vague, unfocused notions of defective moral control 100 years ago to sharper, more specific concepts of hyperactivity, inattention, and impulsivity in recent decades. This evolution of our knowledge from the very general to the very specific has taken us leaps forward in understanding the abnormalities of ADHD children, but it has caused us to lose our perspective on how those behaviors affect the social adaptation of these children over long periods of time.

Now, however, clinical science is stepping back from its microscope on the social moments of ADHD children and once again peering through its telescope at longer-term social development. We are beginning to understand how these "atoms" of momentary ADHD behavior come to form "molecules" of daily life, how these daily "molecules" form the larger "compounds" of weekly and monthly social existence, and how these social "compounds" form the larger stages or structures of a life played out over many years. As a result, we see that ADHD is not just the hyperactivity or distractibility of the moment or the inability to get the day's work done, but a relative impairment in how behavior is organized and directed toward the tomorrows of life.

This larger, longer view of ADHD clarifies why those with the disorder struggle in their adaptation to the demands of social life and so often fail to reach the goals and futures they had tried to set for themselves or that others demand of them. If we remember that the behavior of those with ADHD is focused on the moment, we won't judge their actions so harshly. No one would understand half of what we "normal" adults do if these actions were judged solely by their immediate consequences. Many of the actions we take have been planned with the future in mind. Likewise, we don't understand—and are quick to criticize—the behavior of those with ADHD because we are expecting them to act with foresight when they have always focused instead on the moment. We find it difficult to tolerate the way those with ADHD behave, the decisions they make, and their complaining about the negative consequences that befall them because *we*, who do not have the disorder, can see where it is all leading and use that vision to determine our current behavior while they cannot. Only now is clinical science coming to understand this very important feature of ADHD.

Have You Seen These Children?

The children described in the following cases may be quite familiar to you. They are real cases from my clinic (though their names and identities have been changed to preserve confidentiality), and their stories will give you some idea of the circumstances ADHD children commonly find themselves in today. As you read, you will probably be able to see how their lives might have been different if their parents, teachers, and others had really understood their inability to look toward the future. You also should know, however, how far we have come. To provide some perspective on how much better the prospects are for these children today than in the past, I'll also describe how such children might have been treated during earlier decades.

Amy: A Constant Struggle

Amy is an attractive seven-year-old girl whose parents, Rose and Michael, are quite concerned about her. They tell me they have to repeat their commands to her a lot more than with her brothers or sisters, sometimes having to physically guide her through tasks, such as getting dressed and undressed or picking up her toys. She seems to pay little attention to her homework, chores, or what others are saying to her unless she is interested in the activity at hand. She has great difficulty sitting still through a meal or while the family watches television together and in staying in bed at bedtime. She runs rather than walks everywhere and often climbs up on furniture as she tears about the room.

Amy seems unable to let others finish what they are saying at family meals before she blurts out her ideas and then changes the subject altogether. Her incessant chatter has moved her siblings to nickname her "Motor Mouth."

When her parents tell her not to do something, Amy often becomes angry, resentful, and belligerent. She says, "But I don't care; I want that," repeating her demands and throwing a temper tantrum. When told to pick up toys, put her dirty clothes away, or get ready for her bath, she pouts or crosses her arms over her chest and says, "No, I don't want to do that!"

Her parents have noticed that she does not seem to think before she acts. She lunges into other children's play without considering what they are doing and whether she is welcome to join them. She takes over the activity, bossing others about, and gets frustrated and visibly upset when others do not obey her commands. Her emotions seem to get the best of her during many social activities. At parties she becomes much more excited, giddy, and loud, often being more elated than the birthday child. She becomes even more excited during games and can't wait until others take their turns. Once a game ends, she has great trouble settling down to a quieter activity, such as having birthday cake. She has even been known to start opening the presents for the birthday child.

Amy easily becomes envious of other children and has on occasion taken home someone's new toy that she doesn't have. She brags about her accomplishments, manufacturing many details. Her peers and their parents find her blunt comments rude and her play behavior selfish. Amy has been losing friends and now is not often invited to other children's homes. Neighborhood children have begun to call her "weird" and "hyper." Her parents are worried that she will wind up friendless and that she may develop a poor self-image.

Despite her devil-may-care attitude about most things, Amy depends excessively on her parents or teachers for help with her schoolwork, which she constantly protests with "I'm bored!" and "I hate this!" Amy's completion of schoolwork lags behind her known ability, and she is beginning to fall behind her classmates. She finds it hard to concentrate on what the teacher is saying. Instead she talks to her neighbors, doodles, or gets up and moves about, exploring the aquarium at the back of the room and making frequent trips to the trash can and pencil sharpener.

The school psychologist tested Amy and found her to be of normal intelligence. Her early academic skills are all average or better; no learning disability is causing her poor school performance. She is likely, however, to have to repeat second grade.

When Amy was born, she was premature and weighed less than five pounds. She did not have any other problems but was slow to put on weight. She was a bit late in learning to walk but spoke her first words earlier than most children. Her parents do not remember any serious medical problems during her development. At age four, Amy's preschool teacher reported that she was "wild," always running around the room, climbing on furniture and shelves, taking toys from the other children, throwing things, and fidgeting during group story time. All of the behavior problems she now displays were also noticed during kindergarten.

When I met them, Amy's parents were at their wits' end. Cutting out sugary foods from Amy's diet had had little effect; more discipline had also produced little improvement. Rose feels she has somehow failed as a parent and complains of excessive stress and fatigue when she has had to be with Amy for long periods of time; Michael reports numerous confrontations with Amy over her behavior problems. Both parents fear that their marriage is beginning to suffer and find themselves fantasizing about the early days of their marriage, before children.

Amy's case illustrates the classic symptoms seen with ADHD: inattention and poor ability to stay on a task to completion, impulsiveness and the inability to think about what she does before she acts, and overactivity or frequent restlessness. As for most children with ADHD, Amy's problems began in her preschool years but were not diagnosed until years later. Professional help was not sought until her behavior problems created difficulties outside the family, in this case at school, which is also fairly common. Amy is also fairly typical of many ADHD children because she shows a second pattern of behavior: oppositional, defiant, and hostile behavior toward others, especially parents, known as *oppositional defiant disorder (ODD)*. Up to 70% of ADHD children who are referred to clinics will have this problem.

Over a century ago, in the 1860s, Amy would not have been diagnosed with a psychological disorder, but her "symptoms" might well have been noted. If she lived in Germany, she probably would have been called a "Fidgety Phil" or, more aptly, "Fidgety Phyllis." It was at that time that Heinrich Hoffman, a German physician, wrote a poem about a hyperactive boy by this name. Probably only those raising her would have considered her to be a real problem. With nothing known scientifically or clinically about such children, outsiders would have considered her just a social oddity—a judgment that would not have prevented them from dealing harshly with her. In lieu of the appropriate management methods (such as those discussed in Parts II and III of this book), both her parents and others would have been likely to discipline her often.

Had she been born about 40 years later in England, she might have been referred to Dr. George Still, a British physician who was the first to publish a description of 24 children like Amy. Her parents might have been told that she suffered from a defect of willpower, or volitional inhibition, as Still called it. He might have said that her actions illustrated a serious defect in the moral control of her behavior and might have concluded that its cause was neurological. Even so, little was known about how to treat such a problem, so the prognosis for Amy would have been rather bleak by comparison with today's standards of treatment. Most likely Amy still would not have been diagnosed with any disorder but would have been viewed as ill-mannered, immoral, excessively passionate (emotional), or even an idiot or imbecile despite normal intellectual development. In those days she might very well have faced a life of social rejection and ostracism and educational underachievement. Today, however, early intervention offers hope not only for managing ADHD symptoms but also for possibly minimizing the impact of ODD over the course of a child's development.

"Does my child have ADHD?"

Ricky: A Damaged Self-Image

Ricky is an eight-year-old second-grader whose parents, Richard and Danielle, have tried "everything" to get Ricky to do better at school. He was retained in first grade, and they fear he may be retained again before getting to middle school. Ricky is a noisy, restless gadfly who flits about his home or classroom doing many things at once but not staying long enough to finish any of them. Most days, notes home from his teacher tell his parents he has been "off-task," aggressive, and disruptive of other children's work and play activities. For little apparent reason, just this year he has taken to shoving other children, taking things from them, bullying peers during recess, and sabotaging others' work when he is not being supervised directly. His mother believes that his teacher relies too much on punishment and too little on the positive feedback, one-to-one attention and assistance, and nurturing that Ricky needs. For the first time, his parents are having difficulty getting him to school. He complains of vague bodily aches and pains that are clearly intended to keep him home. Recently he has mentioned hating himself and wishing he were dead and begun referring to himself as stupid.

Ricky's parents have always taken his differences from his older brother and sister in stride as just part of Ricky's unique personality. He frequently responds well to their praise of him and is seen as a loving, affectionate child toward all family members. Yet this year his self-esteem has plummeted, he is easily irritated, and at times he is on the verge of tears when frustrated by the simplest things. His parents see him as really hurting inside yet cannot seem to provide more than temporary relief for him. They have developed an adversarial relationship with his teacher, seeing her harsh discipline and lack of forgiveness as a major contributor to Ricky's downhill slide in self-image.

Ricky met all the typical developmental milestones at a normal age, though as an infant he was always in motion. His parents were forced to put a net over his crib to keep him from wandering around the house while others were asleep. When he was a little older, he was found riding his tricycle in the driveway at 4:00 A.M. one morning with only the garage light to guide him. Ricky seemed accident prone as a toddler and has always been seen as "a talker," easily engaging even strangers in conversation. Ricky's grandmother often remarked on the similarity between Ricky and his father at the same age.

Ricky, unlike Amy, does not have oppositional defiant disorder. Yet like many ADHD children, Ricky's self-esteem has begun to decline as he chronically underperforms at school and increasingly gets into trouble with other children. The unyielding and unsympathetic view of Ricky's teacher seems to have contributed to this decline in self-image and certainly makes for a more conflict-filled school day. That this has led him to the point of being depressed is also not uncommon for ADHD children, although his statements about harming himself at such a young age are extreme for most children with ADHD.

If Ricky had been a child in the 1920s to 1940s in this country, he might have been labeled as having "restlessness syndrome" or "organic drivenness," terms in use in scientific journals at the time. He might even have been diagnosed as having a "postencephalitic behavior disorder" if he had survived a recent serious infection of the nervous system (encephalitis). Some children with Ricky's pattern of behavior were coming to be known as having "brain-injured child syndrome" because injuries to the brain from either disease or trauma could cause children to act this way. Therefore, any child who behaved like this, even if there was no obvious history of a brain injury, was thought of as having a brain-injury syndrome.

Ricky might have been placed in a special classroom where very little extra stimulation was available except for the material related to the lesson being taught. The teachers might have worn rather dull-colored clothing and no jewelry and the classroom kept undecorated to minimize distractions, seen as the greatest problem for children with the brain-injured syndrome. But these classrooms were rare and quite unusual for their time, and as a result, were not available to most families with children like Ricky.

If Ricky had been treated at the Emma Pendleton Bradley home for children in Providence, Rhode Island, in 1936–1938, he might have been tried on a stimulant medication known as d-amphetamine, or Dexedrine (its trade name), being tested with the behavior-problem child by Dr. William Bradley. Note would have been made of the dramatic improvement in behavior and the ability to complete schoolwork that this medication produced. Most likely, however, Ricky would not have had access to this unusual treatment, nor would he have been diagnosed with any psychological disorder. Ricky's parents might have been advised that he was just "all boy" and would likely outgrow the behaviors. When his problems persisted into adolescence, he would have been viewed as a troublemaker or social misfit and probably would have dropped out of school as soon as possible. Onlookers likely would have judged him a young adult lacking in "character," for which his parents would undoubtedly be blamed.

Sandy: Doing Well with Lots of Help

Sandy is a 15-year-old in 10th grade at a small private school for children with learning difficulties. Her parents, Frances and John, placed her there when she began failing in public school years ago despite having above-average intelligence and no signs of a learning disorder. Her greatest problems have always been inability to concentrate on her schoolwork and to apply persistent effort to boring but necessary tasks. She can rarely complete her high school assignments without assistance yet usually knows the answers or the correct steps to get the problem solved. What others seem to provide for Sandy is some external structure, guidance, and discipline. Although she is somewhat restless, her activity level has improved considerably since she was a young child and is now limited primarily to moving her feet back and forth while she is seated, tapping her fingers or pencil while she works, and shifting her posture frequently.

Sandy's schoolwork is often poorly organized, and her notebook is an organizational disaster. She often comes to class without something critical to the classwork, such as pencils, the course text, or her lab equipment. When her many errors in homework are pointed out to her, however, she can quickly say what is wrong with them. Her teachers and parents have tried using daily assignment notebooks and behavior rating cards to support her school performance, with limited and temporary success. In class she typically raises her hand and then blurts out an answer, frequently the wrong answer. Her teachers, nevertheless, enjoy her spontaneity and view her as a bit immature, scattered, and unfocused.

Sandy's problems have existed since at least kindergarten and probably longer. Throughout her schooling, teachers have complained about her inattentive and impulsive style and her poor follow-through on her assignments. Yet she has always had friends, been well liked and included in other children's activities, and had no discipline problems. She has been tested three times by various psychologists and school learning specialists and found to be at the 75th percentile in intelligence and average or better in all academic skills. Her handwriting is often noted to be poor and sluggish, however, and her fine motor coordination has been mildly delayed compared to other children.

Although Sandy gets along well with her parents and siblings, they have all shown academic accomplishments well beyond hers. All of her siblings as well as both her parents are college educated and see this as a necessity for Sandy as well. Sandy's self-esteem is somewhat low, and she is periodically demoralized by her difficulties. She fears that she will continue to disappoint her family and is highly frustrated over what she can do to improve. Sandy represents that rare ADHD child who has gotten into adolescence relatively unscathed by the impact of the disorder. I believe this is because it has had its chief impact on her schooling rather than on her social and family life, because she has had a number of understanding teachers along the way who have tried to help her, and because her parents have tried to protect and assist her as much as possible, including moving her into a private school when the need arose. Not to be overlooked, however, is Sandy's own pleasant disposition, which may have caused others to forgive her the problems she had with organization and completion of schoolwork and which may have allowed her to rebound quickly from any social criticism received. The power of close friendships to help buffer someone like Sandy also cannot be overlooked. Finally, the fact that she is above average in intelligence may have assisted her in finding more socially appropriate ways to cope with difficulties she has faced in school. Much research exists to show that high intelligence predicts a better academic outcome in children with ADHD, just as it does in non-ADHD children.

If Sandy had been in school between the 1950s and 1970s, she might have been diagnosed as having minimal brain damage or minimal brain dysfunction, terms used in the clinical professional journals at that time. These terms came into use because many felt the term *brain-injured child syndrome* was being misused. To appease these critics while still focusing professional attention on a problem in the brain as causing the disorder, the term *minimal brain dysfunction* (or *MBD*) was coined. In the 1960s, the term *hyperactive child syndrome* or *hyperkinetic reaction of childhood* might have been used instead to describe children like Sandy, since it captured one obvious facet of their behavior problems—their incessant movement and restlessness. At about this time, the use of stimulant medication, such as Dexedrine or the new drug Ritalin (methylphenidate), would have been increasingly common, though not as widespread as today. Most likely, if Sandy had been taken for professional help, her parents might have been made to feel to blame for her problems, and she might have received a long-term course of play therapy or psychotherapy to explore what then was thought to be the deep-seated emotional problems giving rise to her "symptoms." Like Ricky, Sandy might have stayed in school only until her early adolescence, dropping out when it became simply too difficult or aversive for her to stay any longer. She might even have been more likely to drift into the 1960s counterculture, where her behavioral problems may even have been viewed positively, reflecting the "free-spirit" attitude of the times.

Brad: A Parent's Puzzle

Brad is a 12-year-old in the sixth grade who consistently begins the school year with excellent grades and acceptable classroom behavior and gradually declines over the fall and winter to Cs and Ds and disruptive classroom behavior. Several times he has come close to having to repeat a grade, but his teachers have always given him the benefit of the doubt because of his above-average intellect and academic achievement skills. At school Brad is restless and hyperactive, concentrates poorly on work, and talks excessively. He is careless in his schoolwork and disruptive at his desk. Consequently, he demands a lot of the teacher's time and attention and is sent to the office once every few weeks. He complains to his parents and teachers that schoolwork is boring and often questions its relevance to what he claims he wants to do as an adult, which is to be a police detective.

Brad's parents noticed that his activity level and attention span were different from those of other children when he was about three or four years old. He was always racing around from one play activity to another, into everything that aroused his curiosity. His mischief included pouring dishwashing detergent into the ventilation grate on his father's new stereo amplifier and decorating the family's new sofa with Hershey's chocolate syrup. He was also known to take apart anything mechanical just to see how it worked—clocks, small appliances such as a Dustbuster, and many toys. He would lose pieces in the process so that most things could never be returned to working order.

At age five, Brad began to argue with his parents over being told to clean up his toys, take a bath, go to church, or stay out of his sister's room. As he grew older, Brad began teasing other children, and gradually they stopped coming over to play or inviting him to their homes. Despite frequent reminders immediately before he began to play with someone not to tease and to control his notorious temper, it would not be long before Brad would come whining to his parents about what the other child was doing that "wasn't fair," or the other child would leave abruptly to go home without much of an explanation. At one point Brad's parents placed him in a summer camp for the advancement of social skills, but he did not seem to carry over any of those skills into his life at home.

Like Amy, Brad's problems are relatively typical of children with ADHD. Unlike the other children described here, however, Brad's ADHD affected his schoolwork episodically rather than more continuously. Brad's unusual pattern may stem from his intelligence, which enabled him to pick up new information at the beginning of the school year with little effort but did not suffice once the workload increased and long-term projects were assigned.

If Brad's parents had gone for professional help during the early 1980s, Brad would have been given a diagnosis similar to the term used today: attention-deficit disorder, or ADD. The treatments typically offered were similar to what are now provided, including counseling his parents on behavior modification methods to use at home, making educational adjustments in his regular classes, drawing on special education services if they were required, and even trying medication treatment, most likely with a stimulant drug such as Ritalin. Brad's parents might even have been told to watch his diet more carefully to remove any substances that contained unusually high levels of additives, artificial flavorings or colorings, preservatives, or sugar.

All of the children you have just met have ADHD. Yes, they are all different—different in their ages, sexes, families, and even in many of their problems. And had they lived in different eras, they would either not have been diagnosed with any psychological disorder or would have been labeled as something entirely different from the diagnosis we use today. Certainly their treatment by professionals would have differed substantially across the decades. Most, however, would not have been diagnosed or treated, and their lives would have been filled with underachievement, missed opportunities, even substance abuse and delinquent or criminal conduct. It is less clear that society's reactions to them would have changed as much. Even today, as described earlier in this chapter, people not familiar with ADHD are likely to react harshly to those with the disorder.

What Is ADHD?

To claim that ADHD is a real developmental disorder, scientists must show that (1) it arises early in child development; (2) it clearly distinguishes these children from normal children or those who do not have the disorder; (3) it is relatively pervasive or occurs across many different situations, though not necessarily all of them; (4) it affects the child's ability to function successfully in meeting the typical demands placed on children of that age; (5) it is relatively persistent over time or development; (6) it is not readily accounted for by purely environmental or social causes; (7) it is related to abnormalities in brain functioning and development; and (8) it is associated with other biological factors that can affect brain functioning or development (i.e., genetics, injuries, toxins, etc.). Addressing these scientific issues has not been easy, and only very recently has evidence for points 7 and 8 become available. It is obvious that the children just described bear out points 1 to 6, and it is safe to say that more than sufficient evidence is available from the thousands of studies on ADHD to show that it meets all of these criteria. This evidence is very compelling, and some of it is described throughout the next four chapters.

The children just described also illustrate how ADHD represents a significant impairment in the ability to inhibit behavior. In its early history as a distinctly recognizable phenomenon (about 1902), ADHD was seen as a problem in how children learn to willfully inhibit their behavior and to adhere to rules of social conduct, not simply social etiquette but fundamental morals of the time. Ironically, despite its rather judgmental tone concerning morality, the essence of this view was not wholly inaccurate and is being revisited in the view of ADHD that I present in this book. That is because one of the many problems that uninhibited behavior leads to is impairment in how well rules, instructions, and the child's internal voice or "conscience" help that child to control behavior.

Over the next few decades, clinical scientists drifted away from defining the disorder and concentrated more heavily on its possible causes. Specifying that the disorder seemed to be in the brain put terms related to brain dysfunction (such as *brain-injured child syndrome*) in favor. But when many children were found to have no underlying brain damage, the term was softened somewhat to *minimal brain dysfunction,* which still implied that something in the brain was awry. Later, clinical research returned to seeking a better description of the behavioral problems. This focus on behaviors such as hyperactivity led to the disorder being called *hyperactive child syndrome.* The concept was then widened in the 1970s to recognize that deficits in impulse control and sustained attention were equally problematic for those with ADHD. Research subsequently shifted away from studies of activity level to studies on the nature of attention, its different types, and which types might be involved in the disorder.

At this point the disorder was renamed *attention deficit disorder* (with or without hyperactivity). As clinical research advanced, it became clear that hyperactivity and the impulsiveness seen in these children were highly related to each other, suggesting that they formed a single problem of poor inhibitory control. In addition, research increasingly showed that this problem was as important as the problems with attention in distinguishing ADHD from other childhood disorders. Consequently the term was amended slightly in 1987 to *attention-deficit hyperactivity disorder,* its current name (there is now a slash between "deficit" and "hyperactivity" as well).

It is important to understand the thinking about ADHD that has prevailed among many scientists and clinical professionals over the last 7 to 15 years because it is the point of view you are most likely to encounter now if you seek professional help for your child. So we will take a closer look at it in the sections that follow. Keep in mind, however, that even this view can stand to be modified to bring it into line with the latest evidence about ADHD emerging from both the behavioral and the neurosciences.

Today most clinical professionals—physicians, psychologists, psychiatrists, and others—believe that ADHD consists of three primary problems in a person's ability to control behavior: difficulties in sustained attention, impulse control or inhibition, and excessive activity. Other professionals (myself included) recognize that those with ADHD have two additional problems: difficulties following rules and instructions and excessive variability in their responses to situations— particularly doing work. I believe that all of these symptoms are associated with a primary deficit in inhibiting behavior that is the hallmark of ADHD. Clinical scientists in other countries have also reached this opinion recently.

Difficulty Sustaining Attention

Parents and teachers often describe their ADHD children in these ways:

"My child doesn't seem to listen."
"My child fails to finish assigned tasks."
"My son daydreams."
"My daughter often loses things."
"My child can't concentrate and is easily distracted."
"My son can't seem to work independently of supervision."
"My daughter requires more redirection."
"He shifts from one uncompleted activity to another."
"She is often confused or seems to be in a fog."

All of these refer to problems with paying attention and concentrating.

ADHD is thought to involve a significant difficulty with sustained attention, attention span, or persistence of effort. In short, people with ADHD have trouble sticking with things for as long as others. They struggle, sometimes mightily, to sustain their attention to activities that are longer than usual, especially those that are boring, repetitious, or tedious. Uninteresting school assignments, lengthy household chores, and long lectures are troublesome, as are reading lengthy, uninteresting works, paying attention to explanations of uninteresting subjects, and finishing extended projects. Our research tells us that although children with ADHD have a shorter attention span for much of what they are asked to do, it is keeping their attention on something over long periods of time that is the most difficult part of paying attention for children with ADHD.

Unfortunately, as children grow up, we expect them to be able to do these things even if they are boring or effortful. The older they become, the more they should be able to do necessary but uninteresting tasks with little or no assistance.

Those with ADHD will lag behind others in this ability, perhaps by as much as 30% or more. That means that a 10-year-old ADHD child, for instance, may have the attention span of a 7-year-old normal child. This will require that others step in to help guide, supervise, and structure their work and behavior for them. So it is easy to see how conflicts could arise frequently between children with ADHD and their parents and teachers.

More than a hundred studies have now measured the attention problems of children with ADHD, and in the vast majority, the ADHD children were found to spend less time paying attention to what they were asked to do than the children in the study who did not have ADHD. For instance, in 1976 I studied 36 boys, half diagnosed as hyperactive (they now would be called ADHD) and half not hyperactive. I asked them to perform a variety of activities in a clinic playroom at the Department of Psychology at Bowling Green State University in Ohio. One activity the boys were required to do was to wait in a playroom for six minutes by themselves before I came to take them to do some other tasks. Toys were available for play. I had placed thin black lines on the floor to form a grid or checkerboard to measure their activity by counting how many lines they crossed as they walked (or ran!) about the room. Through a one-way mirror, I observed and recorded the number of different toys they played with and how much time they spent playing with each toy. The ADHD boys, I discovered, played with three times as many toys as the other boys and spent 50% less time playing with each toy.

I then took the boys to another room and asked them to sit and watch a short movie about a make-believe creature. I told them that I would ask questions about the movie when I returned. While they were watching the movie, I found that the hyperactive boys spent nearly twice as much time looking away from it as the non-ADHD boys. The hyperactive boys also answered 25% fewer questions correctly than did the nonhyperactive boys when I quizzed them afterward. These and other measures I took during this experiment clearly showed that the ADHD boys paid less attention to what they were doing. Many other researchers have found similar results using a variety of procedures.

Filtering Information Is Not a Problem

Interestingly, our research also shows that ADHD children do not have trouble filtering information—distinguishing the important from the irrelevant in what they are asked to attend to. They seem to pay attention to the same things that non-ADHD children would when asked to look at or listen to something. It's just that children with ADHD cannot sustain this effort for as long as other children. They look away from the task more frequently than others. They are also more readily drawn to more rewarding activities. So ADHD children are not really overwhelmed by information or stimulation, as scientists believed in the 1950s. Instead, they cannot persist in their effort and attention and find themselves being drawn away by anything that might be more stimulating or interesting.

Are ADHD Children More Distractible Than Non-ADHD Children?

Scientists are not sure. Parents and teachers say they are, but distractions created in controlled experiments do not seem to draw ADHD children away from their work any more than they do non-ADHD children. I believe ADHD children have two problems that parents and teachers misinterpret as distractibility:

1. *Children with ADHD probably get bored with or lose interest in their work much faster than people without ADHD.* This leads them to go searching intentionally for something else that is more fun, interesting, stimulating, and active, even when their assigned work is not yet finished. Some scientists have argued that these children have a lower level of brain arousal and so need more stimulation to keep their brain functioning at a normal level than do people without ADHD. Other scientists have suggested that rewards lose their value faster over time for those with ADHD, meaning they are less sensitive to reinforcement. For now, the cause of this boredom simply isn't clear. What is clear is that it exists to a great enough degree that some scientists call ADHD children "stimulation seekers."

2. *ADHD children seem to be drawn to the most rewarding, fun, or reinforcing aspects of any situation.* Like magnets, they seem to be pulled toward these more immediately rewarding activities when there is work to be done that does not involve much reward. For instance, Drs. Steven Landau, Richard Milich, and their colleagues at the University of Kentucky studied ADHD and non-ADHD children while they were watching television. When there were no toys in the room, the ADHD children watched the television show as much as the non-ADHD children and were just as able to answer questions about what they watched even though they tended to look away from the TV set more often. However, when toys were placed in the room, the non-ADHD children continued to watch the TV program. The ADHD children were more likely to play with the toys and less likely to watch the TV program. When the program was a typical situation comedy, the ADHD children were able to answer as many questions about the show as the non-ADHD children, but when the program was educational and conveyed the information more visually than verbally, the ADHD children were less likely to answer correctly. The ADHD children were at a disadvantage only when visual attention was needed.

Why would ADHD children be drawn away by toys when non-ADHD children were not? Perhaps ADHD children simply lose interest faster. Or ADHD children may find physical activities more fun, stimulating, and rewarding than passive activities such as watching television.

Yet a third explanation comes from a study on curiosity in ADHD children conducted by former colleagues of mine at Bowling Green, Drs. Nancy Fiedler and Douglas Ullman. They found that ADHD children show more physical curiosity during their play, and so they manipulate objects more, switch from one object or toy to another more frequently, and spend less time with any particular toy or object. Non-ADHD children of the same age, however, show more verbal or intellectual curiosity. They talk aloud about the object or toy, describe a number of different things about the toy they find interesting, invent ways that the toy can be used in play, and even create stories around the toy. Thus the non-ADHD children spend more time with a particular toy given that its intellectual properties seem to interest them.

In 1980 Drs. Ronald Rosenthal and Terry Allen at Vanderbilt University showed that whether or not hyperactive children are distracted more than non-ADHD children depends ultimately on how salient or appealing the source of the distraction happens to be. For instance, if a child with ADHD finds a Nintendo GameBoy on his desk when he goes to his room to do an hour of homework, you can imagine which activity the ADHD child will be doing when you come to check on him 20 minutes later.

Drs. David Bremer and John Stern at Washington University found in a 1976 study that ADHD children were somewhat more likely than non-ADHD children to look away from a reading assignment when a telephone rang with lights flashing or an oscilloscope made patterns of unusual wavy lines on a screen in the same room. However, the groups differed much more dramatically in *how long* they were distracted by the event: an average of 18 seconds for the hyperactive children and 5 seconds for the control children. This indicated that the non-ADHD children found it much easier to return to work after a distraction than the hyperactive children. And so it may be that ADHD children are distracted from activities for longer periods of time than the non-ADHD children and do not return to work as readily as their non-ADHD peers.

A Problem with Deferred Gratification

Inability to persist with a boring task is a sign of immaturity. As children grow, they become better able to resist appealing but competing activities, though psychologists are not sure exactly what mechanism maturity brings that allows them to do so. The children may talk to themselves about the importance of the work, reminding themselves of what rewards they may earn later by completing it or what punishment may result if they don't, and find ways to make the work more intellectually interesting. Non-ADHD children also may learn to arrange consequences to reward themselves for sticking with a difficult task. We know that as children mature, delayed rewards become more attractive to them, and they are likely to value them and work for them more often rather than opting for smaller, more immediate rewards. ADHD children, in contrast, tend to opt for doing a little work now for a small but immediate reward rather than doing more work now for a much bigger reward not available until much later.

This is clearly a problem with deferred gratification, and understanding that is crucial to helping children with ADHD. If we believe that people with ADHD are simply highly distracted by everything, we will use methods that have been recommended for over 40 years—removing sources of distraction—but such attempts to help may actually make these children more restless and less attentive. Reducing stimulation actually makes it even harder for the ADHD child to sustain attention. In fact Dr. Sydney Zentall and her colleagues at Purdue University showed in several studies that adding color to the work materials that were given to ADHD children and adolescents reduced the errors they made during their work. Similarly, when Dr. Mariellen Fischer, of the Medical College of Wisconsin, and I asked adolescents to watch a computer screen while numbers were flashed on the screen at the rate of one per second and to press a button when they saw a 1 followed by a 9, children with ADHD made more errors on this boring task than non-ADHD children. When we repeated this test with distracting numbers flashing to the right and left sides of the test numbers, the ADHD teens matched the performance of the non-ADHD teens. These and many other studies tell us that adding stimulation to a task may increase the ability of ADHD children to pay attention and complete their work with fewer mistakes.

Specifically, then, we should try to increase the novelty, stimulation, or fun involved in the tasks the child with ADHD is asked to do. We might also specify that certain desirable rewards or consequences could be earned immediately by completing the activity, rather than postponing them. We could also break the activity up into smaller segments, letting the ADHD child take more frequent breaks while working.

Difficulty Controlling Impulses

Parents and teachers often describe ADHD children as "blurting out answers to questions before the questions have been finished" and "wanting what they want when they want it." Children with ADHD have a lot of trouble waiting for things. Having to take turns in a game, line up for lunch or recess at school, or just wait until some activity, like a church sermon, is over may make them restless and antsy. They might complain about the waiting and even start in on the activity they have been told to postpone. When a parent promises to eventually take them shopping or to a movie, the child may badger the parent excessively during the waiting period. This makes ADHD children appear to be constantly demanding and very self-centered. So the second problem seen in ADHD is a decreased ability to inhibit behavior or to show impulse control. Those with ADHD have considerable problems with holding back their initial response to a situation so as to think before they finally act. They often blurt out comments that they would not likely have made had they thought first. They also respond to what others say or do to them on impulse, sometimes emotionally, and wind up being judged critically for doing so. They may act quickly on an idea that comes into their mind without considering that they were in the middle of doing something else that should be finished first. They are excessive and loud talkers, often monopolizing conversations.

This behavior is often viewed as rude and insensitive and has negative consequences in both the social and educational arenas. Teachers note that ADHD children often "blurt out comments without raising their hands" in class and "start assignments or tests without reading the directions carefully." They frequently are described as "not sharing" what they have with others and of "taking things they want that don't belong to them."

Knowing that ADHD children already have trouble sustaining attention, imagine how their inability to resist impulses—such as the impulse to abandon a boring task—would exacerbate their problems with working longer for later, larger rewards. In 1986 Dr. Mark Rapport and his colleagues at the University of Rhode Island gave a group of 16 ADHD children and 16 control children some math work to do. When the children were told they would receive a small toy immediately for completing a small number of arithmetic problems, the groups completed the same number of problems. Then the children were given a choice. They could get a small toy for doing a small amount of work or do larger amounts of work for a much larger and more valuable toy. But they would not get the bigger toy until two days later. Under these conditions, more of the ADHD children chose the small, immediate reward for little work, whereas the control children were more likely to choose the larger, deferred reward for more work.

Dr. Susan Campbell and her colleagues at the University of Pittsburgh found similar results with preschool-age hyperactive children in 1982. They hid a small cookie under one of three cups while the children watched. The children were then required to wait until the experimenter rang a bell before they could pick up the cup and eat the cookie. The procedure was repeated for six trials with the waiting period varying between 5 and 45 seconds. The hyperactive children made many more impulsive choices, taking and eating the cookie before the experimenter rang the bell, than did the control children.

Taking Shortcuts

Problems with attention and impulse control also manifest themselves in the shortcuts that ADHD children are notorious for taking in their work. They apply the least amount of effort and take the least amount of time to perform boring or unpleasant tasks.

Taking Too Many Risks

The impulsivity seen in ADHD may also show up in greater risk taking. Failing to consider in advance the harm that could follow an action may explain why people with ADHD—particularly ADHD children, some of whom are also defiant and oppositional—are more accident-prone than others. It is not that ADHD children do not care about what will happen. It *is* that they simply do not think ahead about likely consequences. Constantly "taking the bull by the horns," they are then surprised by the disasters that others foresaw clearly.

> "Our daughter wants her driver's license.
> Yet she seems so immature and distractible.
> Are ADHD kids at greater risk as drivers?"

Such shortsightedness may explain why Drs. Carolyn Hartsough and Nadine Lambert at the University of California at Berkeley found in a 1985 study that hyperactive children were more than three times as likely to have had at least four or more serious accidents than non-ADHD children. In 1988 Dr. Peter Jensen and his colleagues at the Medical College of Georgia found similarly that ADHD children were nearly twice as likely to have had traumas requiring sutures, hospitalization, or extensive/painful procedures than a group of control children. In a more recent study, my colleagues and I at the University of Massachusetts Medical Center found that teens and young adults with ADHD had four times as many auto accidents (average of 1.5 vs. 0.4) and were nearly seven times as likely to have had at least two or more auto crashes than non-ADHD teens (40% vs. 6%). The ADHD youths were four times as likely to have been at fault in the accidents (48% vs. 11%), were nearly twice as likely to have received traffic citations (78% vs. 47%), and received four times as many such citations (four vs. one) in their average of only two years of licensed driving experience. The most common citation they received was for speeding, and the second most common was for failing to obey stop signals.

Lack of impulse control could also explain why teenagers and adults with ADHD may be more likely to take risks drinking alcohol, smoking cigarettes, and using illegal substances such as marijuana. In our study of teenagers with a history of hyperactivity mentioned earlier, Dr. Mariellen Fischer and I found that nearly 50% of hyperactive teens in our study had already used cigarettes by age 14 to 15 compared to 27% of the control teens; 40% of the hyperactive teens had used alcohol compared to only 22% of the control teens; and 17% had tried marijuana compared to only 5% of the teens with no history of hyperactivity.

Money Management Problems

The impulsiveness seen in ADHD may also explain why teenagers and young adults with ADHD have greater difficulties with managing money and credit. They buy things they see and want to have on impulse without much regard for whether they can really afford it now. They do not consider what consequences buying these items will have on their weekly budget or their ability to pay back the debts they already have.

Impulsive Thinking

The impulsiveness of those with ADHD apparently is not limited to their actions but also affects their thoughts. Adults with ADHD have often told us during clinical interviews that they have as much trouble with impulsive thinking as with impulsive behavior. This was demonstrated elegantly in a study by Drs. G. A. Shaw and Leonard Giambra at Georgetown College published in 1993. When college students were asked to press a button when they saw a certain target stimulus (like the 1 to 9 number pattern described earlier), the ADHD students not only pushed the button more often when they were not supposed to than did the students with no history of ADHD, but they also reported, when interrupted by the researchers, significantly more thoughts unrelated to the task than did the other groups of college students. This is clear evidence that those with ADHD find it harder to keep their mind on their work and to inhibit thoughts that are not related to the task at hand.

A Problem with Too Much Behavior

"Squirmy," "always up and on the go," "acts as if driven by a motor," "climbs excessively," "can't sit still," "talks excessively," "often hums or makes odd noises"—are these descriptions familiar? They define the excessive movement or hyperactivity that is a third feature of ADHD. This feature may appear as restlessness, fidgetiness, unnecessary pacing, or other movement and also as excessive talking. It is difficult behavior to ignore, yet it is the behavior that lay observers are most skeptical about. Parents who consistently see their children shifting in their seats, tapping their fingers or feet, playing with nearby objects, pacing, and generally becoming quite impatient and frustrated by waiting periods know this behavior is not normal. Teachers who watch these children constantly getting out of their seats, wriggling or squirming when they should be sitting still, playing with a small toy brought from home, talking out of turn, and humming or singing to themselves when everyone else is quiet know that this behavior is not typical of most children. Yet others often persist in their opinions that parents and teachers are simply "making it up" or being "overly sensitive" about otherwise normal behavior.

ADHD Children Are Hyperactive

The fact that ADHD children really are more active than other children under many different circumstances was demonstrated beautifully in a study published in 1983 by Drs. Linda Porrino, Judith Rapoport, and their colleagues at the National Institute of Mental Health in Bethesda, Maryland. The children in the study wore a special mechanical device that monitors activity or movement every day, all day for one week as they went about their normal daily activities. The scientists found that the boys with hyperactivity (ADHD) were significantly more active than control boys regardless of the time of day, including during weekends and while sleeping. The greatest differences between the groups of boys occurred in school situations.

In my own early studies of hyperactive children, published in 1976 and 1978, I determined that hyperactive children were moving about a room nearly eight times as often as control children, that their arm motions were more than twice those of the non-ADHD children, that their leg movements were nearly four times those of the control children, and that they were more than three times as restless while watching a short movie on TV (as described earlier) and more than four times as fidgety and wiggly during psychological tests while seated at a table.

"We have a lot of problems getting our son
to bed at night. What can we do?"

Studies such as these mentioned directly above have shown clearly
that ADHD children move around far too much relative to others of their
age in similar circumstances, even during sleep. But it is the fact that
ADHD children do not regulate or manage their activity level to meet
the demands of the moment that causes them the most trouble. For instance, children with ADHD may have much trouble lowering their activity level as they move from the fast-paced, active play at recess on the
playground to the restrained, quiet activity in the classroom. At these
times, others may see them as loud, unrestrained, boisterous, rowdy, and
immature. My early studies using a playroom just described showed that
when the boys were told to stay in one corner at one table and play only
with the toys on that table, the hyperactive boys reduced their activity
level much less than the non-ADHD boys. In a 1983 study I published
with Drs. Charles Cunningham and Jennifer Karlsson, audiotaped conversations of hyperactive children with their mothers showed that the
hyperactive children talked about 20% more than the control children.
A surprise to us at the time was that the mothers of the hyperactive children also talked more than the mothers of the control children. We believed that the greater speech of the mothers of hyperactive children was
a response to the excessive talking of their children. We proved this by
giving the hyperactive children the stimulant drug Ritalin and found an
immediate 30% reduction in the speech of the hyperactive children. The
speech level of their mothers was also immediately reduced as well.

ADHD Children Are Also Hyperresponsive

What is most important to understand about ADHD children is not simply that they move about too much—it is that they *behave too much*. They
are much more likely to respond to the things around them in any situation than are non-ADHD children of the same age. Their behavior occurs too quickly, too forcefully, and too easily in situations where other
children would have been more inhibited. Thus a better term for describing
ADHD children is *hyperresponsive*. While such children are certainly more
active than non-ADHD children, the term *hyperactive* misses the point.
Their greater activity level really seems, in large part, to be a by-product
of their greater rate of behaving or responding in a given situation.

*This means that the hyperactivity and the impulsiveness seen in ADHD
children are part of the same underlying problem—a problem with inhibiting
behavior.* I believe that much of their problem with sustaining attention
is due to their poor inhibition as well. As the great psychologist William
James wrote in 1898, it is not possible for humans to pay attention to
any one thing for more than a few seconds. All of us keep adjusting our

eyes and our bodies as we attend to things and often look away from things briefly before returning to them. It is this continual redirection of effort back to the task while resisting the urge to break off our attending to the task to do something else that creates our sustained attention. What those with ADHD have trouble with is not so much that they look away more than those without ADHD (although they do that too); it is that they have much more trouble returning to attend to the task they were doing before their attention was broken. Because the ability to keep returning attention to something requires that a person also be able to inhibit urges or tendencies to do other things, the problem with sustained attention in those with ADHD may actually be part of their problem with inhibiting responses to things around them. So they look away more than others and fail to resist the temptation to leave an uninteresting task for something more interesting and stimulating to do. Those with ADHD find it much more difficult to resist distracting temptations and to sustain this type of inhibition over urges to do other things while they are working on a lengthy task. They also find that they are less likely to return to the task they were working on once they have been interrupted, since they cannot as easily inhibit the desire to respond to other things around them that may be more attractive or compelling. Hence sustained attention is also sustained inhibition, and it is the problem with inhibition that may be at the root of the attention problems in ADHD.

Only recently have many scientists come to believe that, at its core, ADHD is primarily a problem of poor inhibition of behavior. Ultimately the disorder may be renamed to reflect this new view, perhaps as *behavioral inhibition disorder*, or *BID*.

Difficulty Following Instructions

Those with ADHD are also said to suffer from an inability to follow through on instructions and adhere to rules as well as others of their age. Psychologists call this *rule-governed behavior*—when our behavior is controlled more by directions and instructions than by what is actually happening around us. The child with ADHD frequently ends up being "off-task" or engaging in activities unrelated to what he or she has been told to do. For instance, the teacher gives a child with ADHD the simple instruction to return to her seat and start her math assignment. The child may start down the aisle, only to dawdle along the way, poke at other children, talk to others, and slowly wander to her desk, usually taking the long way to get there. Once at her desk, the ADHD child may take out a pencil and begin to draw pictures of flowers on paper or on her math assignment, to stare out the window at other children playing, or to take a toy from her pocket and play with it. The instruction given to the child in this case has clearly had little impact on controlling the child's behavior.

> "My daughter won't do anything I ask.
> How can I get her to listen to me?"

This problem of following through on rules or instructions was made all the more evident to me when I first began studying the parent–child interactions of ADHD children close to 20 years ago with Dr. Charles Cunningham while both of us were in training at the Oregon Health Sciences University. Dr. Cunningham and I evaluated the interactions of a group of hyperactive children with their parents and compared these interactions to a group of control children with their parents. Each parent–child pair was required first to play together in a playroom with toys just as they might do at home. After this period, we gave the parent a list of commands to give the child to obey, such as to pick up the toys and put them back on the shelves. We observed these interactions from behind a one-way mirror and recorded how the parents and children interacted. We found that the hyperactive children were less compliant with their parents' instructions than the control children and that this was especially apparent during the work period. For now, suffice it to say that this finding has been confirmed in many other studies done more recently.

One particularly revealing study, conducted by Drs. Rolf Jacob, K. Daniel O'Leary, and Carl Rosenblad in 1978 at the State University of New York at Stony Brook, examined groups of hyperactive and control children in two types of classroom arrangements. In one arrangement the class was run in a rather informal way with the children being given choices as to what activities they would do during class work periods. Little structure was provided by the teacher except to encourage the children to select what they were going to do with their time from a number of academic activities. Then they changed the classroom procedures to resemble those of a more traditional, formal classroom. The teacher directed the children's academic work and either assigned them math or ditto worksheets or required them to listen to a lesson. The behavior of the hyperactive and nonhyperactive children did not differ very much in the informal classroom arrangement, but when the class arrangement changed to a more formal style, the control children were able to reduce their overall level of activity and inattentiveness and conform their behavior to this more restricted type of situation, and the hyperactive children were much less able to do so.

The result of this inattentiveness is that others frequently have to remind those with ADHD of what they are supposed to be doing. Those who supervise the child with ADHD end up frustrated and angry. Ultimately the ADHD child may fail, be retained in a grade, and eventually drop out. The adult with ADHD may even be fired or fail to get a desired promotion. The general impression left with others, at best, is that the person with ADHD is less mature and lacks self-discipline and organization. At worst, it implies that the person with ADHD is intentionally lazy, unmotivated, and doesn't care or is intentionally trying to avoid his responsibilities.

I believe that these difficulties with following rules and directions are related to the underlying problem with impulsiveness. It is less clear whether the impulsiveness creates the problem by disrupting the rule following when urges to switch to competing activities arise or the impulsiveness stems from an impaired ability of language to guide and control or govern behavior. I have struggled with this dilemma for over a decade, never really being confident which came first, the poorly inhibited behavior or the diminished control of behavior by language, specifically rules or directions. Ample research exists to show that verbal ability and impulsiveness are related. Individuals with better-developed language and verbal skills are usually much less impulsive and more reflective in performing tasks than those with less well-developed verbal skills. The two problems are linked because young children learn to talk to themselves as one means of controlling their own behavior so as to be less impulsive, as mentioned earlier. Talking to themselves helps them inhibit initial urges to respond a certain way. It also allows time for the children to talk over with themselves certain details of the task and various options for responding before choosing which is the best response. We often refer to this as thinking or reflection. In either case, it is the use of self-directed speech that is principally involved in helping to control the children's behavior.

This problem of using self-directed speech to help inhibit behavior was clearly demonstrated in a study by my good friend Dr. Michael Gordon at the Upstate Medical Center in Syracuse, New York. Dr. Gordon was studying the ability of hyperactive and control children to inhibit their responding to a task and learn to wait. He designed a small computer for this purpose and told the children to sit in front of the computer, press the button, and then wait a while before pressing it again. They earned a point only if they waited 6 seconds or more. The points could be cashed in for M & M's at the end of the experiment. The children were not told how long to wait each time before pressing the button, so they had to discover that interval through learning. Dr. Gordon found that the hyperactive children pressed the button much more often than the control children and were not as able to wait for the correct interval of time to pass. What was of more interest, however, was that while they were waiting for the time to pass before pressing the button, over 80% of the control children talked to themselves, counted, or gave themselves verbal instructions and strategies to help pass the time. The hyperactive children, by contrast, sang, hit the sides of the box, spun the button on the box, swung their legs a certain number of times, ran around the table, tapped their foot 16 times, stomped their foot 9 or 10 times, and the like. Only 30% of them reported the use of some verbal strategy like that used by the control children. The more the children used such physical behavior to help pass the time delay, the more hyperactive they were rated by their parents on a behavior rating scale. In other words, the non-ADHD children were more likely to use verbal and thinking tactics to help them inhibit their behavior and wait while hyperactive children used more physical activity.

As you will see in Chapter 2, I now believe that the problem with inhibiting responses in ADHD children arises first, interfering with the later development of the use of self-directed speech for self-control. However, because in later years they are not relying as much on such self-speech to help control themselves, ADHD children are likely to be even more impulsive than non-ADHD children. So the poor impulse control, though it arises first, prevents ADHD children from using self-speech as effectively as non-ADHD children. This then hinders them further in their development of impulse control, self-control, and the use of plans and goals to guide their behavior.

Doing Work Inconsistently

A fifth and final symptom I see in those with ADHD is inconsistent work. Because most ADHD children are of average or greater intelligence, their inability to produce consistently acceptable work often perplexes those around them. On some days, at certain times, these children seem able to complete their assigned work easily, without help. At other times or on other days, they finish little if any of their work and may not get much done even with close supervision. Over time, this erratic pattern creates the impression that the person with ADHD is just lazy. As a child psychiatrist once said, "ADHD children do well in school twice and we hold it against them the rest of their life." Those times when ADHD children completed their work unassisted misleads people into thinking they have no real problems or disabilities. But the problem here is *not that they cannot do the work but that they cannot maintain this consistent pattern of work productivity the way others can.* This once led Dr. Marcel Kinsbourne, a renowned child neurologist, to characterize ADHD as VD, or variability disease.

Scientists are not sure why those with ADHD show this rather striking pattern of inconsistency in their behavior and especially in their productivity. We do know that using our language and self-directed speech to guide us leads to much greater consistency in the way we act and work. Those with ADHD, as we have discussed, are influenced more by the moment than by a preconceived rule or plan. Consequently, their work will be highly variable, depending on the ever-changing conditions that day.

It is quite possible that inconsistent work productivity is a by-product of the other symptoms described already, particularly of the core impairment of impulse control. Consistent work productivity demands the ability to inhibit impulses to engage in other, more immediately fun or rewarding activities, so the more limited and erratic one's impulse control is, the more variable will be his or her work productivity. Productivity will depend more on the circumstances of the immediate situation than being dependent on self-control and willpower.

Where Is My Child's Self-Control?: New View of ADHD

As this chapter has shown, our ability to stop, think, inhibit, plan, and then act as well as to sustain our actions in the face of distraction—the very things we do to help control us—are a problem for children with ADHD. Current scientific research, however, suggests that all of these problems may stem from a core deficit in behavioral inhibition—a developmental delay in impulse control. Scientists sometimes call this problem *disinhibition,* which means that behavior is released from inhibition under circumstances where others would normally inhibit such conduct. It is my considered opinion that all of the five primary characteristics of ADHD reflect a serious problem with inhibiting behavior. This leads to a serious problem with self-control or the way in which our self acts as an executive over our patterns of behavior. The self in an ADHD child, in a sense, is not controlling, regulating, or executing behavior as well as it does in others. So the problems of those with ADHD do not stem from a lack of skill but from a lack of self-control. This means that *ADHD is not a problem with knowing what to do; it is a problem with doing what you know.*

Unfortunately, most people believe that our self-discipline, self-control, and willpower are entirely at our own command. Therefore children without self-control are viewed either as not wanting to control themselves (they are "bad seeds") or as not having learned to control themselves (they are viewed as simply "undisciplined" by their parents). Frankly, this view is out of date. Science is showing us that there are neurological (brain) factors that contribute to self-control and our willpower along with our learning and upbringing. And when these brain systems are functioning improperly or become damaged, normal levels of self-control and willpower are impossible. Those with ADHD are such people. They have a biologically based problem with self-control and the execution of their willpower. This new view is the subject of Chapter 2.

To study ADHD is to gain a glimpse of the will itself and how it comes to be so powerful as an agent in controlling ourselves. This power to show self-control for the sake of directing behavior toward the future is uniquely human; no other animal has it. Those with ADHD, I believe, have a developmental impairment in this power. As a result, *to have ADHD is to have a will disabled and consequently a future in doubt.* This is what makes you as a parent so concerned and alarmed about what you see going astray in your child's behavioral and social development. It may be why you are reading this book.

CHAPTER 2

A New Theory about ADHD

ADHD is probably the best studied of all psychological disorders of childhood. Still, our understanding of the psychology of ADHD is far from complete. While we now know that ADHD represents a problem in the manner in which children learn to control their impulses and regulate their own behavior, these problems are not perfectly well defined.

How do children develop self-control? What are the behavioral or psychological mechanisms and processes that underlie our ability to control our own behavior better than any other species? And which of these processes is impaired or delayed in ADHD? As mentioned in Chapter 1, scientific studies have shown that the problems associated with ADHD can be reduced to poor attention, impulsiveness, and hyperactivity and that the last two seem to be part of the same problem—impairment of behavioral inhibition. Since we have also learned that problems with attention may be part of childhood psychological disorders besides ADHD, it is the problem with behavioral inhibition that seems to be unique to ADHD—its hallmark symptom.

Even what we call problems with attention seem to be problems with inhibiting behavior—inhibiting the urge to do something the child would rather be doing than the task at hand. So when we say that ADHD children have a short attention span, we really mean they have a short interest span. Similarly, when non-ADHD children mature and become better at inhibiting the urge to shift to more rewarding or interesting activities, we say they have acquired a longer attention span, but what we should say is that they have a more developed ability to restrain their impulses and to stay with an instruction. ADHD children are like younger normal children. Their problem does not seem to be with paying attention as much as with sustaining inhibition. So it seems that all three problems thought to be the primary symptoms of ADHD—inattention, impulsiveness, and hyperactivity—can be reduced to a delay in the development of inhibition of behavior.

Everything Comes to Those Who Can Wait

I am not the first scientist to argue that the major problems of ADHD children stem from a fundamental deficit in their ability to inhibit behavior. The English physician Dr. George Still made this point in 1902. Dr. Herbert Quay of the University of Miami has been making this point in his scientific writing since 1986, and more recently so have Drs. Jaap van der Meere and Joseph Sergeant in The Netherlands and Dr. Edward Sonuga-Barke and his colleagues in London. What these scientists have not done, however, is explain how this problem with inhibition leads to the many impairments we find in the academic, social, occupational, mental, language, and emotional domains. Doing so would only strengthen the theory that impaired inhibition is at the root of ADHD. I believe that this can now be done.

The commonly held view of ADHD as a problem with attention and hyperactivity has, over the years, failed to explain many of the findings about ADHD children—what I call "orphan" findings since they have no "parent" theory to account for them. For instance:

- We know that ADHD children do not benefit from warnings about what is going to happen later. They seem to base their behavior on what is at hand rather than on information about future events. How is this explained by the fact that they are impulsive?
- Recent studies have also found that the speech that children with ADHD typically use in talking to themselves while working or playing is less mature than that of other children. Why? What does that have to do with their not being able to inhibit their behavior?
- Dr. Sydney Zentall and her colleagues at Purdue University have found that ADHD children do not do mental arithmetic as fast or as well as other children, despite the fact that they have no problem understanding math. How is this deficiency explained by their immature inhibition?
- Drs. Carol Whalen and Barbara Henker at the University of California at Irvine have found that when ADHD children play or work with other children on a task, the information they communicate to others is less organized, less mature, and less helpful in getting the activity done than in non-ADHD children of the same age. Also, Dr. Stephen Hinshaw and his students recently discovered that ADHD children are less mature in their moral reasoning. Again, how are these problems explained by simply saying that ADHD represents a deficit in attention or inhibition?

These are the questions that must be answered if we are to have a more complete account of ADHD.

My belief that all of these problems can stem from a problem with inhibiting behavior rests on my recent discovery of a theory advanced more than 25 years ago by Dr. Jacob Bronowski, the late philosopher, physicist, and mathematician and author of *The Ascent of Man,* the critically acclaimed book and public television series from the late 1970s. In a brief yet profound essay, Dr. Bronowski discussed how our language came to differ so dramatically from the types of social communication or language used by other animals, especially our relatives, the primates. Dr. Bronowski proposed that everything that makes our language unique (and us human) flowed from the evolution of the simple capacity to impose a delay between a signal, a message, or an event that we experience and our reaction or response to it.

We have the ability to wait for far longer periods of time than other species before responding. This power to wait stems from our greater ability to inhibit immediate urges to respond, and because inhibition takes effort, waiting is not a passive act. Being able to inhibit our immediate urges to respond and instead wait for a while, said Dr. Bronowski, enables us to (1) separate emotion from information in our evaluation of events, (2) create a sense of the past and from it a sense of the future, (3) talk to ourselves and use such speech to control our own behavior, and (4) break incoming information or messages into parts and then recombine those parts into new outgoing messages or responses (analysis and synthesis). If ADHD is a problem with a person's ability to inhibit responses, then according to Bronowski's theory, we might expect someone with ADHD to have problems with these four mental abilities.

Separating Facts from Feelings

Being able to inhibit our urges to respond and to wait gives our brain time to split incoming information into two parts: the personal meaning of the event (our feelings or emotional reactions) and the information or content of the event. We can then deal with the content objectively without introducing a personal bias into our reaction based on our emotions. We certainly do not do this all the time, but we have the power to do it and realize that exercising this ability enables us to deal effectively with a given situation. This is why we tell our children to count to ten before reacting to an upset: It gives them time to settle down and begin to evaluate what has happened more rationally and objectively.

We know from personal experience that responding with emotional behavior is clearly not always in our best interest. Neither is it always bad, but waiting and better evaluating what is happening to us allow us to formulate our reactions, even our emotional ones, so that they are better suited to the situation. This capacity to delay our response permits us to evaluate events more objectively, rationally, and logically as if from the standpoint of an outside, neutral witness. It gives us the power to study our world more objectively than any other species can. In fact, if we could not separate our personal feelings about information from the information itself, we could not pursue science.

This theory seems to explain why ADHD children are so emotional compared to other children. By not inhibiting their first reactions to a situation, they do not permit time to separate their feelings from the facts. They usually live to regret these impulsive and emotional reactions because the behavior drives others away, resulting in social hostility, punishment, rejection, and eventually loss of friendships. It gives them a bad reputation with teachers and coaches, strains relationships with parents and siblings, and in adults can lead to even greater conflicts at home and at work.

Their failure to inhibit their feelings as well as other children of the same age makes us see ADHD children as emotionally immature. A seven-year-old ADHD child may throw a tantrum when denied a snack just before dinner, for example. While we might accept this reaction from a four-year-old, we would expect most seven-year-olds to be able to inhibit the angry reaction for long enough to cool off and evaluate the information conveyed by Mom: the reasons for denying the snack.

Unfortunately, we cannot push that seven-year-old to the maturity we'd like to see simply by telling him or her to inhibit reactions or wait before responding. As Chapter 3 explains, the power to do so is impaired because of a problem in the brain centers responsible for inhibition. Although people with ADHD may be able to learn consciously to inhibit their behavior in certain situations, this takes a great deal of effort.

Consequently, people with ADHD will have difficulty adapting to situations that require being cool, calm, and unemotional or objective. Unfortunately, our society seems to place us in many such situations. Indeed our society highly values the ability to remain calm and rational and often rewards it with greater status, prestige, responsibility, and even income than those without such ability can expect.

There is an upside, however: Those with ADHD will be very passionate and emotional in their actions and thus may do what they do with far more personal conviction than the rest of us. Those with ADHD very well might match or surpass others in performing arts such as music or drama or in the humanities such as writing poetry or fiction, where emotional expression is advantageous. Where passionate conviction is desirable, such as in negotiation or sales, people with ADHD can shine. Combined with their talkativeness and preference for socializing over solitary work, such passion could make for very good salespeople. Remember, it is not their intellect that is impaired. Nor is their *ability* to separate emotions from information impaired. People with ADHD simply do not exercise that ability as well or as efficiently or use it to guide their behavior as much, because they respond too quickly. By not controlling their impulse to act, they do not leave time for the splitting off of facts from personal feeling.

A Sense of Past and Future

Dr. Bronowski claimed that our ability to delay responses also gives us the ability to keep an event actively alive in our mind for some time after the event has passed. That is, we are able to prolong the event or information coming into our brain through our short-term memory. This enables us to think about the event, to study it carefully, and compare it with our memory of past experiences. Doing that gives us a sense of our personal history. Such reference to the past can then guide us in understanding and responding to the events of the moment. Thus our past learning informs our current behavior. We learn from our mistakes and our successes far more effectively than any other species.

Thinking about our past also enables us to create what Dr. Bronowski called *hypothetical futures.* We make educated guesses about what will happen next because we have thought about our past and used it to construct a guess about the future. In doing so we can prepare better for those predicted events. Certainly our guesses won't always be right, but we will be better off making educated guesses than simply failing to think about the future altogether. This way we use our sense of the past to create a sense of the future. Along with that ability to recall images of the past comes our ability to manipulate and combine them, which forms our imagination. And also by recalling the past and sensing the future, we can share that sense of the future with others who have reasoned along with us; we can make plans with others and promises to them, using time as a benchmark for doing things as no other species can.

Referring backward (the past) and forward (the future) creates for us a mental window on time. During our waking hours we are almost continuously aware of this moving window of time in our consciousness. From our sense of immediately past events we are continuously inferring what is likely to happen in the immediate future. We seem to do this almost effortlessly, and so we take it for granted.

If ADHD represents an impairment in inhibiting behavior and waiting for responding as I have suggested, then Bronowski's theory predicts that people with ADHD should show a more limited sense of the past and, as a result, a more limited sense of the future. Their mental window on time should be much narrower. Anyone who has lived with someone with ADHD knows that this is in fact the case. As parents often say, children with ADHD do not seem to learn from past mistakes. Rather than not learning, I think they respond too quickly to refer to their past experiences and consider what those might teach them about the present events.

Those with ADHD will also be less prepared for the future. Because they do not see events approaching, they are likely to carom through life, from crisis to crisis. When a catastrophe strikes, they are caught off guard and react accordingly. They are far too much creatures of the moment.

The upside here is that they do not seem to be as limited by fear of the future as many of us are. We sometimes envy their almost childlike innocence, their happy-go-lucky nature, and their devil-may-care attitude about the moment. Those with ADHD may also take chances that pan out where others would hold back. Life for (and with) the person with ADHD may be more exciting as a result.

Lack of foresight can, however, have negative, even life-threatening, consequences. At the least, the effects can be socially devastating. Promises broken, appointments unmet, and deadlines missed can bring down swift, negative, and unforgiving judgment by others. Reliability is, after all, one of the defining characteristics of a responsible adult in our society. Yet adults with ADHD or with a childhood history of hyperactivity report that they have problems with money management, household organization, management of children's schedules, and working independently on the job, with a commensurately slower upward movement in their social and occupational status—all related to their diminished sense of time.

Because of the neurological deficit in the ability to inhibit behavior, people with ADHD not only do not see what lies ahead as well as others but *cannot* do so as well as others. In essence, holding them responsible for their problem with anticipating and planning for the future is like holding the deaf person responsible for not hearing us or the blind person accountable for not seeing us—it is ridiculous and serves no constructive social purpose. Yet that is exactly what our society tends to do. We respond with disbelief when told that the person with ADHD did not fully understand the consequences of his or her behavior, calling it a cop-out to avoid accepting responsibility. We label these people careless, heedless, unreliable, or risk takers and view them as immature. We hold them responsible for their seeming carelessness and punish them accordingly, sometimes severely.

No wonder so many of those with ADHD are so demoralized upon reaching adolescence or young adulthood. By then they begin to adopt society's view of themselves, holding themselves as much to blame for their failures as do others. This sense of underachievement and of failing oneself and one's family can be so serious in the adult with ADHD as to require separate psychological treatment from what may be needed to deal with their ADHD symptoms alone.

The altered sense of time in those with ADHD has several other interesting effects. First, it makes them feel as if time is passing more slowly than it actually does. This means most things seem to take longer than they expected, which is understandably frustrating. It's not surprising, then, that people with ADHD seem very impatient under many circumstances. Second, without a sense of the future, it's difficult to defer gratification. Studies that have followed ADHD children into adulthood (see Chapter 4) provide clear evidence that they are not as likely to choose pathways in life that involve immediate sacrifice for longer-term, much larger payoffs. Examples include sticking with higher education and saving money. Finally, there is some evidence that this diminished sense of the future causes those with ADHD to be less health-conscious than others. One price we pay for our sense of time is an accompanying sense of our own limited existence and eventual death. So the natural conclusion is that people with ADHD may not have the same sense of their own mortality that the rest of us have. Perhaps they are not part of the wave of increasing appreciation for the health-related consequences of our behavior.

Having less regard for the future consequences of any behavior, are ADHD individuals more likely than others to engage in deleterious habits such as overeating, lack of exercise, smoking tobacco, drinking alcohol to excess, abusing illegal substances, and driving carelessly? One indication that they may be is that follow-up studies have found teenagers and young adults with ADHD to be more likely to smoke tobacco and drink alcohol and to do so more frequently than those who do not have ADHD. They also have a greater risk for speeding tickets and traffic accidents while driving than do others of their age group, as noted in the last chapter.

Self-Directed Speech: Our Mind's Voice and Our Self-Control

A third result that comes from being able to inhibit or delay our responses is that it gives us time to talk to ourselves. Dr. Bronowski pointed out that all other species use their language to communicate with others. Only humans have developed the ability to use language to communicate with themselves as well. We see this ability developing in children. They progress from talking to others as toddlers to talking out loud to themselves while playing during their later preschool years to gradually talking to themselves subvocally so that others do not hear during the early elementary years. Finally they wind up talking to themselves in their "mind's voice" so that no one detects the self-speech at all. This is called *internalized speech*.

Internalization of speech creates the most far-reaching differences between how humans and animals use language. This is what Dr. Bronowski had to say about it:

> When language is internalized, it ceases to be only a means of social communication, and is thereby removed from the family of animal languages. It now becomes an instrument of reflection and exploration, with which the speaker constructs hypothetical messages before he chooses one to utter. In time, the sentences that he makes for himself lose the character of messages, and become experimental arrangements of the images of past experience into new and untested projections. . . . Human beings therefore live with two languages, an inner one and an outer one. They constantly experiment with the inner language and find arrangements which are more effective than those which have become standard in the outer language. In the inner language, these arrangements are information, that is cognitive [mental] assertions; and they are then transferred to the outer language in the form of practical instructions. (Bronowski, 1977, p. 118)

This ability to talk to ourselves does not occur just for the sake of keeping ourselves company. Its greatest consequence is that now our language can serve not only to inform and direct others but also to control ourselves. Psychologists have called this ability to use language to control behavior *rule-governed behavior*. When we develop plans for the future, set goals for ourselves, and then carry out our behavior according to those plans and goals, we are using rule-governed behavior. This capacity largely underlies our sense of free will. We recognize that it frees us from having our behavior controlled by the immediate and momentary circumstances that utterly control the behavior of other species. We can bring our behavior under the control of rules, instructions, plans, and goals so that our sense of the future informs our behavior in the present. We can also *invent* new rules when we have no past experience or immediately available rule to follow. When we inhibit our response and wait, we can take old rules and break them apart, combining their instructions with those of other rules to come up with entirely new combinations. We call this process *problem solving,* and we, as humans, are masters at it.

People who cannot inhibit and delay their responses to what's happening around them should be less adept or efficient at communicating rules and instructions, at using such rules and instructions to control themselves, and at devising solutions to problems encountered. Current research on ADHD does not give us enough evidence to say with certainty that these areas of self-speech and rule-governed behavior are deficient in those with ADHD. What little research there is, however, is highly consistent with this view. This may also help to explain why ADHD children talk too much compared to others—their speech is less internalized or private. Certainly those of us who work clinically with ADHD children, as well as many parents and teachers, have commented on the problems those with ADHD have with using language and rules in the service of self-control.

Dr. Stephen Hayes, a psychologist who has written extensively about the human ability to use rule-governed behavior and its consequences, has identified a number of conditions that result from our ability to use self-speech and the rule-following behavior it permits. These conditions, being diminished in people with ADHD, support the theory that deficiencies in self-speech and rule-governed behavior are part of ADHD:

1. Our behavior in a given situation should be much less variable when we are following rules than when we are being influenced or controlled by the events of the moment. As mentioned earlier, inconsistent work performance is a hallmark of ADHD.

2. A person who is following rules should be less susceptible to control by the immediate consequences or events in a situation and their momentary and potentially unpredictable changes. In ADHD, however, we constantly see people "going with the flow," apparently letting events control them rather than the other way around.

3. Where rules are in conflict with the desires of the moment, the rule is more likely to control our behavior. In other words, we are able to stick to a plan (such as a diet) even though the lure (the ice cream in the freezer) is more attractive right now. The person with ADHD is constantly being controlled by the promise of whatever seems more rewarding at the moment; he or she is more likely than most to give in to the craving for the ice cream even though it means deviating from the diet.

4. At times rule-governed behavior makes us too rigid; the rule we are following is inappropriate for the specific situation we are facing, but we follow it anyway. For example, we prepare a recipe by a cook we trust, and the dish turns out mediocre. Yet we follow it to the letter a second time because the cookbook author is widely known and must be right. It still comes out less than great—because, unknown to us, there is a typographical error in the recipe; the rules were incorrect. The person with ADHD might have tasted the recipe as he went along and modified it to his liking even though such modifications were not part of the recipe. Because he broke the rules and let his tasting of the dish (the im-

mediate feedback or consequences) guide him, the dish may turn out better. So under some circumstances, those with ADHD may actually have an advantage over the person who is too rule-governed.

5. When we follow rules, we should be able to persist at what we are doing and behave "properly" even though any rewards for doing so will be long delayed. That is, we should be able to defer gratification. For instance, a child should be able to stick to homework because the more distant rewards—the consequences of turning in the work the next day or not—are more important than the current reward of avoiding the boring assignment. The child with ADHD is more likely to get off task (off track of the rule) during the homework to pursue things that are more rewarding at the moment.

6. Finally, we should see a steady increase in the ability to use rule-governed behavior over time during a child's development into adulthood. Yet ADHD children are consistently seen as immature precisely because they are more easily controlled by momentary events and immediate consequences than others their age and because they lag behind in the ability to follow rules, to talk to themselves, to use rules to control their own behavior, and eventually to create their own rules when faced with problems.

Breaking Apart and Recombining Information

The fourth important mental ability that Dr. Bronowski attributed to our capacity to inhibit behavior and wait to respond is related to our internal use of speech and consists of two parts: (1) the ability to break information or messages we receive into parts or smaller units (analysis) and (2) the ability to recombine these parts into entirely new outgoing messages or instructions (synthesis). We do not treat instructions or information as indivisible wholes. While we may treat a sentence as one grammatical unit, we recognize that it can also be broken down into nouns, verbs, adverbs, and other parts of speech. Likewise, we know that the idea conveyed can be broken down into the objects in the idea, the actions taken with the objects, the physical nature of the objects (colors, shapes, etc.), and so on. With this fourth mental ability, we can first decompose and analyze the messages and information we receive in the same way that we can parse a sentence. Second, we can reassemble those parts in a nearly infinite number of ways and then choose the outgoing message or behavior that may be most adaptive or successful at that moment. This ability endows us with tremendous powers of problem solving, imagination, and creativity.

Unless we wait and allow enough time for it to happen, this process, called *reconstitution* by Dr. Bronowski, is unlikely to occur. If ADHD involves a deficit in the ability to inhibit behavior and wait before responding, then those with ADHD should not be as good at this process of reconstitution as people without ADHD. Very little research on this idea as it applies to ADHD is available, but what does exist seems to support its being problematic for those with ADHD. The results of psychology experiments in which children with ADHD have been required to come up with as many solutions to a problem as they can think of within a short period of time suggest that they are not able to do so as well as other children. Other studies examining the curiosity of ADHD children during play have shown that they do not evaluate or explore objects as well as other children of the same age. The results suggest that ADHD children do not analyze things they are doing into as many parts or dimensions as non-ADHD children. Such findings seem to hint that the process of reconstitution is not used as well in ADHD as in other children.

The Development of Inhibition and Its Related Mental Abilities

We do not have this tremendous power to inhibit our behavior when we are first born or during our very early development. Studies of infants indicate that it begins to develop toward the end of the first year of life but continues for many years thereafter. As we mature, we can delay our behavior in situations for increasingly longer periods of time before we finally react. Once this ability emerges, the other four mental abilities I have discussed here probably start to mature slowly.

Table 1 presents a hypothetical sequence in which these mental abilities may develop. It is intended only to illustrate a likely sequence and make the point that these abilities do not develop all at once. As you can see, each mental process develops at a different age but overlaps with the previous stages. Dr. Bronowski seems to suggest that the ability to inhibit and separate emotions from information in reacting to events may occur next after inhibition begins to develop. Perhaps it emerges during the second or third year of life. Shortly thereafter a sense of our past begins to mature and, along with it, a beginning sense of the future. The ability to talk to ourselves and to use self-speech likely develops next and slowly becomes internalized so that others no longer hear us doing this. Research on early language development has indicated that the beginnings of self-directed and internal speech probably occur between three and five years of age. The last to develop is the ability to analyze and break messages down into units and then recombine or synthesize them into entirely new ideas or outgoing messages to others. It is not clear when this ability begins to occur in child development.

In my opinion, future scientific studies of ADHD children are likely to show that they develop all four of these mental abilities somewhat later than non-ADHD children. It will likely also show that they are less proficient at them than non-ADHD children of the same age. This occurs because they cannot inhibit their behavior long enough to let these other processes take place. Fortunately for most ADHD children, some research is beginning to show that giving stimulant medication produces a temporary improvement in their ability to inhibit and wait before responding. This seems to lead to improvements in these other four mental powers such that ADHD children behave and think much like their non-ADHD age-mates while they are taking medication. They are now able to show

TABLE 1. A Possible Developmental Sequence of Inhibition and Self-Control

Age of emergence	Mental abilities
1 year	Inhibiting and delaying responses
2–4 years	Prolonging a mental image of an event Developing self-awareness Developing a sense of past (hindsight) Developing a sense of time Developing imagination Developing a sense of future (forethought) Exchanging messages with others about the future
2–4 years	Inhibiting emotions Separating feelings from facts Developing social perspective Developing objectivity Regulating emotions to serve goals Creating motivation to serve goals
3–5 years	Internalization of language Following rules given by others Following rules given by self Creating own rules Exchanging rules with others Diminishing control of behavior by events of the moment Increasing control of behavior by a sense of the future Organizing behavior toward the future
7–12 years	Taking the world apart in our mind Recombining the parts into new ideas Developing creativity

self-control and to direct their behavior toward the future and free themselves up from being controlled purely by events of the moment.

The Neurological Connection: Rethinking Our View of Will

We know that ADHD involves an impairment in the ability of the individual to inhibit responses to situations or events. That is, it is a problem of self-control. As such, the term *developmental disorder of self-control (DDSC)* may be the most accurate name for ADHD. The term ADHD, focusing as it does on attention deficit, clearly falls short. We also know from years of research that this ability to inhibit our behavior is controlled by the very front part of our brain in an area known as the *orbital–frontal cortex*. It was, therefore, not surprising to learn during the past decade of research that this part of the brain is not as active as it is in others who do not have ADHD (see Chapter 3 for more on this subject). Even so, it is a tremendous advance in our understanding of ADHD to finally have a number of different studies that document this underactivity of the brain and relate it to an impairment in impulse control or inhibition.

The theory I have discussed in this chapter indicates that this frontal part of the brain, or other parts closely related to it, must also be involved in the four important mental processes that flow from our ability to inhibit our behavior. Therefore, it is this frontal part of the brain that gives us our powers of self-control and the capacity to direct our behavior toward the future. Time and more research will tell if this is true. But as Dr. Joaquim Fuster has shown in his book *The Prefrontal Cortex*, our knowledge from patients and primates with injuries to this part of their brain strongly suggests that it is likely to be so. Finally, our understanding of the brain and how it functions can now be fitted, like a piece of a puzzle, to what we have come to understand about the nature of ADHD, another piece of the puzzle. From this I believe we can safely conclude that ADHD involves a problem in the development and functioning of the frontal area of the brain.

The developmental–neurological nature of ADHD directly contradicts our strongly held beliefs that self-control and free will are totally determined by the person and his or her upbringing. I believe that this contradiction is what underlies much of society's resistance to admitting this disorder into the class of developmental disabilities for which we have great empathy and on behalf of which we make special allowances and rights. Society has struggled before with scientific advances that contradict the common wisdom of the time, and it has changed to accommodate them. It is my hope that society will come to do the same for ADHD.

The new perspective on ADHD presented here is the cornerstone of this book. The idea that ADHD is a disorder of self-control, willpower, and the organizing and directing of behavior toward the future provides the rationale for almost every treatment recommendation that follows. It also provides a larger framework in which to understand the results of research on the developmental course of ADHD, the problems that are often associated with it, and the social, academic, and occupational problems that are caused by it over time.

This new outlook on ADHD can provide you with the fundamental rationale to accept your child's disabilities, adapt the social and academic demands made on your child to the child's disability, work to strengthen, where possible, your child's weaknesses in the processes involved in developing self-control, and advocate for your child's need for and rights to services for this problem. This knowledge will empower you to act as the scientific, executive, and principle-centered parent that you will have to be to successfully raise a child with ADHD.

CHAPTER 3

What Causes ADHD?

ADHD has multiple causes. Our knowledge of these causes and of how they influence the brain and behavior has increased dramatically since the mid-1980s. Just as important, we have learned that other things once thought to cause ADHD do not. This chapter reviews the chief causes of ADHD and debunks some widely disseminated myths.

As you read, keep in mind how difficult it is to produce direct scientific proof that anything causes a problem with human behavior. The experiments required to give direct, conclusive evidence that, for example, ADHD is caused by damage to the frontal part of a child's brain during development are simply unthinkable. Scientists are not going to damage children's brains just to see what happens. So behavioral scientists who wish to study the biological causes of ADHD are often left searching for information that is highly suggestive of a cause but may never be proven absolutely certain. As a parent attempting to keep abreast of the research, then, it is extremely important for you to understand the possible sources of information and their relative reliability.

One such source is studies that show a consistent *relationship* between a potential causal agent and ADHD or the behavior problems characteristic of it. For instance, smoking by mothers during pregnancy is associated with an increased risk of hyperactivity and inattention in the offspring of that pregnancy. The fact that two events or conditions occur together, however, does not prove that one causes the other. It is merely suggestive.

Another source is studies of accidents of nature involving the cause in which we are interested. For example, when interested in the role of brain injury in ADHD, we may study children who have suffered diseases that attack the brain or children who have had clear-cut head trauma or other neurological injuries. This type of evidence is somewhat stronger because we can see that the accident (the brain injury) changed something in the child (the child shows the behaviors of ADHD), but it still is not definitive proof that brain injury causes ADHD.

Other factors associated with the process of being injured might be the real culprit, and we must remember that most children with ADHD have no evidence of a brain injury.

A third source of evidence comes from studies in which the causal agent is given directly to some animals but not to others in a true experimental test of that cause. To see if exposure of a fetus to alcohol during pregnancy causes hyperactivity, scientists give large doses of alcohol to some pregnant animals, such as mice, rats, or primates, and not to others. They then study the behavior of the animals born of that pregnancy to see how the offspring in these two groups may differ. The scientists may also sacrifice the animals and directly inspect the brain tissue for signs of abnormal development caused by the alcohol. Although such experiments more directly prove that some agent causes hyperactivity or ADHD in the animals, such conclusions cannot be generalized completely to humans. The brains of animals, especially primates, and humans are more similar than different, but they are not identical. So it is likely but not certain that what causes hyperactivity in animals may well cause it or ADHD in humans.

With few exceptions—direct tests of whether certain foods or chemicals in our diet may cause ADHD—behavioral scientists have had to depend on indirect evidence to show that any particular factor is a cause of ADHD. They must consider the totality or weight of the evidence and whether it is logically consistent. They must consider all possible explanations for their findings and justify their conclusions to other scientists. It is this need to convince the widest possible audience of scientists working in the same field through the objective evidence, logical explanation, and public debate that is the basis of the scientific method. And it is through this method that indirect evidence has been mounting that ADHD is related more to biological (neurological and genetic) factors than to purely social ones.

The Causes: Current Evidence

The most probable causes for which there is convincing evidence of association with ADHD are:

1. Various agents that can lead to brain injury or abnormal brain development, such as trauma, disease, fetal exposure to alcohol and tobacco, and early exposure to high levels of lead
2. Findings of diminished activity in certain brain regions
3. Heredity

Neurological Factors

For almost 100 years, scientists have suspected that what we now call ADHD is caused by abnormal development or injury of the brain. They noticed striking similarities in behavior problems between children with ADHD and people who had suffered damage by injuries to the front part of the brain, just behind the forehead, known as the *orbital–frontal region*. This brain region is one of the most well developed in humans compared to other animals and is believed to be responsible for inhibiting behavior, sustaining attention, employing self-control, and planning for the future.

Research in neurology and neuropsychology is replete with case reports and studies of larger groups of patients who have experienced injury to the frontal part of the brain as a consequence of trauma, brain tumors, strokes, diseases, or penetrating wounds, such as by gunshot. An excellent book on this topic for the nonprofessional is *Descartes' Error* (1994) by Antonio Damasio, M.D., an eminent neurologist at the University of Iowa. Earlier in this century this research convinced scientists that injuries to the brain from infections such as encephalitis and meningitis, trauma such as that caused by a fall or a blow to the head, or complications of pregnancy or delivery were the chief causes of ADHD symptoms. More than 20 years ago, however, scientists realized that most ADHD children had no history of obvious or significant brain injuries from these sources. At most, perhaps 5 to 10% were likely to have developed ADHD from some sort of brain damage. As discussed later in this chapter, ADHD children tend to have had more pregnancy or birth complications than non-ADHD children, but evidence that those complications caused brain injury that in turn caused ADHD is inconclusive.

Experiments with animals have served as a second line of research, producing evidence that ADHD may arise from brain injuries. There are many such studies, and they are quite consistent in their results. In these studies, primates such as chimpanzees are trained to perform certain psychological tests, then the scientists disable the frontal region of their brains through surgery or other means, and the tests are repeated. The animals' natural behavior in their environment may also be observed. These studies have shown consistently that the primates' behavior patterns are quite similar or even identical to those seen in ADHD children when these frontal brain regions are altered: The animals become more hyperactive, less able to pay attention for long periods of time, and more impulsive on the psychological tests. They are also less able to inhibit their behavior and delay their responding to events created in the experiments. These animals often develop significant problems in their social behavior with other animals as well. The studies also show that injuries created elsewhere in the brain do *not* produce these patterns of ADHD-like behavior. So the frontal area of the brain can be implicated in producing symptoms of ADHD in primates. Less than 10% of ADHD children can be shown to have suffered brain *injuries*, however, so something else must be disrupting the development of this part of the brain.

Is ADHD Caused by an Immature Brain?

A few scientists once believed that ADHD may arise as a result of a delay in the brain's development. This idea is quite appealing. The social behavior of many

ADHD children resembles that of younger, non-ADHD children, and a neurological exam given by physicians often shows these children are somewhat delayed in motor coordination and development as well. More recent studies have shown that the electrical activity of the brain in those with ADHD is similar to that seen in younger, non-ADHD children. This evidence is discussed in more detail later in this section and is quite convincing. Despite the appeal of this explanation, though, Drs. Bennett and Sally Shaywitz and their colleagues at Yale University concluded from a study using CT scans that if differences in brain structure or anatomy exist between those with ADHD and other children, the differences must be quite subtle and undetectable by this relatively sensitive method. Many other studies taking images of the brains of ADHD children and adults have also not found them to be grossly abnormal or immature in size or slower in development. So whatever is causing the problem in certain regions of the frontal part of the brain is not due simply to slow brain development.

What about Brain Chemistry?

Other scientists have suggested that certain neurotransmitters, chemicals in the brain that permit nerve cells to transmit information to other cells, are deficient in those with ADHD. Support for this idea comes from several sources:

1. Stimulant drugs that are known to affect neurotransmitters (see Chapter 18) temporarily improve the behavior of children with ADHD.
2. Studies with animals suggest that these drugs increase the amount of the neurotransmitters dopamine and norepinephrine in the brain. These stimulants produce significant improvements in the behavior of those with ADHD. This implies that the drugs are increasing the amount of these two chemicals in the brain, and so these two chemicals may be less plentiful in the brains of those with ADHD.
3. When the brain pathways of young animals, such as rats and dogs, that are rich in dopamine are selectively destroyed by a particular chemical, these animals become quite hyperactive as they mature. Such studies have also found that this hyperactivity can be reduced by giving stimulant medications to these animals identical to the stimulant medicines used to treat children with ADHD.
4. Some studies have taken samples of spinal fluid from children with ADHD to see if it contained more or less of certain chemicals related to those in the brain. These studies indicated the possibility that a lower amount of dopamine, once again, may be related to ADHD. Evidence from other studies, however, using blood and urine samples, has not always agreed.

What evidence there is seems to point to a possible problem in how much dopamine and possibly norepinephrine is produced in the brains of those with ADHD. This evidence, however, cannot be considered conclusive. So the idea that ADHD is caused by a reduced amount of one or two brain chemicals remains promising but has not been proven.

Brain Activity

Many such studies to date have measured brain activity in those with ADHD and have found it to be lower in the frontal area than for normal people.

Lower Electrical Activity. A large number of studies have compared the electrical activity in the brains of those with ADHD to those of children without ADHD. A variety of such studies, done easily and painlessly using an electroencephalograph (EEG) while children with ADHD were sitting at rest and also while performing certain mental tasks, found that the brain electrical activity of children with ADHD is less than that seen in non-ADHD children, particularly over the frontal areas.

In 1973, Drs. Monte Buchsbaum and Paul Wender, then at the National Institute of Mental Health, measured EEG activity in response to repeated stimulation to derive average evoked responses. When 24 ADHD children and 24 normal children were compared, the ADHD children responded as younger, non-ADHD children would: Their responses reflected a less mature pattern of brain electrical activity. These researchers also found that giving stimulant medication to the ADHD children reduced these differences.

Less Blood Flow. The more active certain brain regions are, the more blood they require. In 1984, Drs. Hans Lou, Leif Henriksen, and Peter Bruhn, working at the Kennedy Institute in Denmark, published a study comparing the blood flow in the brains of 11 children with ADHD, some of whom also had a learning disability, to the blood flow seen in 9 children without ADHD. They found the ADHD children had less blood flow to the frontal areas, particularly in the *caudate nucleus,* an important structure in the pathway between the most frontal portion of the brain and the structures in the middle of the brain known as the *limbic system.* The caudate nucleus is made up of several bundles of nerve fibers, one region of which is known as the *striatum.* This region is important in inhibiting behavior and sustaining attention. The limbic system to which it is connected is responsible for a variety of human activities, chief among which are controlling emotions, motivation, and memory. Through these connections and pathways, the midbrain limbic system sends signals up to the frontal area of the brain, which sends its own signals back down to the limbic system as a means of regulating and controlling behavior and emotion. In another study, these scientists compared the blood flow of 9 ADHD children to that of 15 non-ADHD children and obtained similar results. In a third study, the same researchers and their colleagues compared 19 patients with ADHD to 9 children without ADHD. Again the results showed decreased blood flow to the frontal brain areas and especially to the striatum region of the caudate nucleus. When stimulant medication like that used to treat ADHD was given to these patients, the blood flow to these underactive areas increased to near normal levels.

Lower Brain Activity Using PET Scans. The most sensational evidence that a problem exists in the brains of those with ADHD came from a recent study by Dr. Alan Zametkin and his colleagues at the National Institute of Mental Health. In this study, the brain activity of 25 adults with ADHD was compared to that of 50 adults without ADHD using a very sensitive instrument known as *positron emission tomography*, or a PET scan. In this procedure radioactive glucose, the sugar used as fuel by nerve cells in the brain, is injected into the bloodstream. A PET scan device then takes pictures of the brain as it uses this glucose. Dr. Zametkin found that adults with ADHD had less brain activity, particularly in the frontal area. The low level of activity was temporarily corrected when the adults took stimulant drugs like those commonly used clinically to treat ADHD children. Dr. Zametkin repeated this study with 20 adolescents with ADHD and again found reduced activity in the frontal region, more on the left side than the right side. The results were especially obvious for female adolescents with the disorder compared to non-ADHD adolescents and less so for the ADHD boys relative to non-ADHD boys.

Comparing ADHD and Other Psychiatric Disorders. In a similar study using brain-imaging techniques, Dr. Karl Sieg and colleagues at the University of Kansas reported in 1993 that they had also found significantly reduced brain metabolic activity in the frontal regions of 10 patients with ADHD compared to 6 patients with other psychiatric disorders but not ADHD. This study is important because it provided some evidence that the reduced frontal brain activity is specific to patients with ADHD and does not just accompany any psychiatric disorder.

In summary, the scientific findings from many lines of scientific research to date clearly indicate that the area in the very front part of the brain, known as the *orbital–frontal region*, and its many connections through a pathway of nerve fibers into a structure called the *caudate nucleus* (which includes the striatum), which itself connects farther back into a deeper area of the brain called the *limbic system*, may be responsible for the development of ADHD. As I described earlier, these brain areas are those that help us inhibit our behavior, sustain our attention, and inhibit our responses. They also let us inhibit and control our emotions and motivation as well as help us use language (rules or instructions) to control our behavior and plan for the future. These areas are the richest in dopamine, which may mean that not enough dopamine is being produced in these areas in people with ADHD. Dopamine is a chemical known to be involved in inhibiting the activity of other cells in the brain. These scientific findings are very consistent with my view that a problem with inhibition or self-control is the hallmark of ADHD and that this arises from a lower level of activity in the regions of the brain responsible for these human abilities.

How is it, many parents still ask, that ADHD children, who are more active and energetic than non-ADHD children, could have brains that are *less* active? Remember that the area of the brain that is not as active as it should be is a part that *inhibits* behavior, delays responding to situations, and helps to maintain our inhibition, and hence our attention, for long periods of time. The less active are these inhibitory centers, the more active (and less inhibited) the child's behavior will be.

Medications and Brain Activity in ADHD. There is some related research that adds to the conclusion that lowered brain activity may be related to ADHD. Drugs such as phenobarbital and dilantin used to treat children who have seizure disorders or epilepsy—that is, drugs that *lower* brain activity—have been shown to increase problems with inattention and hyperactivity in children taking these medications. Considering that very few ADHD children are taking these medications, such drugs cannot be considered to be a major cause of ADHD in the population. However, animal studies and a series of 12 cases reported by Drs. Larry Burd and colleagues at the University of North Dakota in 1987 have provided direct experimental evidence of a link between lower brain activity and behavior problems characteristic of ADHD. (Parents of ADHD children with seizure disorders should discuss this issue carefully with their child's treating physician to determine if their child's seizure medication may be creating or worsening their child's ADHD.)

Returning to our search for causes, we must still ask why these areas of the frontal region of the brain are less active. If it is not damage that causes this pattern of brain underactivity, what is it?

Is Something Wrong with the Structure of the Brain?

Possibly. The fact that the diminished brain activity is localized in the caudate nucleus, especially the striatum, makes it fair to ask whether a structural defect exists there. Drs. George Hynd, Richard Marshall, and Jose Gonzalez at the University of Georgia reported at a scientific meeting in 1993 that, using magnetic resonance imaging (MRI), they had found that the caudate nucleus of 11 children with ADHD was somewhat larger on the right side than on the left, particularly in the males—the opposite of what is found in non-ADHD people. This might mean that the left side of the caudate is not as well developed as it should be in children with ADHD.

In two other studies published in 1990 and 1991, Dr. Hynd and his associates showed that groups of ADHD children had slightly smaller areas of brain matter in the right frontal region than did control children and that the corpus callosum—a large band of nerve fibers that connects the right and left sides of the brain, allowing them to share information—was somewhat smaller in children with ADHD than in children without ADHD. These studies clearly must be replicated, but the findings are consistent with the other scientific information on brain activity suggesting that the frontal regions of the brain are involved in ADHD.

The Causes of Abnormal Brain Development

We know that certain brain regions are underactive and possibly underdeveloped in people with ADHD. We still need to discover why.

Substances Consumed during Pregnancy. Recently nicotine from cigarette smoking and alcohol from drinking during pregnancy have been shown

Can EEG Biofeedback or Neurofeedback Help Treat ADHD?

If ADHD children have low brain electrical activity, teaching them how to increase it should help them alleviate their ADHD symptoms. Almost 20 years ago scientists began to test that theory using EEG biofeedback, and to this day some dramatic claims have been made for this kind of treatment. You may have seen advertisements stating that EEG biofeedback is an effective alternative to medication, that it results in permanent changes in the brain physiology underlying ADHD, that it improves IQ, social skills, and even learning disabilities, and that such improvements can last into adulthood. Those are fantastic claims for any treatment. How much of this should you believe?

The term *biofeedback* means that a child is given back biological information about his or her brain activity through electrodes attached to the scalp that detect brain waves and a computer that classifies them. Over a great number of sessions, typically 40 to 80 sessions over 3 to 10 months or longer—at a cost of several thousand dollars—the child learns through mental exercises and some form of signal from the biofeedback equipment to increase the desired brain activity related to sustained attention and to decrease the undesired activity associated with daydreaming or distraction. The result, supposedly, is that the child's attention, hyperactivity, and impulsivity will then also improve.

Unfortunately, to date no well-controlled large group studies have been done to support the effectiveness of EEG biofeedback for ADHD children. The studies that have been published report on only 7 to 10 cases and do not clarify whether the biofeedback training or the academic tutoring and rewards program that accompanied it were responsible for the improved school and home behavior observed. So although we cannot rule out the possibility that EEG biofeedback training might be of some benefit, we cannot consider it a scientifically established effective treatment. Furthermore, a child could receive 12 years of stimulant medication, 3 years of weekly group–parent training, nearly 3.5 years of twice-monthly classroom consultations by a clinical psychologist, or almost 2.5 years of twice-weekly educational tutoring for the cost of 6 months of this treatment based on current average charges. Which choice would you make for your child?

to cause significant abnormalities in the development of the caudate nucleus and the frontal regions of the brain in children. A 1975 study showed that the mothers of 20 hyperactive children had consumed more than twice as many cigarettes per day during pregnancy as mothers of 20 reading-disabled and 20 control children.

A much larger 1992 study found that direct exposure to cigarette smoke during pregnancy or indirect exposure after pregnancy increased the odds of behavior problems in the children of these pregnancies. The combination of exposure both during and after pregnancy created the greatest likelihood that the children of that pregnancy would have significant behavior problems. Thus, some scientific evidence suggests that exposure to cigarette smoke is related to a higher risk for behavior problems similar to those in ADHD.

Research indicates that children born to alcoholic mothers are more likely to have problems with hyperactivity and inattention and even clinical ADHD. The amount of alcohol consumed by their mothers when pregnant appears to be related directly to the degree of risk for inattention and hyperactivity in four- to seven-year-old children.

Keep in mind, however, that all of these studies merely provide evidence of an *association* between these substances and ADHD, and associations can be misleading. We know, for example, that the number of heart attacks people suffer in a particular region of the country is associated with the degree to which the tar in the macadam driveways in that area is melting. This is a strong relationship, but as it turns out it is only a superficial one; the heart attacks and driveways are each related to a third factor (heat), which is the cause of both.

Similarly, we know that adults with ADHD drink more alcohol than others whether they are pregnant or not. We also know that ADHD is highly likely to be inherited (discussed later in this chapter). Therefore it may very well be the third factor, genetics, not alcohol, that caused ADHD in the children in these studies. So whenever you hear new claims made about the causes of ADHD, try to determine whether the studies have simply found an association between something and a risk for ADHD or really found the specific causal connection between them.

This important point aside, animal studies *have* shown fairly conclusively that nicotine and alcohol cause abnormal development of certain brain regions and that these abnormalities lead to increased hyperactive, impulsive, and inattentive behavior. So perhaps the most significant conclusion is that a mother may increase the risk of ADHD in her children by smoking or drinking during pregnancy, and this risk may be further increased if the mother herself also has ADHD.

Exposure to Lead. There is some scientific evidence that high levels of lead in the bodies of young children may be associated with a higher risk for hyperactive and inattentive behavior. This relationship seems to exist especially when the lead exposure occurs between 12 and 36 months of age. The relationship is rather weak, although it is found consistently in many studies. For instance, on a scale of 1 to 100, the relationship between body lead and hyperactivity rates only 6 to 15. Even at high levels of exposure, a 1979 study found that less than 36% of children with elevated lead levels were rated by teachers as inattentive, distractible, impulsive, and hyperactive. High levels of lead in the body may well cause some cases of ADHD because animal and human studies do show that lead exposure at moderate to high levels injures brain tissue. So lead is a toxin to the brain as are alcohol and nicotine and may therefore be viewed as a potential cause of inattention, hyperactivity, or even ADHD in some cases.

Heredity and ADHD

What else could be causing the brain underactivity? One of the most exciting areas of research on ADHD has been the role of heredity. For many years we've had evidence that the biological relatives of ADHD children have more types of psychological problems—particularly depression, alcoholism, conduct problems or antisocial behavior, and hyperactivity—than relatives of children who do not have ADHD. Such research hints that there may be a genetic predisposition to the disorder.

Clearer evidence that ADHD may be inherited comes from studies that directly evaluate all members of an immediate family for ADHD and determine the risk to other family members if one of them is diagnosed with ADHD. Drs. Joseph Biederman, Stephen Faraone, and their associates at Massachusetts General Hospital have conducted a number of such studies. In one published in 1990, they evaluated the 457 first-degree relatives (mothers, fathers, and siblings) of 75 children with ADHD and compared their results to their evaluation of the family members of 26 control children and 26 children with psychiatric disorders other than ADHD. They found that over 25% of the first-degree relatives of the families of ADHD children also had ADHD, whereas this rate was only about 5% in each of the control groups. This 5% is what you would expect by chance to find in any sample of children since it is the prevalence of the disorder in the population at large. Notice that if a child has ADHD, then, there is a 500% increase in the risk to other members in that family. Other studies have found similar results.

Studies of twins are even more persuasive. Scientists have found that if one twin has symptoms of ADHD, the risk that the other will have the disorder is as high as 80 to 90%. In a study published in 1992 by Dr. Jacquelyn Gillis and associates at the University of Colorado, 79% of identical twins had ADHD when one of the twins had already been diagnosed. For fraternal twins the figure was only 32%, but that is still 6 to 10 times greater than that seen among unrelated children, where the prevalence of ADHD is only 3 to 5%.

Most recently, several very large studies of twins have been able to determine that heredity explains between 50 and 92% of the range of hyperactive–impulsive behavior seen in children. Environmental factors, such as diet, toxins like lead, pregnancy and birth complications, or family life, explained only between 1 and 10%. This clearly supports a very large role for heredity in the expression of ADHD.

What exactly is inherited? It is probably a tendency toward problems in the development of the frontal cortex of the brain and the caudate nucleus, but we still have much to learn. Scientists are now carrying out studies that evaluate all members of a family that include a child with ADHD to determine just how the disorder is transmitted from one generation to the next. Is it a single gene, or are many genes involved? Is it related to the gender of the child? Can the location of the gene(s) on any particular chromosome be identified? Could this lead to a blood test to determine who might be at risk for developing the disorder? It is very possible that these questions will be answered within the next 10 years. The fact that one gene related to the disorder may already have been identified by Dr. Cook and his associates in Chicago is a very promising step in this direction. The work of Dr. Joseph Biederman and his colleagues at Massachusetts General Hospital, as well as that of Drs. Robert Plomin and Craig Edelbrock at Pennsylvania State University, and Drs. Jeffrey Gilger, Bruce Pennington, and John Defries, and colleagues in Denver on the way inheritance works in ADHD have also made significant advances in our knowledge of this topic and no doubt will continue to do so. In your ongoing study of ADHD, be sure to watch for new reports from these and other scientists studying the genetics of ADHD.

ADHD: Simply a Human Trait?

The genetic explanation of ADHD has an important implication that can easily go overlooked: *ADHD may simply represent a human trait and not a pathological condition in most cases.* As we just saw, which of us end up with ADHD seems to be determined much more by genetics than by environmental factors. In that sense, ADHD may be viewed as height, weight, intelligence, or reading ability, to name a few traits that are largely (but not wholly) genetically determined: The trait of behavioral inhibition or self-control represents a dimension or continuum of a human ability, and we differ in how much of it we inherit just as we differ in how much height, weight, intelligence, or reading ability we inherit. What is considered "abnormal" for any trait is simply a reflection of where we draw a line on the continuum. Unfortunately, when people place toward the extreme lower end of the continuum for a trait, we label them as having a disorder. Such labels not only are based on a somewhat arbitrary measure but also obscure the fact that those with ADHD do fall along a dimension of normal abilities. To put it another way, we all have a degree of this ADHD trait, and those with ADHD simply represent the extreme.

The term *disorder* also tends to imply a pathological condition to many lay-people. People can be genetically normal for a trait and "abnormal" only because of some injury or disease, or they can be genetically "abnormal." The evidence to date suggests that most people with ADHD fall into the second group; they have a natural or developmental form of the disorder rather than a pathological condition or a disease state. This means that ADHD should not be considered some grossly abnormal pathological condition—in fact it is a condition not qualitatively or categorically different from normal at all.

Understanding that ADHD is just an extreme form of a trait we all possess and that it is something people "come by naturally" should help everyone view ADHD from a kinder perspective. Your child was born with this problem; it is through no fault of his own that he lies at that position on the continuum. Likewise, you should neither assign blame to yourself nor accept it from others.

The Myths: What Does *Not* Cause ADHD

No doubt you've encountered claims that factors other than those just discussed cause ADHD. Some of these were originally founded in sound hypotheses but have since been disproven. Others are sheer falsehoods; there is not now and never has been any scientific support for them. As we continue to make conclusive findings about ADHD, quackery surrounding the subject should, it is hoped, vanish. In the meantime, use what you know about the scientific method to sort fact from fiction.

It's Not Something They Ate

In the 1970s and early 1980s, it was very popular to view ADHD as resulting from chemical food additives. This theory stemmed mainly from the widespread media attention given to Dr. Benjamin Feingold's claim that over half of all hyperactive children got that way from eating foods that contained additives and preservatives. Most of the substantial amount of research done over the next decade was simply unable to support Feingold's claim. In fact, only a very small number (5% or less) of mainly preschoolers showed a slight increase in activity or inattentiveness when consuming these substances. No evidence has ever been provided that normal children develop ADHD by consuming such substances or that ADHD children are made considerably worse by eating them. In 1983, Drs. Kenneth Kavale and Steven Forness with the University of California published a review of 23 studies investigating the Feingold diet. They concluded that diet modification was not effective for treating hyperactivity.

Despite that view's being shared by many scientists studying ADHD, the popular media continued to tout this now unfounded belief. As late as 1986, in fact, Ann Landers published and personally supported a letter from a parent making such an erroneous claim and directing parents to write to the Feingold Association of the United States (*Worcester Telegram and Gazette*, September 19, 1986). Unfortunately for parents who may have read such nonsense and taken the advice, nothing could be further from the truth. Currently, scientific interest in this theory has diminished greatly, and so has that of the general public.

"Is it sugar that causes ADHD, as I so often hear?"

However, in its place, the public has now adopted a popular view that sugar causes ADHD. So widely accepted had this idea become that in January 1987 it was paired as the correct response to the statement "The major cause of hyperactivity in North America" on the popular television game show *Jeopardy*. Not a single scientific study has been provided by proponents to support these claims. Since 1987 a number of scientific studies of sugar have been conducted, and these have generally proven negative. As an example, a study published in 1988 by Dr. Lee Rosen of Colorado State University and colleagues showed that even when given a beverage with the equivalent of two candy bars worth of sugar, normal preschool and elementary-school-age children may have slightly increased their activity level, but not so as to be detectable by their teachers or the experimenters throughout the school day. No effect of sugar was found on the academic work of the children. Only the girls showed a slight decrease in their attention and learning on one of the psychological tests done within 20 to 30 minutes after they had the drink, but this was a very small change and not noted on any of the teacher ratings or observations. The conclusion of the authors was that sugar does not cause clinically significant or dramatic changes in children's behavior.

Drs. Mark Wolraich, Richard Milich, Phyllis Stumbo, and Frederick Schultz at the University of Iowa Hospital School then conducted two studies of hyperactive children published in 1985. They intensively studied 16 boys in each study who were admitted to the hospital school for three days during which the sugar content of their diet was directly manipulated. To keep the children and other staff from knowing what days the sugar was in the diet, the investigators used aspartame (Nutrasweet) as a placebo. These scientists took 37 different measures of behavior and learning and found no significant effects of sugar on the behavior or learning. In 1986, Drs. Richard Milich, Mark Wolraich, and Scott Lindgren published a review of all of the research conducted up to that time on the adverse effects of sugar on children's behavior. They concluded that "Most studies have failed to find any effects associated with sugar ingestion, and the few studies that have found effects have been as likely to find sugar improving behavior as making it worse" (p. 493).

How could this be the case when nearly half of the parents and teachers queried in one of these studies stated that their children appeared to them to be quite sugar sensitive? One answer has been known to psychological research for decades, and that is the power of psychological suggestion. To evaluate this possibility, Drs. Daniel Hoover and Richard Milich at the University of Kentucky published a study in 1994 using 31 boys aged five to seven whose mothers reported them to be behaviorally "sugar-sensitive." The mothers and children came to the clinic having been told that on the day of the appointment their child would be given either sugar or aspartame (as a placebo, again) in Kool-Aid. Actually, though, none of the children would be given any sugar in their drink. On the morning of the appointment, half of the mothers were told their children were getting sugar and the other half that the children were getting aspartame. The mothers and children were then observed interacting during a period when they played freely and then during a period when they performed work together. The mothers also rated their children's behavior at the end of these periods. Direct measures of the children's activity level were also taken. The scientists found that the mothers who had been told their children received sugar rated their children as being more hyperactive than the mothers who were told the truth, that aspartame was given. The mothers who thought their children received sugar also were more critical of their children's activities, maintained closer physical proximity to their children (hovering), and talked more frequently to their children than the mothers who knew the children had aspartame. This study clearly shows that what parents believe about a dietary cause of hyperactivity (in this case sugar) not only can bias their reports but also can change the way parents treat their children. This study is worth keeping in mind the next time someone tells you that something in a child's diet makes him or her hyperactive or causes ADHD.

> *"I saw a doctor on a talk show who said that food allergies cause ADHD. Can you test my son for that? If not, where can I go to have him tested?"*

Over the years other unsubstantiated claims have been made about the influence of diet on ADHD. Almost 40 years ago, several professionals claimed that large doses of vitamins, particularly vitamins B_3, C, and pyridoxine, would be of benefit to severely mentally ill patients. Nearly 20 years later, another professional published statements that hyperactive and learning-disabled children could benefit from so-called megavitamin therapy or orthomolecular psychiatry. None of these claims has been verified by scientifically rigorous research. In fact, one reasonably well-done study found that the behavior of ADHD children actually became worse on the megavitamin treatment program. Similar claims have been made for large doses of minerals. There is no evidence that megadoses of vitamins or minerals can help ADHD children or that vitamin or mineral deficiencies in any way cause the disorder. *Parents should also be aware that large doses of vitamins (especially fat-soluble vitamins) and minerals can actually be harmful to children.*

You may also have read (or seen on television talk shows) that allergies to substances in foods besides the chemical additives targeted by Dr. Feingold can cause ADHD symptoms (and, incidentally, a raft of other symptoms). Again, I am aware of no controlled scientific studies that support such a claim. Nor does the American Academy of Allergy and Immunology advocate investigating allergies when ADHD symptoms appear.

For the last 30 years Americans have been so fascinated with how foods affect human health that it should come as no surprise when links between diet and ADHD continue to be proposed, but at this point such claims cannot be taken seriously. The burden of proof that food does cause ADHD must rest with those who propose such causes. We have wasted enough valuable scientific time, resources, money, and manhours investigating unfounded claims about diet that could have been better spent pursuing more promising lines of scientific inquiry on ADHD.

Are Hormones Involved in ADHD?

A study published in early 1993 (by Dr. Hauser and colleagues) showing a link between low thyroid hormone levels and ADHD received a great deal of publicity from the media. Some stories even claimed that the "gene" for ADHD had been discovered, because the gene for thyroid deficiency is known and the two must be related in some way. These hormones, chemicals produced in the thyroid gland of the neck, are important in controlling human growth and may have other functions not fully understood. A few people may have a rare condition of thyroid deficiency that may be genetically determined. The study found that 70% of children and 50% of adults who were deficient in thyroid hormone had ADHD. Since then this link has been studied in three additional published papers, and none has found any significant link between problems with thyroid hormone functioning and hyperactivity or ADHD. Thus the initial study appears to have been flawed in some way. Children with ADHD should not be routinely tested for thyroid deficiencies, nor should thyroid hormone treatments be considered to hold any promise for the treatment of ADHD at this time.

No other hormones have been shown to have any relationship to ADHD.

Didn't I Hear Something about Lighting and ADHD?

Probably, if you are as old as I am (45 as of this writing), you may have heard or even read in *Newsweek* in the mid-1970s about a photographic engineer, David Ott, who claimed that cool-white fluorescent lighting gave off certain soft X-rays and radio frequencies that could cause children to become hyperactive and thus that this lighting in school rooms caused ADHD in children. The study proved to be quite poorly designed and seriously flawed, and when researchers attempted to repeat it using considerably better methods, the lighting changes did not result in changes in the children's behavior. No one takes this idea seriously any longer.

Motion Sickness and ADHD

For many years Dr. Harold Levinson of Great Neck, New York, has been garnering media coverage for his theory that ADHD, learning disorders, and other behavioral and emotional problems can occur because of a problem within the vestibular system of the brain, which affects balance, sense of gravity, and head position. This system is located in the inner ear and makes connections with parts of the brain, especially the cerebellum, located at the back lower portion of the skull. Contrary to what most scientists believe, Dr. Levinson claims this system also regulates our energy levels, and so any impairment in this system can lead to hyperactivity and impulsive behavior. He recommends that children with ADHD or learning disorders take Dramamine or dimenhydrinate (an anti–motion-sickness medicine available over the counter) because it is known to have some effects on the inner ear vestibular system. He provides patients with other medicines as well, some of them powerful psychiatric drugs, other vitamin supplements, or herbal extracts.

In their 1994 review of the evidence available on Dr. Levinson's theory and treatment recommendations, psychologists Samuel Goldstein, Ph.D., and Barbara Ingersoll, Ph.D., conclude that the theory is surely inconsistent with what is known about ADHD and the vestibular system and its functions. The vestibular system does not seem to be involved in any way with impulse control, attention span, or regulation of activity level. Dr. Levinson claims to have used this approach to treat thousands of patients with ADHD and learning disorders with at least 70 to 80% of patients responding well. Even so, he has never published a well-controlled scientific study on this issue. Thus, we have only his word to take on how useful this treatment program is for those with ADHD. As with the dietary treatments discussed earlier, parents should avoid this treatment program and view it as entirely unsubstantiated by legitimate scientific research.

Can Yeast Cause ADHD?

Dr. William Crook, a pediatrician and allergist from Jackson, Tennessee, has been a vocal proponent of yeasts, particularly those such as *Candida albicans* that can live in the body, as a major cause of many different learning, behavioral, and emotional problems, especially ADHD. These yeasts are typically kept in check by other bacteria in the body as well as by the body's immune system. Dr. Crook believes that toxins given off by the yeasts can irritate the brain and nervous system and weaken the body's immune system. He recommends that children with ADHD be placed on low-sugar diets because sugar can stimulate the growth of yeasts. Like Dr. Feingold, he also believes that additives and other chemicals in foods may contribute to a yeast problem in the body, and so these should be eliminated from the diets of ADHD children. He believes some children may even need to be treated with an antiyeast medication, such as nystatin, and others may need vitamin, mineral, or other dietary supplements to control their behavior problems.

Presently, not a shred of sound scientific evidence supports Dr. Crook's theory. Given that the American Academy of Allergy and Immunology has found the theory of yeast sensitivity unproven, parents are encouraged to ignore any advice based on it. Certainly, Dr. Crook's recommendations that children take large doses of vitamins and minerals, as noted earlier, can be potentially harmful to children.

Can Bad Parenting or Chaotic Family Life Cause ADHD?

Theories that blame the environment as the major cause of ADHD have not received much support in the scientific literature. Some writers have claimed that hyperactive behavior is the result of poor parental management of the children; these parents are thought to be too permissive and do not provide enough training, structure, or discipline. No studies support this view. I have studied family life and particularly the interactions of parents with their ADHD children for more than 17 years, and my own research shows that the parents of ADHD children are more likely to give commands to their children, to be more directive and negative toward them, and in some instances to be less attentive and responsive to their ADHD children than are mothers of non-ADHD children. Our studies also have found that the ADHD children were less compliant with their mother's commands and directions, were more negative and stubborn, and were less able than non-ADHD children to keep complying over time with the parents' commands. Is it the mother's fault that the child is acting this way or the child's fault that his mother is reacting this way? We simply cannot answer that question from these studies.

> *"My parents think that I spoil my son too much, that I don't discipline him the way I should and that is why he acts this way. How do I convince them he really has a disability?"*

To evaluate this question further, we gave stimulant medication (Ritalin) on some weeks and placebos on the other weeks to the children. Then we observed what happened in these family interactions. Neither the mother nor the child knew which weeks the children were on the real medicine and which weeks they were taking the placebo. We found that when the children were on the real medicine, their behavior toward their mothers was much improved. But we also found that the mothers' behavior toward the children was improved. It even resembled the behavior of the mothers of non-ADHD children. This indicates that the negative behavior of the mothers seemed to be *in response* to the difficult behavior of these children and not the cause of it. After all, by directly changing the ADHD symptoms of the children with medication, we showed that the behavior of their mothers became much more "normal."

You may also have read claims that a chaotic family life or a "dysfunctional" family can cause ADHD based on the fact that parents of ADHD children are somewhat more likely to have psychological problems or even psychiatric disorders. Studies have found that the parents (and immediate relatives) of ADHD children are more likely to have problems with alcohol and substance abuse, antisocial behavior, and depression, and to have had school problems and hyperactivity when they were children. Parents of ADHD children also report more stress in their role as parents and more marital problems than other parents. The families of ADHD children also move more frequently than families who do not have ADHD children. Such things could easily influence how well a household runs, how organized the parents are in managing their personal and family life, and how well they are able to manage their children. These disruptive influences could also create much more stress on the children than would be experienced in the family life of non-ADHD children.

In the minds of many people, including some professionals, this line of reasoning justifies the claim that ADHD can arise out of disorganized, dysfunctional family life, but I believe several lines of reasoning disprove this view. First, the greater problems seen in family members of ADHD children could easily be associated with the genetic or hereditary evidence described earlier. We should expect to see more ADHD and its symptoms in the parents and family members of ADHD children, and we do. This explains why the family members of ADHD children may be having more trouble themselves, may move more often, and may have more marital problems and a higher divorce rate than families with non-ADHD children. It is not the psychiatric problems of these family members and the resulting "bad" family environment that cause ADHD in the child but the genes that the parents and child have in common.

Second, the research by Dr. Mark Stewart and Gerald August at the University of Iowa, Dr. Ben Lahey at the University of Chicago, and me, among other scientists, contradicts this theory. We have all found that these psychiatric problems among the family members of ADHD children occurred most often in only a subgroup composed of ADHD children who have serious problems with aggressive, defiant, and antisocial behavior. It is the parents and relatives of this subgroup who are more likely to have problems with drug and alcohol abuse, depression, and antisocial behavior. Children who are purely ADHD, without significant aggressive behavior, do not seem to have these serious problems among relatives any more frequently than do non-ADHD children. This tells us that these parent and family problems are linked to the development of aggressive and antisocial behavior in the child and not to the child's ADHD. In other words, chaotic or dysfunctional family life due to psychological problems in the parents may be contributing directly to a child's risk of having very aggressive and antisocial behavior. Thus, although chaotic family life and parental psychiatric problems are associated with and may well cause serious defiant and aggressive behavior, they are not causative of the child's ADHD.

Finally there are the findings from my own research: We videotaped the interactions of parents with their ADHD children and compared these to the interactions of non-ADHD children with their parents. But we also subdivided the ADHD children into those who were very oppositional, defiant, and aggressive and those who were not. We discovered that the interactions of the ADHD group that was not aggressive were no different from the interactions of the families of normal children in most respects. It was only in the aggressive group that we found more negative interactions between the parents and their children. Both the aggressive ADHD children and their parents used more insults, putdowns, and commands with each other. They also were less positive in their interactions than were the other two groups of children (purely ADHD and non-ADHD, nonagressive). These families of aggressive children reported the greatest amount and intensity of conflicts with each other at home. The parents of these aggressive children also reported more personal psychological problems in themselves than did the parents of the other groups of children. This is in keeping with the results that parental psychological problems are more common in the families of the aggressive type of ADHD children, confirmed in studies by Dr. James Tallmadge (now at the University of Vermont) and his colleagues and Dr. Arthur Anastopoulos and associates at my university.

All of this evidence makes it highly unlikely that any purely social cause, such as "bad mothering" or a disruptive, stressful home life, creates ADHD in the children of such families. Instead, the research suggests that ADHD children can create stress for their parents and cause some disruption of family life. Where poor parenting and disruptive family life may have some influence on the child, it seems to be one of contributing to aggressive and defiant child behavior, not to ADHD.

Who Is at Risk for Developing ADHD?

Even before a child is born, certain parental or family characteristics increase the odds of producing an ADHD child. These risk factors may not necessarily directly cause the ADHD in a child, but their presence signals that a child born into that family may be more likely to have ADHD than children born into families without those risk factors.

Features of the Parents and Family

As you know, studies tell us that parents who have ADHD are much more likely to have children with ADHD because of hereditary factors. In fact, any family history of ADHD increases the odds of a child having ADHD. For instance, having a sibling with ADHD increases the likelihood that another child in the family will have ADHD to 25 to 35% overall. Scientists estimate this risk to be approximately 13 to 17% for girls and 27 to 30% for boys regardless of the ADHD sibling's gender. It is not clear why boys have a greater risk of having ADHD than girls within the same family. The reasons may lie in the realm of genetics—we know, for example, that it is possible for a characteristic inherited in the genes of both boys and girls in the same family to become manifest only in the boys. Maleness, you might say, has some greater biological risks associated with it, and ADHD may be one of them. Such sex differences are evident not only in ADHD but also in mental retardation and learning disabilities such as dyslexia (reading disorder). Whatever the explanation, it is not likely to rest on purely social factors, such as differences in the ways in which parents treat boys and girls within the same family.

Other family risk factors associated with the early development and persistence of ADHD are (1) less education of the mother, (2) lower social class of the parents, (3) single parenthood, and (4) abandonment of the family by the father. However, these factors produce only a very small elevation in risk for ADHD and obviously do not *cause* ADHD in the children of such parents. They are simply associated with a greater risk for ADHD, most likely because of some third condition that explains both these risk factors and the ADHD itself.

Features of the Pregnancy

Several studies have shown that mothers who experience complications of their pregnancies or deliveries are more likely to have children with ADHD than mothers without such complications. The type of complication does not seem to be as important as the total number of complications. Such complications may cause ADHD by interfering with the normal brain development of the fetus, or a third factor may be involved: ADHD in the mother. In this case, the mother's ADHD would lead to poorer prenatal self-care and thus greater complications; the cause of the child's ADHD would be genetic inheritance. This is an example of noncausal association, discussed earlier in this chapter.

The fact is that there is little evidence that these complications actually cause ADHD. In a large study known as the Perinatal Collaborative Project, conducted by the federal government in the 1970s, the following complications were found to increase the risk to a small degree that children of those pregnancies might have symptoms of ADHD: the number of cigarettes smoked by the mother per day, seizures in the mother, the number of times the mother was hospitalized during pregnancy, breathing problems in the child before or during delivery, and the weight and health of the placenta when inspected after delivery. Higher incidence of problems in these areas increased the odds that the children would have symptoms of ADHD; the worse the mother's problems, the worse the child's symptoms.

Features of Infancy and the Toddler Years

Scientists have also identified some features in the early development of children that may predict a greater risk for the later appearance of ADHD in those children. Delays in motor development, smaller head size at birth and at 12 months of age, meconium staining of the amniotic fluid from the pregnancy, signs of nerve damage after birth, breathing problems after birth, and low birth weight were found in the Perinatal Collaborative Project to be related to risk for later hyperactivity. The risk was still quite low, however, even when these signs were present. Children who were less healthy during their infancy or preschool years and who were slow to develop in motor coordination have also been found to be at a higher risk for early and persistent ADHD symptoms later in childhood.

Certainly young children who were excessively active, even as babies, may have a higher risk for ADHD. Also, children who attended to objects or toys for short periods of time, who could not persist as well in pursuing objects in their field of vision, or who showed a strong intensity of reaction to being stimulated may be at higher risk for having ADHD. Infants or toddlers who are very demanding of their parents are more likely to display ADHD later on. We do not believe that these features of the child or their early development cause the ADHD symptoms to occur later. Instead, many psychologists believe that these are just the early signs of the ADHD itself, which may not be fully formed in its expression at so early an age as infancy or toddlerhood. Very young children display only behavior that is possible for them to show at that early stage of their brain's development. The "seeds" of ADHD may be within these children but will not appear until that stage of development where attention span, inhibition, and the control over activity and behavior normally emerge (see Table 1, p. 53). At those points, we will see that the child with ADHD has fallen behind other children.

Features of the Preschool Years

During the preschool years (ages two to five years), the development of early and persistent problems with overactivity and with getting along with other children marks a child at risk for ADHD. Also, not surprisingly, young children with excessive inattention and emotional difficulties such as frequent anger or temper outbursts or a proneness to becoming easily upset by things may be more likely to have ADHD as they grow up.

Once again, young children whose early temperament is negative and demanding are more likely to be diagnosed as ADHD later on. *Temperament* refers to an early and persistent pattern of personality characteristics, including activity level, intensity or degree of energy in a response, persistence or attention span, demandingness of others, quality of mood (irritability or quickness to anger or display emotion), adaptability or capacity to adjust to change, and rhythmicity or the regularity of sleep/waking periods, eating, and elimination (bowel and bladder control). These features appear to be as important as predictors in the preschool years as they were in infancy. These characteristics, especially overactivity, high intensity, inattention, negative mood, and low adaptability, have also predicted the continuation of ADHD into later childhood once it developed. Certainly children whose inattentive or hyperactive symptoms are sufficiently severe to get them a diagnosis of ADHD in early childhood are quite likely to continue to receive this diagnosis up to 5 to 10 years later.

The presence of these personality characteristics early in life is a very strong predictor of later risk for ADHD. For instance, Dr. Susan Campbell at the University of Pittsburgh studied 46 children who were reported by their parents to be excessively active, inattentive, and defiant at ages two to three years. She also studied 22 non-ADHD children who had no significant behavior problems. She then followed all of the children until age six and reevaluated them. At age six, approximately 50% of the children with early behavioral problems were still hyperactive or had ADHD, which suggests that children who are hyperactive and difficult to manage at age two have at least a 50% chance of being labeled as ADHD or hyperactive by entry into school at age six.

Still, 50% of the children did *not* persist in their behavior problems. Dr. Campbell found that where this pattern of early hyperactive and defiant behavior combines with other factors in the child's life ADHD is more likely to develop. What are these other features? One important one is the characteristics of the parents' personality, especially the presence of psychiatric or psychological problems that may interfere with caregiving and raising the child. Dr. Campbell studied this issue and found that a negative, critical, and commanding style of child management by mothers of young children with hyperactivity was likely to predict persistence of those problems into later years. Parents who are very hostile or who are having marital problems may also contribute to the risk for ADHD in preschool children with negative temperament. Thus it appears that child temperament, while an important early risk factor, can be either improved or worsened by the type of home environment parents create and the manner in which they respond to this difficult child. This environment combines with the child's early temperament problems to increase the risk for *later* ADHD.

Taken together, these research findings suggest that it is possible to identify children at risk for developing an early and persistent pattern of ADHD symptoms prior to their starting kindergarten and perhaps even as early as two or three years of age. A combination of both child and parental variables seems the most useful in making such predictions. The following factors, listed in descending order of importance, would appear to be useful as potential predictors of the early emergence and persistence of ADHD in children:

1. The early emergence of high activity level and demandingness in infancy or preschool years
2. Critical/directive behavior by mothers in the child's early years when combined with Item 1
3. Family history of ADHD
4. Smoking and alcohol consumption by and poor health of the mother during pregnancy
5. A greater-than-normal number of complications during pregnancy
6. Being a single parent and have less education than normal
7. Poor health of the infant and delays in motor and language development

If any of this seems to contradict earlier statements in this chapter that ADHD is not *caused* by the manner in which parents manage and raise their children, understand that here I mean that how parents respond to and manage a child may contribute to the *persistence* of ADHD. (These studies have not even proven that it is what the parents are doing that *causes* the persistence of the ADHD.) The research suggests that once symptoms of ADHD have developed, how severe they may become and how much they persist is partly related to how parents manage the children. In other words, parents may not have initially caused the problem through how they raise a child, but they can make the problem somewhat better or worse by how they choose to respond to that child. It may also be that the parents' own child-management skills are being affected by ADHD in the parent and that it is this genetic presence of the ADHD in the parent that contributes to the child's ADHD *and* to the poor parenting behaviors, rather than just the poor parenting alone or at all.

To summarize, it is primarily biological factors that are most closely associated with and may perhaps be causal of ADHD. So far studies indicate a very strong genetic contribution to ADHD—one that is much greater than the contribution of environmental factors. Everything we know points to the idea that children with ADHD have less brain activity in the frontal regions, precisely those brain centers known to be involved in behavioral inhibition, persistence of responding, resistance to distraction, and controlling one's activity level. The precise cause of this underactivity is not known, but lower levels of several brain chemicals in this region may be at the root of the problem, or portions of these brain regions may be somewhat smaller in those with ADHD.

Where the environment seems to be important, as in the case of poor child-management skills by parents, is in predicting which children may have more severe and persistent forms of ADHD and, especially, which are at risk for more aggressive and defiant behavior. Even the existence of this relationship, however, does not mean that how parents are managing a child with ADHD is the cause of the increased severity or persistence of that child's disorder.

We have much more to learn about ADHD and its potential causes. When we fully comprehend what causes this disorder, perhaps we will also discover how to cure it. In the meantime, the information that is available, along with what we know about the nature of ADHD (see discussion in Chapter 4) has brought us a long way toward successful management of ADHD, the subject of Parts II through IV (Chapters 6–19).

What to Expect: The Nature of the Disorder

As all parents know, ADHD is a perplexing disorder that can make day-to-day coping a unique challenge. By its very nature it seems to create adversarial relationships between the ADHD child and everyone else. The mundane routines of a normal day can seem like a series of battles. It *is* possible to make life easier, and a good way to begin is to stop fighting the inevitable. Know all you can about the nature of this disorder—what you can and cannot change.

ADHD is found in about 3 to 5% of all children. That means more than 2 million of all those under age 18 in the United States could have the disorder. In several ways, though, the label ADHD is relative. In Chapter 3 we discussed the idea that most cases represent just one end of a continuum for a normal trait that we all have. This means that there are degrees of the disorder in the population; some people have mild or even borderline ADHD, whereas others have moderate or severe ADHD. Typically people today are diagnosed with ADHD when their symptoms occur more frequently and with greater magnitude than in 93% of those of their age and sex, but even within that group, the frequency and severity of symptoms will vary. How professionals determine the severity of the condition in any given case is explained in Chapter 7.

> "I've heard that other countries don't have as much ADHD
> as we do. Is that true? Why is it that in Great Britain
> they hardly ever diagnose ADHD and don't use medications at all?"

We also know that the definition of ADHD is ever evolving. Other countries may not even recognize the disorder as such. It may be called a conduct problem in Great Britain, or children simply may be branded undisciplined in eastern Europe and the countries of the former Soviet Union. It's unfortunate that such labels perpetuate the misperception of ADHD as a problem of personal character; the fact remains that ADHD is a neurologically determined disorder and is found throughout the world. When it comes to diagnosis, however, methods of quantifying the symptoms vary.

ADHD Is Difficult to Quantify

To arrive at a figure for total cases of ADHD, a common approach is to conduct surveys of parents and teachers about children under their care using behavior rating scales that measure the symptoms of ADHD. The number of children in that population who probably have the disorder is then determined by establishing a certain cutoff score for the questionnaire, above which a child will be considered to have ADHD. This is not the same as doing a careful evaluation of all the children in a given region, which would not be feasible. But it is one way of getting a rough idea of how many children might qualify for the disorder. These studies have turned up a range of less than 1% to as high as 14%. Obviously, though, where you place the cutoff score on these rating scales will determine how many children get labeled as ADHD.

In one of the largest studies of this type ever conducted, Drs. Peter Szatmari, David Offord, and Michael Boyle at the McMaster University Chedoke Hospitals in Ontario surveyed the majority of households in the entire province using a behavior rating scale and other survey forms. They determined in their study what score on the questionnaire was likely to result in that child being diagnosed as ADHD when seen by a child psychiatrist and then used that score to decide which children in the survey had ADHD. They discovered that 10.1% of the males aged 4 to 11 years and 3.4% of the males aged 12 to 16 would have had the disorder. Overall, the prevalence was 3.3% for all females. You can already see from these numbers that boys are approximately two to three times more likely to have ADHD than girls. You can also see that the likelihood of having ADHD declines with age, at least for males in this particular study. Some children truly outgrow the disorder, while others improve to the point where they drop below the cutoff score on the rating scale yet are still impaired by their symptoms, which remain at the high end of normal. In this study the overall rate for all children regardless of sex was 6.3%.

Using a different approach, Drs. Nadine Lambert, Jonathan Sandoval, and Dana Sassone with the University of California at Berkeley asked parents, teachers, and physicians in 1978 to identify children they considered hyperactive out of a population of 5,000 elementary school children in the East Bay region of San Francisco. They found that approximately 5% were identified as hyperactive, or ADHD, by at least one of these: parent, teacher, or physician. However, the percentage of children called hyperactive by each source differed greatly, and when all three sources had to agree, the prevalence of hyperactivity fell to about 1%. This study points to a crucial issue: When no definition of hyperactivity is given, as was the case here, the judgments become quite subjective.

The average of the rates produced by the many other studies examining the U.S. and Canadian populations is approximately 5% of school-age children. Remember, though, that the figure is higher for boys and lower for girls. The estimate means that roughly 1 out of every 20 to 30 children is hyperactive or has ADHD. This makes ADHD one of the most prevalent disorders seen in children. Given that 50 to 65% of these children will continue to have the full disorder into adulthood, ADHD should be present in about 2 to 3% of adults, or 1 in every 33 to 50 individuals.

ADHD is seen in all social classes, ethnic groups, and nationalities. As just mentioned, it is seen more often in males than females—three times more frequently. Mental health clinics that specialize in the disorder may see as many as six to nine boys for every girl who comes into their clinic because of a referral bias: People tend to refer children who are more aggressive and difficult to manage to such clinics, and boys with ADHD are typically more aggressive than girls. One obvious lesson from this is that more ADHD girls may go unrecognized and untreated.

ADHD Changes with Development

One of the most vexing aspects of ADHD for parents is that it evolves as the child grows up. What worked at age 6 may not work at age 16. Up to 80% of school-age children given a clinical diagnosis of ADHD will continue to have the disorder in adolescence, and between 30 and 65% will have it into adulthood, depending on how the disorder is defined in any particular study. Parents are likely to notice it first when a child is three to four years old or younger. Some children with ADHD, however, may have been difficult to care for, active, and irritable or temperamental since infancy. Others may not have shown such difficulties until entering preschool, kindergarten, or even first grade. In these latter cases, the child probably had some features of the disorder earlier, but these either did not create problems for the parents or did not interfere with the mastery of relatively simple developmental tasks.

Preschool ADHD Children

A great deal of research has shown that up to 57% of preschool-age children are likely to be rated as inattentive and overactive by their parents by four years of age. As many as 40% of these children may have sufficient problems with inattention to be of concern to their parents and teachers. Yet the vast majority of these children get better within three to six months. Even among those children whose problems may be severe enough to receive a clinical diagnosis of

ADHD, only half will have the same diagnosis by later childhood or early adolescence. This tells us that the appearance of symptoms by age three to four by itself does not guarantee that ADHD will persist. However, in the majority of those in whom this early pattern of ADHD lasts for at least a year, ADHD is likely to continue into the childhood and teenage years. This tells us that both the degree of early ADHD symptoms *and* how long they last in early childhood determine which children are likely to show a chronic course of ADHD.

Children with this durable pattern of ADHD in this age group are described by their parents as restless, always up and on the go, acting as if driven by a motor, and frequently climbing on and getting into things. Persistent in their wants, demanding of parental attention, and often insatiable in their curiosity about their environment, ADHD preschoolers pose a definite challenge to the child management skills of their parents, particularly their mothers. Such children require far more frequent and closer monitoring of their ongoing conduct than do other preschoolers. Sometimes they even have to be tethered to allow parents to complete necessary household chores that require their undivided attention. Those ADHD children with excessive moodiness, quickness to anger, and low adaptability are likely to prove the most distressing to their mothers. Disobedience of mothers' instructions is common, and at least 30 to 60% are seriously defiant or oppositional, especially if they are boys. Even though temper tantrums may be common even for normal preschoolers, they occur more often and with greater intensity in young ADHD children.

Although the mothers of ADHD preschoolers are likely to report feeling competent in managing these children, this confidence will decline progressively as the children grow older and parents find that the typical techniques used to manage other children are less effective with ADHD children.

Placing a young ADHD child in day care is likely to bring additional distress to parents. Day-care staff are likely to begin to complain about the child's disruptive behavior, and it is not uncommon to find the more active and aggressive among these ADHD children "kicked out" of preschool—so begins the course of school adjustment problems that afflict many of these children throughout their compulsory schooling. Other ADHD children, especially those who are not oppositional or aggressive and who have milder cases of ADHD, and perhaps those who are intellectually brighter, might have no problems in day care, particularly when it is only for a half-day program for a few days each week.

Many mothers of young ADHD children have also told us how difficult it can be to find babysitters, which severely limits the parents' mobility—a particularly difficult problem for single parents. No wonder parents with ADHD children tell us that the preschool years were often the most stressful and demanding in their life as parents.

ADHD at School Age

Once ADHD children enter school, a major social burden is placed on them that will last for at least the next 12 years. It will prove to be the major area of impact of their handicapping condition and will create the greatest source of distress for many of them and their parents. The abilities to sit still, attend, listen, obey, inhibit impulsive behavior, cooperate, organize actions, and follow through on instructions as well as to share, play well, and interact pleasantly with other children are essential to negotiating a successful academic career. It is not surprising that the vast majority of ADHD children are identified as deviant in behavior by entry into formal schooling, particularly first grade. Parents will now have to contend with not only the ongoing behavioral problems at home but also the burden of helping their children adjust to the academic and social demands of school. Regrettably, these parents must also tolerate the complaints of many teachers who see the child's problems at school as stemming entirely from home problems or poor child-rearing abilities in the parents.

Often at this stage parents must confront decisions about whether to retain the children in kindergarten because of "immature" behavior and possibly slow academic achievement. The fact that many schools now assign homework, even to first graders, makes an additional demand on both the parent and the child to accomplish these tasks together. Homework time becomes another area of conflict. For those 20 to 25% of ADHD children likely to have a reading disorder, these will be noted as the child tries to master the early reading tasks at school. Such children are doubly handicapped in their academic performance by the combination of these disabilities. For those who will develop math and writing disorders, these problems often go undetected until several years into elementary school. Even without learning disabilities, almost all ADHD children will be haunted by their highly erratic educational performance.

At home, parents often complain that their ADHD children do not accept household chores and responsibilities as well as other children their age. They need help with these daily chores as well as with dressing and bathing. While the frequency of temper tantrums is likely to decline, as it does in non-ADHD children, ADHD children will show such behavior when frustrated more often than normal children. Often, ADHD children are barely tolerated or ejected outright from social activities such as clubs, music lessons, sports, and scouts. Their overall pattern of social rejection will start emerging during the school years if it has not done so already. Overwhelming, intrusive, and even aversive to others, the ADHD child who is attempting to learn appropriate social skills becomes confused by peers' avoidance, and by late childhood, he or she is commonly developing low self-esteem. Yet many children with ADHD will place the blame for these difficulties on their parents, teachers, or peers because of their limited self-awareness.

By later childhood and preadolescence, patterns of social conflict are well established for many ADHD children. Between 7 and 10 years of age, at least 30 to 50% are likely to develop symptoms of conduct disorder and antisocial behavior such as lying, petty thievery, and resistance to authority. Twenty-five percent or more may have problems with fighting with other children. Those who have not developed some other psychiatric, academic, or social disorder by this time are in the minority, and it is these children who are likely to have the best adolescent outcomes, experiencing problems primarily with academic performance and eventual attainment. The majority of ADHD children by this time will be placed on a trial of stimulant medication, and over half will participate in some type of individual and family therapy. Approximately 30 to 45% will also be receiving formal special educational assistance by the end of sixth grade.

The Adolescent with ADHD

Follow-up studies published since the late 1970s have done much to dispel the idea that ADHD is typically outgrown by the adolescent years. Seventy to 80% of children clinically diagnosed with ADHD are likely to continue to display symptoms, and as many as 25 to 35% of the adolescents display antisocial behavior or conduct disorder. As many as 30% may be experimenting with or frankly abusing substances such as alcohol and marijuana. Up to 58% have failed at least one grade in school, and at least three times as many hyperactive teenagers as non-ADHD children have failed a grade, been suspended, or been expelled from school. Almost 35% of ADHD children quit school before completion. Their levels of academic achievement on standard tests are well below normal on tests of math, reading, and spelling.

The same issues that make these years difficult for non-ADHD individuals— identity, peer group acceptance, dating, and physical development—erupt as a second source of demands and distress with which the ADHD adolescent must now cope. Sadness, depression in a minority of cases, poor self-confidence, diminished hopes of future success, and concerns about school completion and social acceptance may all develop.

The ADHD Child as an Adult

Research to date suggests that 50 to 65% of ADHD children continue to have symptoms as they reach adulthood. Although many ADHD children will be employed and self-supporting, their educational level and social class tend to be lower than those of others, even their own siblings. Antisocial behavior is likely to be troublesome for at least 20 to 45%, with as many as 25% qualifying for a diagnosis of adult antisocial personality—a pattern of repetitive antisocial behavior beginning in early adolescence.

Only 10 to 20% of ADHD children reach adulthood free of any psychiatric diagnosis, functioning well, and without significant symptoms of their disorder. The rest continue having many of the same problems they had as children and then teenagers, and dealing with those problems for so long can take a tragic toll: A Canadian follow-up study by Gabrielle Weiss and Lily Hechtman found that almost 10% will have attempted suicide within the past three years and about 5% will die from either suicide or accidental injury—much higher rates than for control groups.

It is fair to say that perhaps 25% are persistently antisocial in adulthood: ADHD adults are four times as likely as others to have committed acts of physical aggression toward others within the last three years.

In the undemanding part-time jobs typically held by teenagers, ADHD adolescents function as well as their non-ADHD peers, but in the adult working world, they are likely to have problems that add up to a poorer work record and lower job status than other adults.

We have known for a long time that children diagnosed with ADHD have a number of significant additional problems to contend with as they get older. Some of these may be preventable with prolonged treatment, but keep in mind that children with ADHD should not be dismissed as having little or no future risk. What determines who will outgrow ADHD is not clear at this time. Certainly children whose ADHD was quite mild in childhood seem to have a better chance of outgrowing it. We do know that ADHD children benefit from the same advantages that non-ADHD children do—intelligence, lack of aggression or defiance, good care and supervision from parents who do not have their own serious psychological problems to deal with, and sufficient affluence to have access to economic and community resources.

The Symptoms of ADHD Change with the Situation

To make life even more challenging for parents of ADHD children, all of the primary symptoms of ADHD change not only with the child's growth but also with the situation: where the child is, what he or she is asked to do, and who must care for the child. Table 2 shows the results of a study I did in the late 1970s to examine those situations in which ADHD children were most likely to have problems when with their parents. The table illustrates that the less restrictive the setting and the less demanding the tasks required, the less distinguishable ADHD children are from non-ADHD children.

Interestingly, the table also indicates that ADHD children are more compliant and less disruptive with their fathers than mothers. There are several possible reasons for this, discussed in the following chapter (see Chapter 5).

Research also has shown that ADHD children do better under the following conditions.

Unfamiliar Surroundings or New Tasks

ADHD children do much better at the beginning of the academic year, when teachers, classmates, classrooms, and even school facilities are new. Their behavioral control deteriorates over the initial weeks of school. Similarly, they may be less troublesome when visiting with grandparents whom they have not seen frequently. These grandparents are likely to provide them with more one-on-one attention than the parents and are unlikely to make demands of the children's self-control. At such times, it is likely that ADHD children would be at their best. Research also suggests that more colorful, highly stimulating, bright, cheerful, fun educational materials presented differently from the usual dry textbook or workbook format may be important in helping ADHD children to work better at school.

TABLE 2. Percentage of Hyperactive- and Control-Group Children Displaying Problems in 14 Home Situations and the Average Severity Rating in Each Setting

Situation	Hyperactive group		Control group	
	Percent	Average severity[a]	Percent	Average severity
While playing alone	40.0	4.3	0.0	0.0
Playing with others	90.0	5.4	10.0	1.6
Mealtimes	86.7	4.7	13.3	3.0
Getting dressed	73.3	6.1	10.0	2.3
Washing/bathing	43.3	5.1	16.7	1.2
When parent is on phone	93.3	6.6	33.3	1.3
While watching television	80.0	5.0	3.3	2.0
When visitors are in home	96.7	6.1	30.0	1.6
When visiting others	96.7	5.4	13.3	1.5
Public places	96.7	5.4	23.3	2.7
When father is at home	73.3	3.9	6.7	2.5
When asked to do chores	86.7	5.6	36.7	2.0
At bedtime	83.3	5.0	20.0	1.5
While riding in the car	73.3	4.8	20.0	1.7

Note. From R. A. Barkley (1981), *Hyperactive children: A handbook for diagnosis and treatment.* New York: Guilford Press. Copyright 1981 by The Guilford Press. Reprinted by permission.
[a]Severity was rated by parents on a scale from 1 (mild) to 9 (severe).

Immediate Rewards for Complying with Instructions

Few ADHD children show deficits in attention to popular video games, such as Nintendo. They perform better when special rewards such as money are promised immediately upon completion of a task, perhaps even as well as non-ADHD children do. However, when the timing and amount of the reward are changed, the behavior of ADHD children worsens significantly. These dramatic changes have led scientists to question whether ADHD is actually a deficit in attention at all, as discussed in Chapter 2.

Individual Attention

During one-to-one encounters with others, ADHD children may appear less active, inattentive, and impulsive. In group situations, ADHD children may appear at their worst. Again they may be at their best with grandparents, who are likely to give them this individualized attention. They work more effectively under close supervision and when instructions are repeated frequently.

Most Demanding Schedule in the Morning

Fatigue or the time of day may determine how problematic a child's ADHD symptoms are likely to be. ADHD children seem to do better on schoolwork in the mornings, more so than non-ADHD children. This means not only that educators would do well to schedule repetitive, boring, or difficult tasks requiring the greatest powers of attention and self-control for morning but also that trying to do homework with an ADHD child in late afternoons or early evenings is sure to meet with trouble.

Other Problems Are Associated with ADHD

It is rare in a clinical practice to see children who have only one disorder; probably less than 20% of the children who come to my ADHD clinic, for example, have only ADHD. Being diagnosed as having ADHD raises the odds of having several other problems as well, a phenomenon called *comorbidity*. In particular, people with ADHD may be more likely than others to have additional medical, developmental, behavioral, emotional, and academic difficulties.

Intelligence

ADHD children are likely to represent the whole spectrum of intellectual development. Some but not all studies have found that children with ADHD are more likely to be behind the general mental or intellectual development of non-ADHD children, to a not very large, but scientifically significant, degree. Children with ADHD may score an average of 7 to 10 points below others on intelligence tests, but the differences may be more a reflection of the problems ADHD imposes on the test-taking abilities than of intelligence.

There is some evidence that the IQ test scores of ADHD children may decline as much as 7 to 10 points over the years, but any real decline very well may be due to educational shortfalls that are preventing them from keeping pace with their peers. If so, this gradual drop in IQ ought to be preventable by designing educational environments to suit ADHD children's needs, though that theory has not been tested.

School Performance

One area of tremendous difficulty for ADHD children is academic performance: the amount of schoolwork they are able to perform and their general conduct in the classroom. (Achievement, in contrast, means the level of difficulty of work they are able to accomplish.) Almost all ADHD children referred to clinics are doing poorly at school. They seem to have at least two main problems with academic work: (1) They are not getting as much done as other children or as would be expected from their known abilities and so have lower grades and are retained more often in their grade levels. (2) Their ability levels are also somewhat below those of non-ADHD children and may even decline somewhat over their years in school. Consequently, it is not surprising to find that 40% or more of ADHD children may eventually be placed in special educational programs for learning or behaviorally disordered children. Nor is it unexpected that as many as 35% will have been retained in a grade at least once before reaching high school. Being inattentive and impulsive in a setting where self-control and sustained effort are crucial for success, as in school, can be devastating for these children.

ADHD children are also more likely than non-ADHD children to have learning disabilities. A learning disability (LD) is a significant discrepancy between a child's intelligence and his other academic achievement test scores. Between 20 and 30% of ADHD children have at least one type of LD, in math, reading, or spelling.

Why do nearly three to five times as many ADHD children as non-ADHD children have these learning disabilities? Scientists are not sure, but possible explanations are emerging from studies on the genetics of ADHD and LD. Both disorders have a strong hereditary predisposition. Recent studies suggest that at least for reading disorders the two do not tend to be inherited together; that is, the genes for ADHD are not the same as those for a reading LD. We don't know why reading disorders occur more often in those with ADHD at this time.

In the case of spelling/writing disorders, a recent study by Dr. Bruce Pennington and his colleagues at the University of Colorado suggests that the genes for ADHD and this type of LD may in fact be the same ones. Much more research is needed on this issue before this relationship can be taken as proven, however. No one has yet looked at the inheritance of math disorders, so we have no clues as to how these come to coexist with ADHD.

Although most ADHD children are not seriously delayed in the development of language, they are more likely to have specific problems in speech development than normal children. ADHD children also are more likely to have problems with expressive language and fluency. These findings might be explained by my new theory, discussed in Chapter 2, but this is only an educated guess.

Other Mental Abilities

ADHD children also tend to be less skilled in the use of complex problem-solving strategies and organizational skills needed for solving intellectual or social problems. Their impulsiveness is a disadvantage to them in most problem-solving situations, as discussed in Chapter 2. They also use less efficient strategies in searching their memory when they need to think about how to react to a situation. We often refer to this as hindsight, and again Chapter 2 discusses how I believe ADHD precludes the use of adequate hindsight. Children with ADHD do not have memory problems. Their problems in doing intellectual work come when they must apply thoughtful strategies in their work—when they must inhibit the urge to respond and reflect on the problem. Little wonder, then, that many studies also show that ADHD children are less organized or planful in their approach to learning and performing school work in general.

Physical Development

Several relatively large studies have indicated that ADHD children have more problems with physical development than non-ADHD children. Table 3 summarizes one done by Drs. Carolyn Hartsough and Nadine Lambert of the University of California at Berkeley, who in 1985 published their findings on the medical histories of 492 hyperactive children from the East Bay area of San Francisco. The percentages of the hyperactive and the control or normal children having each developmental problem are shown in this table. If a Yes appears next to the item or problem, then that difference is considered to be statistically significant—that simply means that the groups can be considered to be reliably different on that item. Where a No appears, even though the numbers are not quite the same, the groups should be considered to be the same. This study found that the hyperactive children were more likely to have problems than the other children with 19 of the 30 problems listed, but we should keep in mind that other studies have disagreed. Let's look at some individual problems.

Congenital Problems

The table shows that mothers of hyperactive children were much more likely to have experienced complications of their pregnancies than mothers of control children. The hyperactive children were also more likely to have experienced medical problems shortly after birth (congenital problems) and to have had general health problems during infancy.

Hearing and Speech

While there is no evidence that ADHD children are any more likely than non-ADHD children to have difficulties in the development of their hearing, some studies show that more will have otitis media, or middle ear infections, than other children, which can reduce hearing and create problems with speech development. The findings are not very consistent across studies, however.

Vision

ADHD children seem somewhat more likely to have vision problems than non-ADHD children, but again research findings are inconsistent.

Motor Skills

Drs. Hartsough and Lambert found ADHD children to be slightly more likely to be delayed in crawling than non-ADHD children (6.5% vs. 1.6%), but over 93% of the hyperactive children had no such delays. Nevertheless, as many as 52% of ADHD compared to up to 35% of non-ADHD children are likely to have poor motor coordination, especially fine motor coordination, such as buttoning, tying shoelaces, drawing, and writing.

Physical Appearance

One fascinating finding is that ADHD children seem to have more minor or slight deformities in their physical appearance than non-ADHD children, such as an

TABLE 3. Percentage of Hyperactive- and Control-Group Children Having Medical Problems

Medical problems	Hyperactive group	Control group	Significantly different?
Pregnancy/birth problems			
1. Poor health of mother	26.4	16.2	Yes
2. Young mother (under 20 years of age)	16.3	6.7	Yes
3. At least one previous miscarriage	21.1	24.4	No
4. First pregnancy	42.7	32.8	Yes
5. Rh factor (blood) incompatibility	14.9	12.4	No
6. Premature delivery (under 8 months)	7.9	5.4	No
7. Postmaturity (over 10 months)	7.9	1.5	Yes
8. Long labor (13 or more hours)	24.8	15.7	Yes
9. Toxemia or eclampsia during pregnancy	7.8	2.5	Yes
10. Fetal distress during labor or birth	16.9	8.0	Yes
11. Abnormal delivery	26.6	20.2	No
12. Low birth weight (under 6 lbs.)	12.2	7.8	No
13. Congenital problems	22.1	13.2	Yes
14. Problems in establishing routines during infancy (eating, sleeping, etc.)	54.6	31.7	Yes
15. Health problems during infancy	50.9	29.2	Yes
Developmental milestones			
16. Delay in sitting up	0.4	0.0	No
17. Delay in crawling	6.5	1.6	Yes
18. Delay in walking	1.5	0.5	No
19. Delay in talking	9.6	3.7	Yes
20. Delay in bladder control	7.4	4.5	No
21. Delay in bowel control	10.1	4.5	Yes
Childhood illness and accidents			
22. Chronic health problems	39.1	24.8	Yes
23. One or more acute illnesses or diseases in childhood	78.0	79.0	No
24. Four or more serious accidents	15.6	4.8	Yes
25. More than one surgery	27.3	19.5	No
Childhood health status			
26. Poor general health	8.9	2.4	Yes
27. Poor hearing	11.1	7.6	No
28. Poor vision	21.6	13.4	Yes
29. Poor coordination	52.3	34.9	Yes
30. Speech problems	26.6	14.8	Yes

Note. Adapted from C. S. Hartsough and N. M. Lambert (1985), "Medical factors in hyperactive and normal children: Prenatal, developmental, and health history findings." *American Journal of Orthopsychiatry, 55,* 190–201. Copyright 1985 by the American Orthopsychiatric Association. Adapted by permission.

index finger that is longer than the middle finger, a curved fifth finger, a third toe that is as long as or longer than their second toe, ears that are set slightly lower on the sides of the head than normal, no earlobes, or a furrowed tongue. However, recent research shows that all children with psychiatric disorders tend to have more such anomalies, so these anomalies are not just a sign of ADHD alone.

Health or Medical Problems

ADHD children seem to have more problems with their general health than do non-ADHD children. Up to 50% were described by their mothers as having been in poor health during infancy, compared to less than half this number in non-ADHD children. We do not yet understand why ADHD children are more likely to have medical problems, but children with other psychiatric disorders also have a greater tendency toward general health problems.

Similarly, nighttime bed-wetting (enuresis) and problems with toilet training plague ADHD children more than other children, but the same can be said of all children with psychiatric problems.

Parents often complain that their ADHD children do not sleep well, and several studies have confirmed that these children take longer to get ready for bed or to fall asleep, wake up more frequently during the night, and may be unusually tired upon awakening.

Some studies have found that children with ADHD are more accident prone than non-ADHD children. Recent studies using much larger groups of children have found this truer for children who are defiant and stubborn than for hyperactive children.

Behavioral and Emotional Problems

ADHD is often associated with other behavioral and emotional disorders. From early infancy, children with ADHD are often reported to be more demanding and difficult to care for in their general temperament than are non-ADHD children (see Table 3). Up to 45% of ADHD children have at least one other psychiatric disorder besides ADHD and many have two or more additional disorders. ADHD children display more symptoms of anxiety, depression, and low self-esteem than do other children.

It is widely accepted by scientists that ADHD children have more difficulties with oppositional and defiant behavior. Up to two-thirds (or more) can be very stubborn and argue with their parents more than other children. Many of these defiant children are also aggressive toward others. They may be quick to get angry, verbally attack others, or even physically assault others more than other children of their age. These conduct problems can progress to more severe forms of antisocial behavior such as lying, stealing, fighting, running away from home, destroying property, and other delinquent or criminal behavior. My own research shows that up to 65% will eventually have a diagnosis of oppositional defiant disorder, and as many as 45% may progress to the more severe level of conduct disorder.

How Do ADHD Children Get Along with Other Children?

Not usually very well, I'm afraid. Drs. William Pelham and Mary Bender at the University of Pittsburgh Western Psychiatric Institute studied the social relationships of ADHD children. They estimated that over 50% had significant problems in their peer relationships. Research shows that the inattentive, disruptive, off-task, immature, and provocative behaviors of ADHD children quickly bring out a pattern of controlling and directive behavior from their peers when they must work together. And, despite talking more, ADHD children are less likely to respond to the questions or verbal interactions of their peers. It is easy to see why many ADHD children have few, if any, friends with whom to play.

This can be very painful for a parent to witness. We all want our children to be liked by others, to have friends, to be invited out with other children, and to develop close relationships with their peer group. We know that such relationships can sustain us through other difficulties we may experience as we grow up. When parents notice that their ADHD children are having great troubles in forming and keeping friendships, they have reason for concern.

This chapter should have shown you that ADHD children are not all alike. Some will exhibit different patterns of behavior, development, and later risks than others. Some will have only ADHD; others will have this disorder as well as learning problems, aggression, antisocial conduct, and poor peer relations. All share the problem of reduced ability to inhibit behavior and to sustain effort to activities. And, of course, all are children in need of our care, support, guidance, nurturance, and love, though they can be challenging to raise and do not always appear grateful for our efforts to guide and raise them to adulthood.

CHAPTER 5

Family Life with an ADHD Child

Children with ADHD do not exist in a vacuum. They occupy specific places within a social network or system, the most significant of these being the most immediate one, the family. Forgive me for stating the obvious, but traditionally our theories, assessment, and treatment of these children focus so heavily on them as individuals and their behavior in isolation from others that we forget this important point. No one can fully appreciate the disorder, its causes, impairments, course, and outcome without recourse to this social environment and the interaction of the child with it. The very diagnosis of ADHD hinges on our understanding this point. It is the reports of others within this social network that determine which children get referred, diagnosed, and treated. The prognosis of ADHD for any given child surely revolves around this factor as well. To understand who becomes ADHD, who stays ADHD over development, which ADHD children develop additional problems, which will fare well despite these problems, and which individuals will fare poorly in adulthood requires reference to this social network. Therefore, knowing that children are ADHD is of limited importance in predicting their future or in designing treatment for them. We must refer further to the various contexts in which specific children live and interact, with whom they interact, and who, in turn, act on them.

Knowing what impact children with ADHD have on their families, how their families act on them, and how their behavior is managed by parents will help you understand not just your child but also yourself, and even your family. The journey of discovery that led you to this book must also be a journey of self-exploration for you as a parent. As you read this chapter, consider how you typically respond to your child's appropriate behavior and especially to inappropriate, disruptive, or demanding behavior. Also consider how your child treats you, what reactions your child brings out in you, and the overall quality of your relationship. Then examine, in turn, how your ADHD child affects others in the family and how they treat this child. Are you married? If so, do you have marital problems that spill over into your relationships with your children, particularly the ADHD child? Or is your marriage a source of strength for you in dealing with the day-to-day demands of raising children and managing a household? Do you work outside the home? Does this bring stress into your home and affect your relationship with your children? Or is your job also a source of personal growth and success that feeds your strength as a parent? Although I will describe here the results of research on the family interactions of ADHD children, the ultimate purpose of this chapter is to encourage you to examine your own family relative to these scientific findings. See if there are things about *your* family that you would like to change. Then make a commitment to change them. Hopefully the later chapters of this book will help you with that goal. In any case, it should be obvious that you are at least seeking to change the quality of your relationship with your ADHD child, or you probably would not have started reading this book.

The family context of an ADHD child is critically important in understanding these children for several reasons. First, the social interactions of these children with and reactions from their parents and siblings have been shown to be inherently more negative and stressful to all members than in typical families without an ADHD child. Despite the view taken in this book that the development of ADHD has a strong biological–hereditary predisposition, not even the strongest advocate of this view could deny the powerful effects this difference in social interaction must produce on the expression of ADHD in a child.

Second, much evidence exists that the parents and siblings of ADHD children are more likely to be experiencing their own psychological distress and psychiatric disorders than families of non-ADHD children. In fact, there is about a 40% chance that at least one of the parents of an ADHD child also has the disorder. These difficulties that other family members are experiencing surely have some influence on the manner in which the ADHD child is perceived, managed, reared, loved, and then launched into adulthood. This influence acts in unique ways that seem to have long-lasting effects for the adolescent and adult outcome of these children. Perhaps it starts a vicious cycle much like the following:

1. Parents who are having personal problems often perceive their children as showing more disruptive behavior, and that behavior is more difficult for them to manage than it is for parents without such problems.
2. These perceptions affect the way the parent reacts to the child's behavior, sometimes resulting in unnecessarily harsh punishment or a general irritability toward the child no matter what the child does.
3. The child may also receive much less encouragement, praise, and general warmth than would otherwise be given.
4. This treatment of the child in turn influences how the child behaves toward that parent, perhaps increasing the level of defiance, stubbornness, argument, and general conflict.

5. This may reinforce the parent's view that the child is a problem or difficult to manage.
6. The cycle starts anew.

This does not mean that the parent is the chief cause of the child's ADHD or defiant behavior; it only suggests that the parent–child relationship can affect the severity of the child's problems and the parent's perceptions of how stressful the child is to raise.

Since 1980 or so, a large number of scientific studies have been published on the manner in which ADHD children interact with their parents and the reactions of parents to them. I have devoted much of my own scientific career to understanding these interaction patterns and how they are changed by various treatments. What does the research tell us?

The Interactions of ADHD Children with Their Mothers

The first studies to directly observe the behavior of mothers with their ADHD children were done by Dr. Susan Campbell at the University of Pittsburgh in 1975. Dr. Campbell observed that hyperactive boys initiated more interactions than other boys when working with their mothers to complete a task. These children also talked more with their mothers and requested more help. In short, hyperactive children seem to require more attention from, talk more to, and seek more help from their mothers during interactions with them. The mothers of the hyperactive children gave them more suggestions, approval, disapproval, and directions on impulse control than the mothers of the control children. In other words, mothers of ADHD children had to manage the behavior of their children more and involve themselves in their children's self-control more than mothers of non-ADHD children. Extended over time, this degree of interaction can be quite stressful and exhausting to the mothers.

In my own early studies, I found that hyperactive children were much less compliant, more negative, more likely to get off task, and less able to persist in complying with their mothers' directives. Their mothers gave more commands, were also more negative, and at times were less responsive to their children's interactions than I observed in the relations of other children. I also found, as did Dr. Campbell, that hyperactive children talked more during these exchanges.

Later I found that these interaction conflicts changed with age (though not with gender). Younger children had far more mother–child conflicts than older children in both the ADHD and non-ADHD families. However, at none of the ages studied did the hyperactive children behave like their non-ADHD peers—and, of course, neither did their mothers. So there is hope that these family relationships improve somewhat, but there is some evidence that they do not become fully normative.

The Interactions of ADHD Children with Their Fathers

"I have a lot of problems in managing my child, but my husband has far fewer problems. Why?"

One of the things I have heard repeatedly from mothers of ADHD children is that the child seems to behave better for their husband. When Dr. James Tallmadge and I compared videotaped interactions between mothers and ADHD children with those between the fathers and children, overall we did not find much difference. We did notice, however, that the ADHD children were less negative with their fathers and were more likely to stay on task than when with their mothers.

I am not sure why this should be so. It might have to do with the fact that mothers still typically carry more of the responsibility than fathers for interacting with the ADHD child at home, especially in getting work and chores done, even when the mothers work outside the home. The parent who taxes the behavioral deficits of the ADHD child will clearly have the greater conflicts with that child (an illuminating example of this is related in Chapter 17). Mothers also appear to rely somewhat more on reasoning and affection in gaining their children's compliance with instructions. With an ADHD child who does not follow instructions or reason very well and is not as sensitive to praise, this approach is less likely to motivate. Fathers may reason and repeat commands less and may impose swifter punishment for noncompliance. So perhaps the parent who acts quickly to provide some consequence for the child's good and bad behavior may get more compliance. We can also not rule out the fact that the greater physical size and strength of the father may be intimidating to the ADHD child.

Regardless of why the discrepancy exists, the fact that it does exist can cause problems in the parents' marriage. The father in such a case might attribute his wife's reports to exaggeration or decide that the child's worse behavior with her results from her being too permissive. He might then conclude that it is the mother, not the child, who needs professional assistance. I have also heard of similar scenes being played out in the pediatrician's office: When the male physician has no difficulty managing the ADHD child, he labels the mother as hysterical and incompetent. It is time for fathers and male professionals to realize that children, especially ADHD children, differ in their response to mothers and fathers. If you doubt this, let the father assume greater responsibility for the day-to-day care of the ADHD child for a while and see if his view of the child's behavior problems begins to resemble the mother's more closely.

The Interactions of ADHD Children with Their Siblings

The relationship of ADHD children to their brothers and sisters also seems to differ from that seen in other families. ADHD children argue more, play more disruptively, yell at siblings more, and are more likely to encourage inappropri-ate behavior or mischief, so it's no surprise that conflict is greater than normal. Again, this difference is more marked when the ADHD children are younger.

> "How do we get our other kids to understand why their sister
> acts the way she does, that she is different from them?
> They think she's lucky for all the help she gets."

How does the non-ADHD sibling feel? Brothers and sisters tend to grow tired and exasperated by living with such a disruptive—and baffling—force, with some coming to resent the greater burden of work they often carry compared to their hyperactive siblings. Certainly, the greater time the ADHD children receive from their parents is often a source of envy, especially when the non-ADHD sibling is younger.

Little additional research exists to tell us how these sibling interactions might contribute to problems for both the ADHD child and the sibling(s). But let's not forget that the siblings of ADHD children have approximately one chance in three or four of having ADHD themselves. When they do, it exacerbates the problem for the whole family.

How Does ADHD Affect Family Interactions?

The answer cannot be given with much certainty at this time, but an obvious starting place is the ADHD symptoms themselves. The inattentive, impulsive, and overactive behavior patterns of ADHD children often conflict with the de-mands all parents must make on their children. Many daily tasks place heavy demands on the child's ability to sustain attention, persist in effort, and ignore things that might be more fun to do at the moment. When these children have trouble complying, their parents cannot help reacting with greater direction, con-trol, suggestion, encouragement, and ultimately anger. But even when no task is required of the child, the excessive behavior, activity, speech, and vocal noises are likely to be viewed as intrusiveness and aversive by others, especially over extended periods of time.

So who is causing this cycle of interaction conflict? Both the child and the parent contribute to the upward spiral of conflict, but the ADHD child contrib-utes more than you may have realized. Keep in mind, of course, that the child does not do this intentionally. Research on the interactions of ADHD children with other adults and children outside the family, such as teachers and peers, shows that when an ADHD child is placed in a classroom, teachers, like mothers, are likely to increase their commands to, reprimands of, and discipline of the child. Likewise, when ADHD children first enter a new play group, the other children will start to act like little mothers of ADHD children—giving more com-mands, directions, and help to the ADHD child. When this doesn't squelch the

ADHD child's hyperactive and disruptive behavior, the other children may get angry, tease, or insult the ADHD child. Failing this, they will pull away from the ADHD child to find some peace from this unruly, intrusive, and domineering person.

Studies using stimulant medications with ADHD children have shown that when ADHD children are placed on such medication, the use by mothers, teachers, and peers of commands, disapproval, and general control diminishes to that seen with non-ADHD children, and the interactions become generally more positive. If the parents of ADHD children were the major cause of the conflict, medicating their children should produce little change in the parents' behavior or little decline in the conflicts. This was hardly the case in our studies.

How Parents Seem to React to Child Misconduct over Time

Although there is little research on the issue, I have been impressed clinically that parents may move through several steps in their efforts to control their ADHD children's disruptive behavior. When one strategy fails to work, they move on to the next step in this sequence. My experience suggests that parents initially try to ignore or withhold attention from their children when the children show disruptive behavior. Perhaps they believe that some of this behavior is intended merely to get attention and so ignoring the child should decrease the problem. But the ADHD child's behavior is not merely the result of bids for attention, so these techniques are unlikely to succeed. As the disruptive behavior continues or intensifies, parents give more commands and directives, especially those aimed at controlling the children's impulses. These commands are often restrictive, calling for the children to stop what they are doing, and parents will find themselves repeating them frequently.

At some point frustration and exasperation may result in the parents issuing threats along with these repeated directives. When this approach fails (as it often does) to motivate the ADHD children to listen and obey, parents may then move to the actual use of physical discipline or other forms of punishment (loss of privileges or time-out) to regain control over the children's unruly behavior. Some parents may simply give up at this point, giving in to the child and perhaps even doing the child's task themselves or simply walking away, leaving the task undone. If the children have begun to comply but the quality of compliance is poor, parents step in and assist the children in doing the chore.

With time, parents do not start at the beginning of this sequence whenever they have to step in to control their ADHD children. Instead, they may proceed straight to the last strategy of management that produced some partial success. This could readily lead to immediate negative reactions toward a child or harsh physical discipline when the child starts to show even minimal disruptive behavior. Some parents appear to have reached such a severe state of failure in their management of their children that they could best be described as being in a state of "learned helplessness." They make no, or minimal, effort to give or enforce commands to their children, leaving them to do as they please. They begin to withdraw from the children, ultimately providing little if any supervision. At this point many such parents report depression, low self-esteem in their role as parents, and little satisfaction with or involvement in their parenting responsibilities. In some cases such parents may shift between complete disengagement and overly harsh reactions to their children's misbehavior, depending on their own mood and irritability at the time. In short, living with an ADHD child can seriously tax a parent's mental health and commitment to parenthood. If that parent is already experiencing personal emotional problems, it can make them far worse.

Parental Psychiatric Problems

Parents and relatives of ADHD children are in fact more likely to have psychological problems than those of children without ADHD. Some of these come about from the difficulty of living with someone who has ADHD; others are rooted in biology.

Parenting Stress

There is no question that parents of ADHD children, especially mothers and particularly when the children are young, experience greater stress than do caretakers of non-ADHD children. Mothers of ADHD children tell us that they have lower levels of parenting self-esteem and experience markedly more depression, self-blame, and social isolation than mothers of non-ADHD children. The more severe the child's behavior problems, the more severe the stress. Obviously, other factors that are affecting the mother's psychological well-being can distort how she views her children and thus how much stress she feels, but our studies show that the major source of parenting stress comes from the child's ADHD and its disruptiveness rather than from other sources in the family.

> "I'm at my wits' end with him. I'm afraid I'm going to hurt him.
> He's driving me crazy and won't listen. I can't cope with him anymore.
> I may have to send him away."

We also have found that both the stress of raising an ADHD child and the greater risk for personal emotional problems in the parents can greatly strain a marriage, especially when the ADHD child has serious oppositional, defiant, or aggressive behavior. My associates and I have found that over an eight-year period, during which we followed a large number of families of ADHD children, their parents were three times more likely to have separated or divorced than in families of non ADHD children.

Parents of ADHD children also may be deprived of the encouragement, warmth, and assistance of a supportive family. They tell us that they have fewer contacts with their extended family members than in families without ADHD children and that these contacts are less helpful to them as parents and more aversive or unpleasant. So parents of ADHD children may experience a form of social isolation that is detrimental both to their caretaking abilities with their children and to their own emotional well-being.

Psychiatric Disorders

As I have said, the biological parents of ADHD children are themselves more likely to have ADHD or at least some of the residual characteristics of the disorder. About 15 to 20% of the mothers and 20 to 30% of the fathers of ADHD children may have ADHD at the same time as their children. The biological siblings of ADHD children also share this risk. Approximately 26% of brothers and sisters of the ADHD child may have the disorder. In general, the risk of ADHD among the first-degree biological relatives of ADHD children is between 25 and 33%.

Parents of ADHD children are more likely to experience a variety of other psychiatric disorders as well, the most common being conduct problems and antisocial behavior (25–28%), alcoholism (14–25%), hysteria (excessive emotional responding to distress) or mood disorders (10–27%), and learning disabilities. Even if they are not abusing alcohol, parents of ADHD children consume more alcohol than those of non-ADHD children. Recall, though, that these psychiatric problems are associated mainly with aggressive and antisocial behavior in the children and not so much with the children's ADHD. The more aggressive and antisocial the child is, the more numerous and severe are the psychiatric problems among the relatives. Only ADHD and a history of school problems seem to be more common in the family members of ADHD children who are not seriously aggressive or antisocial. This certainly suggests that parent and family psychiatric problems may be giving rise to the child's aggressive and antisocial behavior. They do so by the influence these parental problems have on the child-rearing skills of the parents and the emotional climate of family life in the home.

What Does All of This Mean for Me as a Parent?

All of the preceding information can be boiled down to the simple fact that having an ADHD child places great stress on parents, particularly mothers. This stress is as great as or greater than that experienced by parents who have children with autism, a far more serious developmental disorder than ADHD. The excessive, demanding, intrusive, and generally high intensity of behavior of ADHD children and their clear impairment in self-control naturally elicit greater efforts at direction, help, supervision, and monitoring by parents that is far in excess of what parents of non-ADHD children need to do. Parents with more than one child with ADHD are assured that their stress levels will be more than twice those of any other family with just one ADHD child. It therefore is easy to see how you could become overwhelmed by the demands these children place on you as a parent. I am sure you are aware that when people are exposed to high levels of chronic stress they are more likely to have medical problems, especially those related to immune disorders, such as colds, flus, and other infections. So you may find yourself similarly affected and find your overall energy level lower since having a child with ADHD.

Short of placing your ADHD child up for adoption, which no one would suggest, there are many ways to make life at home easier that we consider in Parts II and III of this book (see Chapters 6–19). Above all, do not give up as a parent. ADHD children do have a positive side, and raising them to adulthood can give you tremendous satisfaction, provided you learn to cope with the extra stress such parenting brings with it. Draw on the seven principles of effective parenting discussed in the Introduction, and, particularly, do not ignore opportunities for your own personal renewal (see Chapter 10). Strive to be a principle-centered, executive, and scientific parent, and you should find that the stress of raising a child with ADHD is substantially diminished.

PART II

Taking Charge: How to Be a Successful Executive Parent

CHAPTER 6

Deciding to Have Your Child Evaluated for ADHD

Deciding to seek a professional evaluation for a child is a major decision for any parent. Most parents reach this turning point when they realize that their child's problems exceed the capacity of family and school resources to solve them and when their frustration in trying to help and get help has reached a peak. Consequently many parents who are taking that first tenuous step toward help already feel overwhelmed. The goal of this chapter is to make the transition from self-help to professional help a smooth one.

When Should You Consider Getting a Professional Evaluation?

Many parents notice on their own during the preschool years that their child seems to behave differently from others. Excessive activity, lack of attentiveness and control over emotions, aggressiveness, excitability, and the other symptoms described in Chapter 1 become difficult to ignore. Sometimes it's also obvious that the tried-and-true methods used to manage other children's disruptive and temperamental behavior are not having much impact. It's often when these two factors converge, and parents perceive the continuing need to help their child more than other parents do, that they conclude something is wrong.

In many other cases the child's problems are pointed out by school staff. Parents often learn their child is behaving differently and disruptively before kindergarten, from day-care personnel or preschool staff. Sometimes, however, staff members don't say anything, so the parents, who only suspect a problem, do not seek immediate assistance. It is, in fact, in the formal school setting, usually during the first year or two, that the vast majority of parents learn their child has a behavior problem that needs attention. In the more structured setting of the primary grades a child who can't sit still or be quiet when appropriate is impossible to overlook. In a small but significant minority, the parents have not sought professional help for their child's ADHD or have not been advised to do so by the time the child has gone through several years of school. At some point these parents encounter media stories depicting ADHD children, and this sparks the recognition that their own child may well have this disorder. Frequently parents call our ADHD clinic after seeing or hearing me on a TV or radio program or reading an article, desperate for help now that they finally have an idea of what may be wrong with their child.

At whatever point in their child's life parents begin to suspect a problem in development, they are likely first to confide in friends or relatives. They may also make a trip to the library to get the latest paperback on child development. Invariably they begin to hear a lot of the folklore surrounding ADHD. They may try cutting back on the child's sugar intake, taking the child for allergy testing, exercising firmer discipline—all to no avail.

If they're lucky, they stumble across an informative, factual article on ADHD, or an astute preschool or primary-grade teacher recognizes the signs of ADHD. As a result these parents seek the advice of their family physician, who may recognize the hallmark characteristics of the disorder and make a diagnosis of ADHD. More often, the physician suspects that the child may have ADHD and refers the child to other professionals in the community—child psychologists or psychiatrists, developmental pediatricians, or child neurologists—who may be more expert at the assessment and diagnosis of the disorder. The doctor may also suggest, for school-age children having significant behavioral problems at school as well as at home, that the parents solicit a school evaluation to determine whether the child should receive special educational assistance.

If you're beginning to suspect that your child has a problem that may be ADHD, don't ignore it in the hope that it will go away. Consider seeking a professional evaluation when any of the following conditions exist:

1. For at least six months the child has displayed activity, inattentiveness, and impulsiveness far greater than in other children of the same age.
2. For at least a few months other parents have been telling you that your child has much poorer self-control or is far more active, impulsive, and inattentive when with other children than is normal.
3. Far more of your time and energy is required to manage and keep the child safe than other parents invest.
4. Other children do not like to play with your child and avoid him or her because of the child's excessively active, emotional, or aggressive behavior.
5. A day-care staff member or schoolteacher has informed you that your child has been having significant behavioral problems for several months.

6. You frequently lose your temper with this child, feel as if you are on the verge of excessive physical discipline or might even harm the child, or are greatly fatigued, exhausted, or even depressed as a consequence of managing and raising this child.

What Type of Professional Should You Call?

Generally, the professional to call is the one in your area who seems to know the most about ADHD. Whether you consult a pediatrician, child psychologist, child psychiatrist, child neurologist, social worker, school psychologist, family practitioner, or other mental health professional seems to matter less than finding someone who is familiar with the substantial scientific and professional literature on ADHD. Parents' support groups, such as CHADD or ADDA (see the back of the book), can provide recommendations based on their experience in your region. If no local chapter exists, ask your child's teacher or physician for a referral to someone who has a solid reputation in the area for dealing with ADHD children.

In specific circumstances, however, you may need the services of a particular type of professional.

Physicians

Any child who is to be evaluated for ADHD should first have a standard pediatric checkup to rule out medical causes of the symptoms. Epilepsy is relatively rare, even in ADHD children, so you should not routinely seek out a neurological evaluation just because a child has ADHD. But if there are other indications that your child may be having medical problems such as seizures, you will want to call a pediatrician or child neurologist for an appointment. If it is already clear that seizures are occurring, you can take your child to a local emergency room for an evaluation.

Sometimes you might need to consult a physician after your child has already been diagnosed as having ADHD. If you've been working with only psychologists, social workers, and educators, you'll need to find a physician who knows ADHD and how to use medications with the disorder in cases where you're considering a trial of medication for your child (see Chapters 18 and 19). Not all pediatricians, child neurologists, and child psychiatrists are knowledgeable in this area, so your best bet may be to contact either a child psychiatrist who specializes in medications for children or a developmental and behavioral pediatrician who knows about ADHD. Then when you call for the appointment, ask the office staff whether the doctor sees a lot of ADHD children or knows a lot about medications used with ADHD.

Psychologists

These professionals are trained not only to evaluate psychological problems in children but also to give psychological, learning, or neuropsychological tests that can help pinpoint the type of learning or behavior problem your child has. For this reason the majority of parents seeking an evaluation of their child consult a psychologist.

If you have already had your child evaluated and diagnosed properly but are seeking a particular kind of treatment, then of course you will want to seek out a professional specializing in that type of therapy. There are, to name just a few, family counselors, psychotherapists, group therapists, and school counselors.

Before You Choose . . .

Again, just be sure that the person you contact knows something about ADHD and its treatment. Ask these questions:

- Are you licensed? (If necessary, contact the state licensing board to be sure.)
- Do you see ADHD children frequently?
- Do you consider yourself well informed about the disorder and well trained in how to manage it?
- What types of treatment for ADHD do you routinely provide? (If the answer does not include the ones you are after, try again elsewhere.)
- Have any malpractice complaints been filed against you?

Don't be embarrassed to ask such pointed questions. Find another professional if the one you ask is offended.

What about the Cost?

You'll want to get the very best professional help that suits your unique situation, but on a purely practical level you have to consider the expense. Take these steps to avoid unpleasant surprises:

1. When you're calling a professional's office for an appointment, ask what the cost is likely to be. Most professionals accept insurance payment, but a few do not, so be sure to inquire.

2. Then contact your insurance carrier to be sure that it will cover this type of evaluation. Most insurance companies classify an evaluation for ADHD as a mental health service and will limit how much they will pay for such services, usually to $500 or $1,000 per year. A rare few have no such limits, while other companies will not cover evaluations at all.

If your insurance carrier tells you that it will not pay for your child to be evaluated and/or treated for ADHD, ask if it pays for evaluation or treatment of other mental disorders. Specifically ask if it covers the disorders listed in the

Diagnostic and Statistical Manual of Mental Disorders, known professionally as the *DSM-IV*, published by the American Psychiatric Association. If it does but won't cover your child's evaluation, try giving this explanation (diplomatically, of course): They may not be aware that ADHD was recently recognized as a disability by the American Dental Association, by the Social Security Administration, and by the Office of Civil Rights (OCR), which administers the laws that protect the disabled against discrimination based on their disability. If the company is paying for services for other mental disorders but not for ADHD, is it aware that this could be construed as discriminating against those with ADHD because of their disability? The Americans with Disabilities Act considers ADHD a disability and protects children with ADHD from discrimination because of it. Indicate that you may need to contact the OCR about a complaint of discrimination against the company because of its policy not to cover services for ADHD. The company may change its mind; it may not have been aware of these recent legal developments. If the company does not provide coverage thereafter, you may wish to file such a complaint with your local branch of the OCR.

3. If you're in a managed care program, such as a health maintenance organization (HMO) or preferred provider organization (PPO), you may end up having to pay for a professional of your choice if you're not satisfied with the expertise available within your program. Usually you will have to see a professional within your plan first. Should you wish to go outside your plan, your HMO or PPO will then decide whether it will cover such expenses. If not, you'll have to pay the entire bill.

Your Child's School

If your child has already entered school, your local school district can be one of your greatest sources of professional help. Either before you make an appointment with a professional or while waiting for one, ask your local school district to perform an educational evaluation. Federal Law PL 94-142 requires your child's public school district to provide a free evaluation if the child's school performance is being affected significantly by ADHD or other behavior or learning problems. Ask your child's school or central school district offices about your child's rights under this law and the state law that has been created to implement the federal law. This evaluation will be done by several school professionals who have expertise in the areas in which your child is having problems. Usually a school psychologist, social worker, your child's teacher, and the school principal or a member of the school's office of special education will be part of the team to evaluate your child. Often teachers with special training in learning or behavior disorders will serve on this team as well.

> "I want him in special education. He needs help at school.
> The school says he doesn't qualify for such services.
> Is that true? How can I get him the help he needs at school?"

If this evaluation seems like an extra step to you, understand that no public school is likely to give your child special education services without it. You might as well, in fact, request a school evaluation *before* going to an outside professional so the psychological testing of your child's intelligence, learning abilities, and other areas of psychological development are done by the school at no cost to you. If you've already had this evaluation done, be sure to send it to the professional who is to see your child *ahead of the appointment date* so that he or she can digest its contents before seeing your child.

If you're unhappy with the school evaluation or the recommendation based on it, be sure to tell the chairperson of the evaluating team to see if the problems can be corrected. If not, you may wish to appeal the team's decision to the local school superintendent. Your school office can tell you your rights of appeal and the process you will have to follow. You can also request a second opinion or evaluation from an outside professional. Some school districts—the minority—will pay for such second opinions; be sure to ask.

Parents of ADHD children whom I have met have reported a tremendous range and variety of experiences in getting their child evaluated for educational assistance. Some report dealing with sensitive school personnel who initiated an evaluation within a month or two, treated the parents as equals and valued members of the evaluation team, made sure the parents understood their findings, and implemented reasonable recommendations quickly. Others report quite a different experience. With school budget problems and limited educational staff, it's no surprise that parents have found evaluations completed six months after requested, so the child gets no help until the next school year, and that school staff members have been harried and insensitive, condescending and disrespectful, unwilling to describe the procedures, findings, and recommendations from the evaluation in terms a parent can comprehend. Add to this the fact that some school districts in this country are still trying to deny that ADHD is a real problem for children and are continuing to refuse to take any responsibility for helping such children, and that some school staff may be completely ignorant or out of date in their understanding of ADHD, and it is small wonder some parents feel compelled to bring lawsuits against their school districts for violating the rights of ADHD children to a free, *appropriate* public education.

Helpful Hints for an Effective School Evaluation

What can you do to make this evaluation process a more positive and constructive experience?

1. Ask the central office of your child's school district for literature describing the procedures the school must follow in initiating an evaluation of a child for special education. This literature will explain the federal and state laws that govern the evaluation process, the rights you and your child have, the timetable the school system must adhere to in conducting an evaluation, and the appeal process. Most school districts have prepared such literature; be sure to take advantage of it.

2. Read *ADD and the Law* and *Learning Disabilities and the Law* by attorneys Peter and Patricia Latham (1993, Latham & Latham, 1016 16th Street N.W., Washington, DC 20036) for more information on your child's rights within the school system (and in other areas, such as employment and insurance).

3. Speak with your child's teachers about their concerns about your child's school performance and take notes. This will prepare you to give specific information to school administrators who question the purpose and focus of the evaluation.

4. Once the evaluation has begun, monitor the school system's adherence to the required timetable. If it looks as if the school is going to miss a deadline, ask about it immediately. Do not agree to sign a waiver unless the school has a very good reason for missing a deadline.

5. Throughout the evaluation, be cooperative but also firm in your conviction that your child needs assistance. For example, if unfinished classwork is being sent home, say you wish the practice to stop; if your child is not completing classwork at school, the problem is at school, and that is where the solution to the problem is to be found. Don't let the school shift the burden of correcting the problem to you.

6. Attend the team meeting convened to review the results of all of the different professional evaluations with tape recorder in hand. State up front that you will find it easier to absorb everything if you can focus on listening without having to take notes. Nevertheless, take a few written notes during the meeting as well—many parents find it helps to relax them and buys them some time to think. Always ask for clarification of terms; it is the job of these professionals to communicate results effectively and clearly to you.

7. Pay particular attention to the team's recommendations: Do they square with your impressions of what kind of assistance your child may need? Be sure to ask about timelines for implementing these recommendations. What is the school recommending? When would it begin? Who is to implement the recommendations? How will progress during the intervention be monitored? Before the meeting adjourns, set a date to reconvene after the recommendations have been in effect for a few months to discuss how your child is responding to the treatment programs.

8. Always begin this evaluation process being as gracious, cooperative, and diplomatic as possible. Even if you have reason to be somewhat hostile, starting the evaluation process by making demands, challenging school officials, and insulting personnel may very well slow the process down and get you labeled as a troublemaker, a reputation that can hurt your effectiveness with the school system and may even spill over to affect your child's treatment at school. Bring any concerns to the attention of school administrators by having a frank discussion in which you are diplomatic, open to discussion, yet firm in your convictions that your child may need help.

9. If you are unhappy with the evaluation process, seek a second opinion. Have a clinical professional outside the school system, who is experienced in evaluating ADHD and learning-disabled children, attend the school team meeting with you when the results of the evaluation are discussed. Let him or her

advocate for your child's needs. In many cases, school personnel seem more inclined to respect the opinions of another professional than those of a parent.

10. If you are not happy with the results of the evaluation, file an appeal with the school administration following the guidelines set forth in the literature provided by the school district.

Moving On

Armed with as much information as you can gather about your local resources, you can choose what you feel is the best course of action for evaluation of your child. The next chapter will tell you what to expect from an evaluation by a psychologist or a physician and how a diagnosis will be made.

CHAPTER 7

Preparing for
the Evaluation

A thorough evaluation and accurate diagnosis are the stepping-stones to successful management of your child's ADHD. Whether you are seeking a professional evaluation in place of or as a result of a school evaluation, try not to postpone taking action. Many professionals have long waiting lists, and you want to get in to see the appropriate person as soon as you can. While you're waiting for the appointment date, there's much you can do to ensure that the evaluation by a psychologist—as well as the medical checkup—answers all your concerns and serves your child's particular needs.

Preparing for a Psychological
or Psychiatric Evaluation

Sit down and make up a list of answers to the following questions to help clarify your thoughts about your child's difficulties. This task, done in advance, can make the evaluation proceed more smoothly and quickly, perhaps even saving you money in the process. (Professionals usually charge by the hour or quarter hour for their time.)

1. What most concerns you now about your child? At the top of a sheet of paper, write headings such as "Home," "School," "Neighborhood," "Peers," and other areas where you see problems. Then, under each, list precisely what concerns you, sticking to the major problems that you feel occur more often or to a greater degree than they should for children at this age. Also write down those that concern you even if you're not sure they are deviant for your child's age, but note that fact next to that item. Save this list to take to your appointment.

2. On the back of that sheet of paper or on a new one, write down the headings "Health Problems," "Intelligence or Mental Development," "Motor Development and Coordination," "Problems with Senses," "Academic Learning Abilities," "Anxiety or Fears," "Depression," "Aggression Toward Others," "Hyperactivity," "Poor Attention," and "Antisocial Behavior." Then list anything that comes to mind that might indicate your child has a problem in these areas: chronic or recurring medical problems; problems with eyesight, hearing, and so forth; problems with reading, math, and so forth; lying, stealing, setting fires, or running away from home. You may already have listed some of these on the front of the paper, but it can help to reorganize them into these new categories for your child's professional evaluation.

3. Fill out the Home Situations Questionnaire shown in Figure 1. Then, on another sheet of paper, list each situation for which you circled Yes, and briefly write down what problem arises in that situation. For instance, if you said Yes to "When you are on the telephone," what does your child do at that time? Interrupt? Get into mischief out of your sight? Pick fights with siblings? Also jot down what you try to do to handle the situation. Make a photocopy of your completed questionnaire and take it and your descriptions of the problem situations to your appointment.

4. Understandably, parents sometimes hold back information that they find embarrassing to divulge to a stranger. Most often people are reticent about family problems that one or both parents believe are contributing to the child's problems—alcoholism or substance abuse in the family, marital conflict that spills over into mistreatment of the child, excessive discipline or physical punishment, or suspected sexual abuse, for example. No matter how difficult it is to talk about these problems, you must understand that withholding such information increases the possibility of mistakes in diagnosis, the formulation of the important issues in the case, and treatment planning. These matters have a direct bearing on a complete understanding of the case.

5. If at all possible, speak with your child's teachers and write down their major concerns about your child's school adjustment. Again, save this list to take to your appointment.

6. Now take one more sheet of paper and make a list of any problems you think are occurring in your family besides those of your child. Use the following headings if it will help: "Personal" (things that are troubling you about yourself), "Marital," "Money," "Relatives," "Job" (yours or your spouse's), "Other Children," and "Health" (yours or your spouse's). Take this list with you to your appointment.

These lists address the areas most likely to be covered in your interview with the professional. Keep them handy before your appointment and add items as you think of them. They should help to focus the evaluation quickly on the areas of greatest concern to you.

7. *Be sure to take along your child's baby book.* It will provide valuable information about your pregnancy and your child's birth as well as the ages at which the child achieved important developmental milestones. If you don't have a baby book, write down any of the following information that you can recall: (a) any

Child's name _____ Date _____

Name of person completing this form _____

Instructions: Does your child present any problems with compliance to instructions, commands, or rules for you in any of these situations? If so, please circle the word yes and then circle a number beside that situation that describes how severe the problem is for you. If your child is not a problem in a situation, circle No and go on to the next situation on the form.

Situations	*Yes/No*		Mild			(Circle one)			Severe		
	(Circle one)					*If yes, how severe?*					
Playing alone	Yes	No	1	2	3	4	5	6	7	8	9
Playing with other children	Yes	No	1	2	3	4	5	6	7	8	9
Mealtimes	Yes	No	1	2	3	4	5	6	7	8	9
Getting dressed/undressed	Yes	No	1	2	3	4	5	6	7	8	9
Washing and bathing	Yes	No	1	2	3	4	5	6	7	8	9
When you are on the telephone	Yes	No	1	2	3	4	5	6	7	8	9
Watching television	Yes	No	1	2	3	4	5	6	7	8	9
When visitors are in your home	Yes	No	1	2	3	4	5	6	7	8	9
When you are visiting someone's home	Yes	No	1	2	3	4	5	6	7	8	9
In public places (restaurants, stores, church, etc.)	Yes	No	1	2	3	4	5	6	7	8	9
When father is home	Yes	No	1	2	3	4	5	6	7	8	9
When asked to do chores	Yes	No	1	2	3	4	5	6	7	8	9
When asked to do homework	Yes	No	1	2	3	4	5	6	7	8	9
At bedtime	Yes	No	1	2	3	4	5	6	7	8	9
While in the car	Yes	No	1	2	3	4	5	6	7	8	9
When with a babysitter	Yes	No	1	2	3	4	5	6	7	8	9

FIGURE 1. Home Situations Questionnaire. From R. A. Barkley (1987), *Defiant children: A clinician's manual for parent training.* New York: Guilford Press. Copyright 1987 by The Guilford Press. Reprinted by permission. This form may be reproduced for personal use.

problems during your pregnancy with this child; (b) problems with the delivery; (c) your child's birth weight; (d) problems your child had shortly after birth; (e) any serious health, medical problems, or injuries your child has had since birth; and (f) any delays the child had in sitting, crawling, walking, learning to talk, or toilet training.

What to Expect

Probably the most important components of a comprehensive professional evaluation of a child with ADHD are:

1. The clinical interview with the parents and child
2. The medical examination (where necessary)
3. The completion and scoring of behavior rating scales completed by the parents
4. An interview with the child's teacher(s)
5. Completion of similar behavior rating scales about the child by the teacher(s)

Where feasible, I recommend that the evaluation also include some methods for objectively measuring the ADHD symptoms such as psychological tests of attention or direct behavioral observations of the child in school or in the clinic while doing schoolwork. However, these additional steps are not critical to reaching a diagnosis.

Before any professional can diagnose a child as having ADHD, he or she must collect a great deal of information about the child and family, sift through this information looking for the symptoms of ADHD, determine how serious the problem is likely to be, and rule out other disorders or problems. You can expect an evaluation to run an average of two and a half to four hours—longer if your child also needs educational or psychological testing for learning or development problems.

When You Make the Appointment

When you call for an appointment, you'll be asked for basic information—your name, address, child's sex and date of birth, child's school and grade placement, and so forth—and possibly your reasons for seeking an evaluation. You may also be asked to:

1. Give your permission for releases of information from previous evaluations
2. Allow the professional to contact your child's treating physician for further information
3. Provide the results of the most recent (if any) PL 94-142 evaluation from your child's school
4. Initiate a school evaluation if not already done
5. Complete and return before your appointment a packet of behavior rating forms about your child
6. Grant permission for your child's teacher(s) to complete similar forms
7. Give permission for the professional to obtain information from any social service agencies working with your child

You should agree to these requests in all cases except possibly when you're seeking an unbiased second opinion because you strongly disagree with the first one obtained. In that case you may want to ask the professional not to request the records from the first evaluation—and explain why—but never deny access to your child's teachers, even when you disagree with them. The information from teachers is too important to omit; just mention your disagreement beforehand.

In this initial phone meeting, beware of professionals who are willing to give specific treatment advice over the phone, who tell you that only they have the expertise to evaluate and treat your child, who ridicule other professionals in your community, who promise a cure, and who will schedule an evaluation appointment that will take only an hour or less. In all such cases, find another professional.

The Day of the Appointment

Several things will happen during your appointment: A psychologist will interview both you and your child and perform tests if he or she needs information about the child's intelligence, language, academic skills, or other mental abilities. If a physician is conducting the evaluation, your child is not likely to receive any extensive psychological testing, and the interview with you may be much shorter, perhaps 30 minutes to an hour. Instead, your child may be given a more thorough physical exam and may be referred for a vision and hearing exam if one has not been done before or for the past few years.

The Interview with You

The interview with you is indispensable. Whenever possible, both parents should attend since each has a unique perspective. If that's not feasible, the parent who can't be there can write down concerns and opinions that can be taken to the evaluation.

The interview with you serves several purposes: (1) It establishes a necessary rapport among you, the examiner, and your child. (2) It gives the professional your view of your child's apparent problems and narrows the focus of later stages of the evaluation. The more information you provide, the better appreciation the professional will have of your child's problems and the more accurate the diagnosis. Use the lists you constructed so you don't forget anything you wanted to discuss. (3) It shows how the child's problems are affecting the family and gives the professional some sense of your own psychological integrity. (4) It can reveal information about your relationship with your child that could be important in pinpointing potential contributors to your child's problem. (5) But the most important purpose is to determine a diagnosis of your child's problem(s) and to provide you with reasonable treatment recommendations.

The examiner will take notes throughout the interview, including observations of you and how you are dealing with your child while at the clinic. A wise professional will know, however, that behavior in the office, particularly your child's, is not likely to mirror typical behavior elsewhere. Research with ADHD children has shown that many behave normally during this evaluation. If this happens, don't accept any statement that it means your child *is* normal.

> "The pediatrician says my daughter doesn't have ADHD. The day we took her for an appointment, the doctor spent 20 minutes examining her, and she behaved just fine. Why do you say she is ADHD when our doctor says she isn't? Why do you disagree?"

Some professionals like to have the child present. This is fine as long as the subject of discussion will not upset your child or make you uncomfortable. Be sure to state your feelings on this matter.

The interview should begin with an explanation of the procedures to be undertaken, the time it is expected to take, the estimated cost and manner of payment if not already discussed, and the fact that most of what you say will be confidential (many states' laws require professionals to report child neglect or abuse to the department of social services).

Information about Your Child

The interview will probably then proceed to a discussion of your concerns about your child. Here is where your notes are helpful. The professional will ask for specific examples of behavior that concerns you, such as examples of your child's impulsive behavior. You may also be asked how you are presently trying to manage your child's behavior problems and whether your spouse is using a different approach. You will surely be asked when you first noticed your child's problems. This naturally leads to questions about any professional assistance you have already obtained. Some examiners like to ask parents what they believe has led their child to develop these problems. Feel free to give your opinion, but also don't hesitate to say you don't know.

If you completed behavior rating forms before the appointment and returned them, the professional may want to review some of your answers now, especially any that were unclear. Similarly, *you* may want to ask if the professional has any questions about your answers. You may also be asked about some answers on the forms that were sent to your child's teacher(s). If you are curious, ask to see the teacher's answers on these forms; it is your right to see them. Ask the professional to explain anything on these forms that is confusing to you.

The examiner will also talk with you about any developmental problems your child has. I customarily ask parents about the child's development so far in physical health, sensory and motor abilities, language, thinking, intellect, academic achievement, self-help skills like dressing and bathing, social behavior, emotional problems, and family relationships. Many professionals will also review with you a variety of behavior problems or symptoms of other psychiatric problems to see if your child also may be having these difficulties. Simply be truthful and indicate whether or not these other symptoms are present and to what degree.

The examiner may ask you about the symptoms of ADHD that were discussed in Chapter 1. If not, politely ask if the examiner typically uses the DSM guidelines for diagnosing ADHD (see sidebar, pp. 118–120). Most professionals now use them. Ask the professional to review them with you just to be sure all the criteria have been covered. I think professionals should also take care to ask you about any strengths and interests your child has. If yours does not, then mention some yourself. This information not only provides a more complete and balanced picture of your child but gives helpful information to be used later in treatment.

At some point in the interview, the professional should conduct a careful review of your child's developmental and medical history and school history.

I always ask parents about their relationship with school staff. Knowing if it's friendly, supportive, or filled with conflict, whether communication has been open and reasonably clear or limited and hostile, greatly helps me in preparing for later contacts with the school staff if needed.

Information about You and Your Family

Professionals know that many families of ADHD children are under more stress than other families and that the parents may be having more personal problems than most. Don't be offended if you're asked such personal questions. This information can be of great assistance in understanding your child's problems and developing more useful treatment recommendations for you. You will probably be asked about your own background, education, and occupation as well as those of your spouse. The examiner may ask if you, your spouse, or your other children have had any psychiatric, learning, developmental, or chronic medical problems.

Before the interview is over, take a minute to review your notes. Share anything not yet covered or any other information you feel might be helpful. The vast majority of professionals will respect and appreciate your candor.

The Interview with Your Child

The professional will interview your child during the appointment and make some informal observations of your child's appearance, behavior, and developmental skills. How much time he or she devotes to this will depend on your child's age and intelligence. Again, neither you nor the professional should place too much importance on the information obtained in this interview since so many children behave atypically in the psychologist's office.

Psychologists usually ask children a lot of general questions dealing with these areas:

- Their awareness of why they are visiting the examiner today—their own feelings and what their parents have told them
- Their favorite hobbies, television shows, sports, or pets
- Where they go to school, who their teachers are, what subjects they take and like most, and the reasons for any specific difficulties
- Whether they see themselves as having any behavior problems in the classroom and what types of discipline they get for misconduct

Diagnostic Criteria for ADHD: Loose Guidelines or Law?

Most professionals will base their diagnosis of ADHD on guidelines in the American Psychiatric Association's *Diagnostic and Statistical Manual of Mental Disorders*. If your child has already been diagnosed, the professional probably based the diagnosis on the criteria in the third edition, revised (DSM-III-R), in use since 1987. If you are about to seek an evaluation, the professional may use DSM-IV, published in 1994. Those for DSM-IV are reprinted below for your information only; they are intended to be used only by a highly trained clinical professional.

The Guidelines for Diagnosis of ADHD from DSM-IV

A. Either (1) or (2):

    (1) six (or more) of the following symptoms of **inattention** have persisted for at least 6 months to a degree that is maladaptive and inconsistent with developmental level:

    Inattention
    (a) often fails to give close attention to details or makes careless mistakes in schoolwork, work, or other activities
    (b) often has difficulty sustaining attention in tasks or play activities
    (c) often does not seem to listen when being spoken to directly
    (d) often does not follow through on instructions and fails to finish schoolwork, chores, or duties in the workplace (not due to oppositional behavior or failure to understand instructions)
    (e) often has difficulty organizing tasks and activities
    (f) often avoids, dislikes, or is reluctant to engage in tasks that require sustained mental effort (such as schoolwork or homework)
    (g) often loses things necessary for tasks or activities (e.g., toys, school assignments, pencils, books, or tools)
    (h) is often easily distracted by extraneous stimuli
    (i) is often forgetful in daily activities

    (2) six or more of the following symptoms of **hyperactivity–impulsivity** have persisted for at least 6 months to a degree that is maladaptive and inconsistent with developmental level:

    Hyperactivity
    (a) often fidgets with hands or feet or squirms in seat
    (b) often leaves seat in classroom or in other situations in which remaining seated is expected
    (c) often runs about or climbs excessively in situations in which it is inappropriate (in adolescents or adults, may be limited to subjective feelings of restlessness)
    (d) often has difficulty playing or engaging in leisure activities quietly
    (e) is often "on the go" or often acts as if "driven by a motor"
    (f) often talks excessively

(cont.)

Diagnostic Criteria for ADHD (*cont.*)

Impulsivity
(g) often blurts out answers before questions have been completed
(h) often has difficulty awaiting turn
(i) often interrupts or intrudes on others (e.g., butts into conversations or games)

B. Some hyperactive–impulsive or inattentive symptoms that caused immediate impairment were present before age 7 years.

C. Some impairment from the symptoms is present in two or more settings (e.g., at school [or work] and at home).

D. There must be clear evidence of clinically significant impairment in social, academic, or occupational functioning.

E. The symptoms do not occur exclusively during the course of a Pervasive Developmental Disorder, Schizophrenia, or other Psychotic Disorder, and are not better accounted for by another mental disorder (e.g., Mood Disorder, Anxiety Disorder, Dissociative Disorder, or a Personality Disorder).

Code based on type:
    314.01 **Attention-Deficit/Hyperactivity Disorder, Combined Type:** if both Criteria A1 and A2 are met for the past 6 months
    314.00 **Attention-Deficit/Hyperactivity Disorder, Predominantly Inattentive Type:** if Criterion A1 is met but Criterion A2 is not met for the past 6 months
    314.01 **Attention-Deficit/Hyperactivity Disorder, Predominantly Hyperactive–Impulsive Type:** if Criterion A2 is met but Criterion A1 is not met for the past 6 months

Coding note: For individuals (especially adolescents and adults) who currently have symptoms that no longer meet full criteria, "In Partial Remission" should be specified.

Note. From American Psychiatric Association (1994), *Diagnostic and statistical manual of mental disorders* (4th ed.). Washington, DC: Author. Copyright 1994 by the American Psychiatric Association. Reprinted by permission.

As a scientific parent, your main concern should be understanding the role that these criteria should play in a diagnosis. *Never view these guidelines as cast in stone; they are merely suggestions for how clinicians can identify a child as ADHD at this time.* The guidelines have several problems:

1. DSM-IV criteria make no adjustments for age. Since children are less likely to show the listed behaviors as they mature, using one cutoff score for all ages means too many young children and too few older children will be diagnosed as ADHD.
2. The guidelines make no adjustment for gender, despite the fact that we know little girls show the listed behaviors less than little

(cont.)

Diagnostic Criteria for ADHD (*cont.*)

boys. So little girls will have to have more severe behavior problems compared to other girls to be diagnosed as ADHD than boys compared to other boys will.

3. DSM-IV requires that the behavior problems show up in two of the three settings of home, school, and work. In practice this means that parents and teachers must agree that the child has ADHD before the child can be given that diagnosis—and experience shows that parent–teacher disagreement is quite common.

4. The DSM criteria do not tell us just how deviant from normal a child's "developmentally inappropriate" behavior must be, which makes diagnosis difficult in borderline or mild cases.

5. DSM-IV categorizes ADD or those with only attention deficits as just another type of ADHD, whereas I strongly believe that the differences are significant enough to classify the two as separate disorders.

There are, of course, ways to compensate somewhat for the failings of such criteria. At my clinic, for example, it is enough that the child meet all of the criteria through either the parent *or* the teacher. We, among many other scientists, use our behavior rating scales to help us solve the problem of how much ADHD is enough to get a diagnosis: We compare the child's behavior with tables of scores received by normal children and classify as developmentally inappropriate any rating that puts the child above the 93rd percentile for his or her age and sex. Still, the important point to remember is that this and other measures are somewhat arbitrary. So the answer to our opening question is that these criteria are best considered loose guidelines, certainly not law.

- How they think they are accepted by other children at school
- Their perceptions of any problems the parents have reported
- What they would like to see changed or improved at home or at school
- Whether they see themselves as having the symptoms of ADHD (as included in the DSM criteria and/or in general terms)

Particularly with young children, some examiners find it helpful to let them play, draw, or simply wander about the office. Others may ask the child to fill in the blanks in a series of incomplete sentences.

The Interview with the Teacher

Few adults spend as much time with your ADHD child as his or her teacher, so the teacher's opinions are a critical part of the evaluation.

In person or by telephone, the professional will ask the teacher about your child's current academic and behavioral problems, relationships with classmates, behavior in various school situations, especially those involving work, as well as those with limited or no supervision, such as recess, lunch, in hallways, or on the bus. The professional should also find out what the teacher is currently doing to manage your child's problems and should go over any school evaluation done.

The Medical Examination

It is essential that children being evaluated for ADHD have a complete pediatric physical examination. Usually this has been done as part of annual school or summer camp physicals, but it may have to be repeated with more careful attention to medical problems that could be contributing to the child's current school difficulties.

The Interview

The medical interview about your child will be similar to the psychologist's interview with you, but the doctor will devote more time to reviewing the child's genetic background, your pregnancy and birth events, developmental and medical history as well as current health, nutritional status, and gross sensory–motor development.

The main distinction, however, is the attempt to distinguish ADHD from other possible medical conditions, particularly those that may be treatable. In rare cases, ADHD develops as a result of a clear medical problem, such as severe Reye's syndrome, a near-drowning or severe smoke inhalation, serious head trauma, or recovery from a brain infection or disease. In other cases, the ADHD may be associated with a high lead level in your child's body or with other metal or toxic poisonings. Any of these may require treatment in their own right separate from the ADHD. If your doctor strongly suspects that your child has a seizure disorder, additional tests such as an EEG or brain scans may be ordered for your child.

Besides searching for possible causes, the doctor will thoroughly evaluate any coexisting conditions that may require medical management, especially problems such as motor uncoordination, bed-wetting, soiling, and middle ear infections, for which ADHD children are at higher risk. He or she will also determine whether your child has any physical conditions that would contraindicate the use of medications to treat ADHD.

The physician's written recommendation will normally be required to document any need for physical or occupational therapy at school. For this and other reasons, the role of your child's physician in the evaluation of ADHD should not be underestimated. However, by itself it is usually inadequate to make a diagnosis of ADHD.

The Physical Exam

In the course of the child's physical examination, the doctor will follow up on any findings from the interview, looking for thyroid problems, lead poisoning, anemia, or other illnesses. He or she may also do a brief neurological exam to screen for relatively gross neurological problems. Your child's height, weight, and head circumference will be measured and compared to standard charts for normal children. Hearing, vision, and blood pressure will also be screened.

Don't be surprised if your child's routine physical exam is normal, his or her height and weight are normal, and the routine neurological exam is normal. Abnormalities in these areas are not necessarily signs of ADHD; the goal is to rule out the rare case of visual, hearing, or other deficits giving rise to symptoms that look like ADHD.

Laboratory Tests

Misled by research reports that lab measures have found differences between ADHD and non-ADHD children and by the fact that ADHD is a biologically based disorder, many parents ask for medical tests to confirm the diagnosis of ADHD. At present, there are no lab tests or measures that are of value in making a diagnosis of ADHD, so blood work, urinalysis, chromosome studies, EEGs, averaged evoked responses, MRIs, and computed tomography (CT) scans should not be used routinely in the evaluation of ADHD children.

Certain limited tests may be required if your child is going to take particular medications (see Chapter 19) but not the more popular stimulants, such as Ritalin (methylphenidate) or Dexedrine (d-amphetamine).

The Final Step: Making a Diagnosis

During the evaluation the professional you have chosen has collected a wealth of information about your child and your family. He or she has probably already made a *differential diagnosis,* a preliminary step employing DSM guidelines to differentiate what disorders your child may have from those your child does not seem to have. Now, using the behavior rating scales filled out before or during the appointment, as well as everything culled from the interviews and observations, he or she will make the best possible educated guess about which disorders your child has. As mentioned in the sidebar, a diagnosis of ADHD most likely will be based at least in part on either the DSM-III or DSM-IV criteria, but understand that diagnosing psychiatric disorders in children is far from an exact science. The absence of entirely objective evaluating methods and the reliance on the observations and opinions of others such as parents introduce some uncertainty into the diagnostic process.

During the evaluation, the professional has also been formulating possible treatment recommendations, which she or he will present to you along with the diagnosis. You and the professional *together* must then discuss which of these *you* will agree to have implemented. As an executive parent you view the profes-

The Difference between ADHD and ADD

In recognition of the fact that some children have attention problems but are not hyperactive, in 1980 the American Psychiatric Association created two subtypes of attention deficit disorder (ADD), and we now call the subgroup with hyperactivity *ADHD*. Research conducted since then suggests that ADD without hyperactivity and ADHD actually may be two different psychological disorders. This book concentrates on ADHD; in fact my new theory presented in Chapter 2 does not apply at all to what I still call ADD—what the DSM-IV now calls ADHD, Predominantly Inattentive Type.

Children with ADD are often described as more anxious or as somewhat fearful and apprehensive about things compared to other children of their age. They also are more daydreamy or "spacey" than others, acting as if they are often in a mental "fog" and not very attentive to what is happening around them. Parents of ADD children tell us that they are not only not hyperactive but are actually lethargic, sluggish, or slow moving compared to other children. These children seem to wander through their daily lives only half-attending to events around them, acting like little absent-minded professors. As a result, they often miss a lot of the information in situations that other children are attending to and so seem "out of it." They make more mistakes than other children in following oral or written instructions—but not because they go headlong or headstrong into their work and make impulsive mistakes as ADHD children do. ADD children seem to have a problem with sifting through the information given in instructions; their mental filter seems less able to sort out the relevant from the irrelevant. Unlike ADHD children, they are likely to be quiet while working, yet mentally they are "not all there"—not fully processing the task and its instructions.

In a study at our university, Drs. George DuPaul, Mary McMurray, and I found that ADD children differed from those with hyperactivity or ADHD in having considerably less problems with aggression, impulsivity, and overactivity at home and school. The kids with ADD also had a lot less trouble in their relationships with other children. Even more telling, however, was the finding that children who were ADD performed much worse on tests involving perceptual–motor speed or eye–hand coordination and speed. The ADD children also made more mistakes on a memory test. In particular, they had more trouble consistently recalling information they had learned as time passed. These problems were not seen in the ADHD children. The findings tell us that ADD may be more of a problem with memory, perceptual–motor speed, and the speed with which the brain processes incoming information in general. In contrast, those children with hyperactivity, or ADHD, show far more problems

(cont.)

The Difference between ADHD and ADD (*cont.*)

with impulsiveness and distractibility during work in addition to their overactivity. Both groups may do poorly at school. But it is the ADHD children who are going to have more social problems because of their impulsive and aggressive behavior.

Surveys that have been conducted on large populations of children have shown that the percentage of children having these two disorders may be quite different, especially at ages 6 to 11. ADD appears to be considerably less prevalent than ADHD. In a study discussed in Chapter 2 that surveyed a large population in Ontario, Canada, Dr. Peter Szatmari and his colleagues found that only 1.4% of boys and 1.3% of girls in one such survey study had the ADD, or nonhyperactive, type. By contrast, 9.4% of boys and 2.8% of girls had the ADHD, or hyperactive, type. These figures changed considerably when the scientists looked at the adolescent age groups. There 1.4% of male teens and 1% of female teens had ADD, while 2.9% of male teens and 1.4% of female teens had ADHD. In other words, the rates for the nonhyperactive or ADD type remained approximately the same across these age groups, whereas the hyperactive or ADHD type showed a remarkable decline with age, especially in boys. Also important here was the finding that ADD seems to occur at nearly the same rate or prevalence in boys and girls. In contrast, as discussed earlier, ADHD seems to occur nearly three times more often in boys than girls.

Unfortunately, at present much less is known about treating ADD than ADHD. The little research done has studied the stimulant medications and shown that a lower dose is more useful with ADD, whereas higher doses appear to be more effective with ADHD. More telling was the finding that up to 30% or more of those with ADD did not respond at all to this drug, compared to less than 10% of those with ADHD.

sional as your consultant. As a scientific parent you weigh the information received against your own sense of your child and the other information you have gathered about ADHD, determine if the conclusions and recommendations make sense, then ask questions about anything that confuses or concerns you. Be sure to ask the professional to define any diagnosis rendered. What he or she calls ADHD or ADD may not coincide with the way I have been using those terms in this book (see sidebars). If you're left with much doubt about the diagnosis, thank the professional and seek a second opinion.

As a principle-centered parent, you will go about the entire evaluation process with dignity and diplomacy, guided by Dr. Covey's seven principles (summarized in the Introduction) not only with your child but in your interactions with others.

CHAPTER 8

Coping with the Diagnosis of ADHD

How You Are Likely to React

Having your child evaluated was a big step, and you invested your mental, physical, and emotional energies into doing it right. Now you've received a diagnosis: Your child has ADHD. What next?

First, stop and try to acknowledge how you feel. From the several thousand parents I have counseled personally about ADHD as well as the thousands of others I have heard from at my public speeches, I have come to realize that parents' emotional reactions to information about ADHD are an important part of their adjustment to their child's disorder. They also influence the quality of the investment they are able to make in helping and advocating for their ADHD child.

Denial or Relief?

Some parents may initially engage in *denial* of the label or diagnosis or the neurological basis of it. They hold desperately to their original view that nothing was so wrong that it could not be righted by counseling or some simple behavior management methods. This reaction is likely to occur when the parents did not suspect that much was wrong with their child in the first place. Typically it is a day-care worker, a preschool teacher, or even a friend whose child plays with the ADHD child who broaches the possibility that a problem exists. When parents are the last to know that their child has ADHD, it is natural for them to deny or minimize the extent of the problem until they can reevaluate the information they are receiving and come to see the problems of their child on their own. If you find yourself resisting a diagnosis, the best way to erase your doubts is to seek a second opinion from someone you trust who knows about ADHD.

Other parents willingly accept the information they receive about ADHD, embracing its message as the answers they have desperately sought for so long. Finally they have a name for their concerns about their child and can pursue ways to help.

These families welcome *relief* from the burden of uncertainty and often of guilt as well. Knowing that ADHD has a biological basis allows them to let go of the previous sense that they personally created the problem.

Anger

For some parents a diagnosis of ADHD evokes *anger*—anger aimed at anyone who may have assured them that nothing was wrong, anger at those who blamed the problem on the parents' mismanagement or on family problems. All too often practitioners in my field chastise and shame parents in their quest to lay blame. When the parents finally realize they are not at fault, anger and resentment are not unreasonable reactions.

Grief

It is both natural and healthy to have a mild *grief* reaction to the information about your child's ADHD. Almost all parents, when confronted with the news that their child is handicapped in some way, will grieve for this loss of normalcy. Some parents grieve over their child's future risks; others are reacting to the alterations the family must make to accommodate ADHD.

For most people this grieving will pass as they reframe their views of their child and his or her problems. I have been told by others, however, that they never fully resolve this grief. They adapt to it and for a time seem to put it behind them as they confront the day-to-day responsibilities of child rearing and work. But when the child has been doing particularly well for a long period and then has a regression or a significant crisis, the feelings of mild sorrow return. This may happen to you as well. If so, talking with other parents who have ADHD children can help, perhaps through your local parent support group. If the grief reaction persists, consider undertaking some short-term counseling with a professional knowledgeable about ADHD or therapy with parents of disabled children.

Acceptance

The natural and desired outcome of dealing with information on ADHD is *acceptance*—acceptance of what your child is and may become and, equally critical, what your child is not and may never be. There is peace of mind at this stage, as if a cloud has been lifted, allowing the parents to see their child's problems and their own reactions to these problems more clearly. From this new perspective you can clearly see that your child has a problem that he or she did not ask for, cannot help having, and needs your help in dealing with, including protection from those who will not understand. The child needs your advocacy to obtain what is rightfully his or hers among the community and school services. This change in perspective can be profound and moving, both to the parents experiencing it and to anyone who has the privilege to witness it as I have.

If you've reached this stage, you may now thirst for knowledge about how best to help your child. Perhaps you are now motivated to enter a support group, counseling, or a formal child management training program that provides you with the skills and techniques that may help your child succeed. You will also find yourself seeking ways to modify the environment, not the child. For your child an appropriate "prosthetic device" may be an organizing chart or a home point system instead of a wheelchair; access may mean a special seating arrangement rather than a ramp to a doorway. In both cases the goal is to permit the disabled child to succeed given his or her circumstances.

Acceptance also means, however, recognizing that some things simply cannot be modified to permit ADHD children to succeed maximally or adapt as well as do non-ADHD children. Failure to accept some limitations for your child will instill intolerance, anger, and frustration in you, as well as put undue pressure on the ADHD child.

The bottom line is that your acceptance of your child's ADHD and all it could entail frees you to fulfill the role so crucial to your child's progress. More than other parents, you must actively support your child's self-esteem, perhaps via less traditional routes, whereas non-ADHD children build their own through academic and social success. You need to exercise creativity to find successful outlets for your child, whether in organized sports, fine arts, hobbies, or science or mechanical projects. Once you've truly accepted your child's ADHD, you can look beyond the child's limitations and see—as no one else can—his or her unique strengths and talents.

Getting Educated about ADHD

It's fortunate that acceptance leads to a thirst for knowledge, because staying educated is the most fundamental ongoing task of the executive, scientific parent. In the thousands of cases of ADHD seen at our clinic at the University of Massachusetts Medical Center, we have in fact learned that the single most important intervention we have provided is up-to-date information about the disorder. Here are a number of things you can do to get and stay educated about ADHD:

1. Read as many books about ADHD as you can. Some of the best, in my view, are listed at the end of this book. Remember, truth is an assembled thing. The more you read and learn about ADHD, the closer to the truth about its nature, causes, and proper treatment you will come. You can obtain many of these books by ordering them through your local bookstore. The majority are

also available through the ADD Warehouse in Plantation, FL (1-800-233-9273). Or go to your local library, keeping in mind that smaller libraries rarely have current books. If a book was copyrighted more than 10 years ago, you should assume the information is not current enough. For current scientific articles and professional books on ADHD, check a local university library or medical center library. Look up the names of researchers mentioned in this book for reports on the latest scientific studies. Some school professionals or districts have also developed lending libraries on materials for parents; ask if your school district has anything on ADHD, ADD, or hyperactivity.

2. Watch specially made videos on this subject. Some are listed at the end of the book, including four of my own (available from The Guilford Press or the ADD Warehouse), but if the expense is prohibitive, see if your local school district has any you can borrow. Also check libraries and video rental stores, some of which are now setting aside shelf space for health, self-improvement, and psychology video programs.

3. Make an appointment with a local professional expert on the subject to get opinions and any educational materials available for loan. Be prepared to pay for this time spent with you or to have this billed to your health insurance program as a therapy session.

4. You can also join a local parent support group, such as CHADD or ADDA (see Chapter 18), both of which publish informative newsletters and feature expert guest speakers at their frequent meetings. Your local group may also receive brochures and notices on one-day seminars and workshops held in your area. Although such workshops are often aimed at professional audiences, parents may be permitted to attend. Ask any professional you're working with to let you know about these events too.

5. The national arms of these parent support associations are also great resources. Both CHADD and ADDA hold two- to four-day annual conventions where you can hear numerous speakers on most aspects of raising a child with ADHD. Call the national organizations to find out when and where such conferences are held. It can be tremendously inspiring and reassuring to attend a three-day conference with hundreds of other parents of children with ADHD, all striving to learn more about caring for and raising these children.

Throughout this process of self-education, remember that your child is struggling with a developmental disorder and that you're undertaking this somewhat monumental task to help the child surmount as many of the problems that disability poses as you can. Bolstered by the empathy that naturally flows from acceptance and armed with all the knowledge you can amass, you are prepared to help your child as no one else can. The next chapter will give you some fundamental principles to follow in that endeavor.

CHAPTER 9

Ten Guiding Principles for Raising a Child with ADHD

Part I (Chapters 1–5) explained that ADHD is a deficit in self-control, what some professionals call the *executive functions* critical to planning, organizing, and carrying out complex human behavior over long periods of time. That is, in ADHD children the "executive" in the brain that is supposed to be organizing and controlling behavior, helping the child plan for the future and follow through on those plans, is doing a very poor job. The ADHD child is not suffering from a lack of skill or knowledge, so showing the child how to do something to correct his or her problems will not be of much help. Instead you will find it more effective to give clear instructions, rearrange work so it's more interesting and motivating, redirect the child's behavior toward future goals versus immediate gratification, and provide immediate rewards for a completed task or adherence to rules.

Sound simple? It *is* relatively simple—in theory. In practice it's not always easy to implement. Over almost 20 years of clinical experience I've found that parents benefit greatly from 10 general principles distilled from our current understanding of ADHD. As touchstones in the daily behavior management of ADHD children, these principles have served parents well in designing both home and classroom management programs for ADHD children. Brief illustrations of some of the principles are given here; specific techniques are detailed in Chapter 11.

Remember that principle-centered parenting of a child with ADHD means (1) pausing before reacting to the present misconduct of the child, (2) using this delay to reflect on the principles contained in this book, and (3) choosing a response to the child that is consistent with these principles. To keep you grounded in this approach to rearing your ADHD child, I suggest you tape a photocopy of page 136 to both your bathroom mirror and your refrigerator door (or a wall in your workspace if you work outside the home as I do). Glancing at the list of 10 guiding principles when you get up and seeing them throughout the day gives you a gentle reminder of what you are striving for.

1. Give Your Child More Immediate Feedback and Consequences

As Virginia Douglas, Ph.D., a renowned Canadian psychologist and expert on ADHD, and others noted long ago, children with ADHD seem much more un-der the control of the moment than normal children. Either you become part of that moment or you will have little influence over your ADHD child.

As already explained, when confronted by a job that they find tedious, bor-ing, or unrewarding, ADHD children will feel the urge to find something else to do. If you want them to stay at a task, you'll have to arrange for positive feed-back and consequences that will make the task more rewarding as well as mild negative consequences for shifting off task. Similarly, when you're attempting to change negative behaviors, you must provide quick rewards and feedback for behaving well and swift negative consequences for acting inappropriately.

Positive feedback can be given in the form of praise or compliments as long as you state expressly and specifically what the child did that was positive. It can also be in the form of physical affection. In some instances it will have to involve rewards, such as extra privileges, or systems by which the child earns points toward privileges, because your praise will not be enough to motivate the child to stick with the assigned task. Whatever type of feedback you give, however, the more immediately it can be provided, the more effective it will be.

For example, if an ADHD child normally has problems playing nicely with a younger sibling, the most effective reinforcement of cooperative play would be for you to be on the alert for any instances of cooperation, sharing, and kind-ness shown by the older child with ADHD and then give immediate praise when you spot it. Likewise, the child should receive immediate and mildly negative feedback and consequences after bullying the younger child. You tell the child exactly what he has just done wrong (rather than yelling) and why it is not ac-ceptable, then you remove a privilege the child had access to that day or some earned tokens in such a program (see Chapter 11).

2. Give Your Child More Frequent Feedback

ADHD children need feedback and consequences that are not just swift but also frequent. Immediate consequences or feedback can be helpful even when given occasionally, but they are even more beneficial when given often. Admittedly, going too far with this can get irritating and intrusive to your child and tiring for you, but it is necessary to do this as much as your time, schedule, and energy permit, especially when you're trying to change some form of significant misbehavior. For instance, rather than waiting to praise a child who has considerable trouble finishing homework when all of the homework is finally done, or punishing the child for not finishing after several hours when it should have taken 20 minutes, instruct the child that she can now earn points for completing each math problem, with the points adding up toward purchasing a privilege. A reasonable time limit—say 20 minutes—is also set for the whole assignment, and when the time expires the child is fined (loses) one point for each problem not done. During the work period you praise the child frequently for remaining on task and provide words of encouragement to keep working hard at the same time you're tallying points.

Often parents get very busy with their own household responsibilities and forget to check frequently on the child. One way to remind yourself is to place small stickers with smiley faces on them around the house in locations where you frequently look—in the corner of bathroom mirrors, on the edge of the face of a kitchen clock, and so on. Whenever you spot a sticker, comment to your child on what you like that the child is doing at that very moment—even if it's just sitting quietly watching television. You can also set a cooking timer or watch for various brief intervals or use the device called a MotivAider (available from the ADD Warehouse), which is worn on a belt or in a pocket and vibrates at the programmed intervals.

3. Use Larger and More Powerful Consequences

Your ADHD child will require more salient or powerful consequences than other children to encourage him or her to perform work, follow rules, or behave well. These can include physical affection, privileges, special snacks or treats, tokens or points, material rewards like small toys or collectible items, and even occasionally money.

This may seem to violate the common wisdom that children should not be materially rewarded too often because such rewards may replace intrinsic rewards such as the pleasure of reading, the desire to please parents and friends, the pride of mastering a job or new activity, or the esteem of peers for playing a game well. But these forms of reinforcement or reward are much less likely to influence ADHD children to behave well. They also do not consistently motivate ADHD children to start working, to inhibit their urges to do inappropriate things, and to persist in their work. The nature of your child's disability dictates that you use larger, more significant, and sometimes more material consequences to develop and maintain your child's positive behaviors.

4. Use Incentives before Punishment

It is common for parents to resort to punishment when a child misbehaves or disobeys. This may be all right for the non-ADHD child, who misbehaves only occasionally and thus receives a small amount of punishment. It is not all right for the ADHD child, who is likely to misbehave much more often and could receive a great deal of negative consequences. Punishment, when used alone or in the relative absence of ongoing rewards and positive feedback, is not very effective at changing behavior. It usually leads to resentment and hostility in your child and eventually the child's avoidance of you. Sometimes it can even lead to efforts at countercontrol: Your child tries to find ways to strike back, retaliate, or get even for the excessive punishment.

It is critical that you avoid this all-too-common drift toward using punishment first. Frequently remind yourself of the rule *positives before negatives*. It might help to remember that your child receives more than enough reprimands, punishments, and rejection from others who do not understand the child's disability and that only rewards and incentives teach what you expect your child to do.

The rule of using incentives before negatives is simple: When you want to change an undesirable behavior, first decide what positive behavior you want to replace it with. This will instinctively lead you to start watching for that positive behavior. When it occurs, you will be more likely to praise and reward it.

Only after this new behavior has been rewarded consistently for at least one week should you begin punishing the undesired opposite behavior. Even then, try to use only mild punishment such as the loss of a privilege or special activity or a brief time-out, and keep the punishments in balance with the rewards: only one punishment for every two or three instances of praise and reward. Punish consistently but selectively, only for the occurrence of this particular negative behavior. *Do not punish your child for everything else he or she is doing wrong.*

Let's look at the example of a child who frequently interrupts, intrudes, and blurts out comments at the dinner table. You would speak with the child just before the next family mealtime about what you would like to see the child do more of at the table: try not to talk so much, wait until others are finished before talking, and talk after finishing chewing your food. You explain that the child can earn points for following these rules. Throughout the meal, you mark points on a small card and make sure the child sees this occur, at the same time giving some nonverbal cue such as a wink that lets the child know you appreciate how hard the child struggles to adhere to these rules. You ignore rule violations for a week or so and then let the child know just before the next meal that from now on breaking a rule means losing a point. Remember that a fine or penalty should be imposed no more than once for every two or three rewards.

5. Strive for Consistency

You must use the same strategies for managing your child's behavior every time. Applying consistency means four important things: (1) being consistent over time, (2) not giving up too soon when you are just starting a behavior-change program, (3) responding in the same fashion even when the setting changes, and (4) making sure that both parents are using the same methods. Being unpredictable or capricious in your enforcement of the rules is a common invitation to failure. So is losing hope when your new method of management fails to yield dramatic, immediate results. Try a behavior-change program for at least two weeks before deciding it isn't working. Don't fall prey to the trap that snares many parents: responding to behaviors one way at home but an entirely different way in public places. Finally, try to maintain a united parental front as much as you can granted the inevitable differences in parenting styles.

6. Act, Don't Yak!

Sam Goldstein, Ph.D., a psychologist and expert on clinical work with ADHD, said it beautifully when he advised parents to stop talking and use consequences: *act, don't yak.* As said at the beginning of this chapter, your child does not lack intelligence, skill, or reasoning, so simply talking to the child won't change the underlying neurological problem that makes him or her so uninhibited. Your child is much more sensitive to the consequences and feedback you use and much less sensitive to your reasoning than is a non-ADHD child. So act quickly and act frequently, and your ADHD child will behave better for you. Keep talking, and all you will get is aggravation, not compliance.

7. Plan Ahead for Problem Situations

I'm sure you're familiar with the scenario: You're in a store and your ADHD child begins to tear open packages, pull things off shelves, and generally create havoc, despite your repeated threats and commands. You become flustered and frustrated, unable to think quickly and clearly, so a solution eludes you. Your dismay is intensified by the disdainful glares of salespeople and other shoppers, and you try to skulk out of the shop, pulling your screaming child behind you.

I am often struck by parents' ability, when pressed, to predict where their children are likely to misbehave. So I am surprised by how few seem to put this information to good use. Why not use it in preparing for such problems to arise again? You can save yourself much anguish if you learn to anticipate problem situations, consider ahead of time how best to deal with them, develop a plan of action before entering that problem situation, share the plan with your child beforehand, and then follow through on your plan should a problem arise. People may find it hard to believe that even just sharing the plan with the child before entering a potential problem setting greatly reduces the odds that behavior problems will arise. But it works!

Try these five simple steps before entering any problem setting:

Step 1: *Stop* just before entering the site of a potential problem, such as a store, restaurant, church, or friend's home.

Step 2: *Review with your child two or three rules* that he or she often has trouble following in that situation. For a store the rules could be "Stay next to me, don't ask for anything, and do as I say." No long-winded explanations, just a brief statement of the rules. Then ask the child to repeat these simple rules back.

Step 3: *Set up the reward or incentive*—stopping for a frozen yogurt on the way home, for example—that your child can earn by obeying the rules.

Step 4: *Explain the punishment* that may have to be used, such as a loss of points or a privilege.

Step 5: *Follow your plan* as you enter the situation and remember to give your child immediate and frequent feedback while there. If you must, punish your child swiftly for any acts that violate the rules.

8. Keep a Disability Perspective

At times, when faced with a difficult-to-manage child with ADHD, parents may lose all perspective on the immediate problem. They may become enraged, angered, embarrassed, or at the very least frustrated when their initial attempts at management do not work. They may even stoop to the level of the child and argue about the issue as another child might do. You must remember at all times, *you are the adult;* you are this disabled child's teacher and coach. If either of you is to keep your wits about you, it clearly has to be you.

One way to keep your cool in trying circumstances is to try to maintain some psychological distance from your child's problems. Pretend you are a stranger so you can view the situation for what it really represents—a parent's attempt to deal with a behaviorally disabled child. If you can do this, you are likely to react to your child more reasonably, fairly, and rationally than if you let your child's problems upset you.

This is hard, so you may have to remind yourself of your child's disability each day, perhaps even several times a day, and especially when you are trying to deal with disruptive behavior.

9. Don't Personalize Your Child's Problems or Disorder

Don't allow your own sense of self-worth and personal dignity to become wrapped up in whether or not you "win" an argument or encounter with your child. No one is keeping score here. Stay calm if possible, maintain a sense of humor about the problem, and by all means try to follow the other principles listed here when you respond to your child. Sometimes this may even mean removing yourself from the situation for a moment by going to a different room to gather your wits and regain control over your feelings. Don't conclude that you're a bad parent when a situation goes wrong or does not turn out as you wanted.

10. Practice Forgiveness

This is the most important principle but often the most difficult to implement consistently in daily life. Practicing forgiveness means three things. First, each day, after your child is put to bed or before you retire for the night, take just a moment to review the day and forgive your child for transgressions. Let go of the anger, resentment, disappointment, or other personally destructive emotions that have arisen that day because of your child's misconduct or disruptions. The child cannot always control what he or she does and deserves to be forgiven.

Do not misunderstand this essential point. It does not mean your child should not be held accountable for misdeeds. It means that you should let go of any bitterness over them.

Second, concentrate on forgiving others who may have misunderstood your child's inappropriate behavior that day and acted in ways offensive to you and your child or simply dismissed your child as lazy or morally defective. You know better; don't buy into what others think about your child. Take any corrective action that's needed and continue to advocate for your child, but let go of the hurt, anger, and resentment such instances may have inflicted on you.

Finally, you must learn to practice forgiving yourself for your own mistakes in the management of your ADHD child that day. ADHD children have the capacity to bring out the worst in us as parents, which frequently results in parents feeling terribly guilty over their own errors. Without giving yourself license to make the same errors repeatedly without consequence, let go of the self-deprecation, shame, humiliation, resentment, or anger that accompanies such acts of self-evaluation. Replace them with a frank evaluation of your performance as a parent that day, identifying which areas to improve and making a personal commitment to strive to get it right the next day.

You will find this principle the hardest to adhere to but the most fundamental to the art of effective, and peaceful, management of your child with ADHD.

1. **Give Your Child More Immediate Feedback and Consequences**
2. **Give Your Child More Frequent Feedback**
3. **Use Larger and More Powerful Consequences**
4. **Use Incentives before Punishment**
5. **Strive for Consistency**
6. **Act, Don't Yak!**
7. **Plan Ahead for Problem Situations**
8. **Keep a Disability Perspective**
9. **Don't Personalize Your Child's Problems or Disorder**
10. **Practice Forgiveness**

CHAPTER 10

Just for Parents: How to Take Care of Yourself

Undoubtedly you already know how stressful it can be to raise a child with ADHD. These children require a lot more monitoring and supervision than other children as they launch headlong into life with all its hazards. They can be demanding, defiant, loud, selfish, and aggressive; even their more benign incessant talking takes its toll. As a result, one recent study showed, parents of ADHD children, especially those of preschool/kindergarten age, suffer higher levels of stress, depression, and self-blame than parents of non-ADHD children. Another study showed, in fact, that parents of ADHD children endure the same stress levels as parents of children with severe disabilities such as mental retardation and autism. To make matters worse, many parents also end up socially isolated as relatives, friends, and neighbors try to avoid contact with the family.

As I've seen all too often, this pattern can carry parents along on a downward spiral that leaves them drained and exhausted, demoralized and in despair. Taking care of their ADHD child has left them nothing for themselves, and ultimately that leaves them with no resources to care for the child either. Obviously that's a situation that serves no one.

I can't pretend to give you a panacea for all of the ills that can strike a family struggling with ADHD. A certain amount of stress is inevitable. It does not, however, have to destroy you or anyone else in your family. So this chapter is just for you: some specific tips and general suggestions for preventing stressful events, minimizing the impact of the unavoidable ones, and giving yourself the break that you richly deserve.

Heading Off Stressful Events

The first thing you need to do to reduce the number of stressful events that you have to cope with is identify the exact sources of your stress. Many parents I've worked with seem to focus on their reactions to stress rather than on the sources of the stress. They in fact mistake one for the other and believe they need to eliminate the feelings of depression and sadness, the fatigue and the headaches rather than the events that are precipitating them. Granted, there are stressful events that can't be avoided—more of them for you than for parents of non-ADHD children. For these you will have to resort to stress reduction techniques such as formal relaxation methods, meditation, exercise, perhaps even medication in extreme cases. But in other cases—and you might be surprised by how many— you can identify and avoid or at least reduce the source of the stress and head it off. Try this simple method:

1. When you have some quiet time, sit down with paper and pencil and think back over the times in the last few weeks when you felt stress reactions— irritability, anger, or hostility. Then list the stressors—not how you felt but the events that immediately preceded that stress reaction. What did your child or someone else do that elicited this negative reaction from you? What did others do to your child? What might your spouse have done? What event came up that made you feel this way? Leave a few blank lines after each stressor identified.

2. Now look closely at the first event. What could you have done to avoid or eliminate that event or problem? Did your reaction worsen the situation? Would any of Dr. Covey's seven principles (see Introduction) have helped you eliminate the stressor? Or would any of the 10 principles for raising an ADHD child (see Chapter 9) have helped you avoid the situation? Can you see how any of these principles might help you eliminate or avoid this stressor the next time around? Or can you simply plan to avoid the stressful event or person altogether? Write down at least one coping method after each of the stress events listed.

3. Now focus on one (or a few) of these stressors and resolve either to avoid it in the future or, if unavoidable, to use your coping method the next time the event arises. Close your eyes and visualize yourself responding differently and more effectively in just that situation.

4. Remind yourself of your plan by posting small notes to yourself around your home and work space.

5. Take a few minutes each day to practice visualizing your use of this new action plan. This practice will fortify your confidence that you can in fact head off the source of stress when it threatens to rise again.

6. Once your confidence has been built up or you have actually tried the new plan, move on to another stressor or two. Work on only one or two stressors at a time until you've mastered or eliminated them; then move on to one or two more.

Coping with the Inevitable

Because stress seems to be a part of life for everyone these days, many effective techniques have been devised for reducing its deleterious impact. Any professional you're working with can steer you to sources of more information on the subject, but so can your local librarian or bookseller. You can even find audiotapes and videotapes that will teach some of the best-known methods. Space limitations make it impossible to go into depth here, so only a few brief suggestions follow.

1. Delay Your Response

Most of us respond quickly and impulsively to a stressful event. When we're emotionally aroused—angry or anxious—we get physically aroused as well: our pulse quickens, we might feel flushed, and adrenaline readies us for "fight or flight." Unfortunately, none of this contributes to mental acuity. In fact it's those impulsive responses that we usually end up regretting. So sometimes the best thing to do is nothing. If the only way to delay your response is to get away, just leave the room for a brief time or send your child away with a calm "I'll discuss this with you in a few minutes."

When you're confronting a stressful encounter with your ADHD child, try simply waiting to let your mind play on the situation and its possibilities. This doesn't mean filling your mind with thoughts like "Oh, what will I do? What will I do?" or "This won't work, I have no options, and I don't know what to do." Rather, try to remain calm and let your mind engage the problem. That's the wonderful thing about the human mind: The only thing you have to do to help it come up with ideas is not interfere with its natural problem-solving ability. Just give it a little time.

2. Practice Relaxation

Many people use relaxation techniques on a regular basis to lower their overall stress level. Because these techniques can have a considerable preventive effect, they'll serve you well when you're facing an upcoming stress event that can't be avoided. For example, say the school has called to say your ADHD child is being sent home for starting a fight with another child and you must meet with the principal the next day. Stress is likely to build before the meeting as you ponder the possible repercussions. Practicing techniques like progressive muscle relaxation can keep you from blowing the situation way out of proportion. There are many books that sum up this method and others (Dr. Jon Kabat-Zinn of our university has a bestselling book on relaxation and meditation called *Full Catastrophe Living*—sound like your home?), which involves deep breathing and progressive relaxing of each muscle group, followed by mental imagery of yourself in a relaxing, beautiful place. It's easy to learn but is most effective when you've had some practice, so anticipate stress and start practicing ahead.

3. Broaden Your Focus

Another way to avoid blowing things out of proportion is to broaden your focus when you are involved in a stressful situation. Try to avoid zeroing in on the small details and instead focus on the entire situation from the perspective of your or your child's lifetime. This can often help you realize that the stress event is not as important as you are making it out to be, that it can be managed, and that even if it does not go well, it is not as big a deal as you may think. At the school meeting in our earlier example, you could listen to the details of what the principal is saying while concentrating on the fact that this is just one school meeting, that the opinions expressed are not final and will not cause havoc in your life or your child's, and that as an executive parent you are ultimately in charge of this meeting and of what happens to your child.

4. Begin with the End in Mind

Before and throughout a stressful situation, visualize how you want the situation to turn out for your child. Keeping your positive goals in mind can lessen the impact of negative remarks, decrease the intensity of your own reactions, and thus avoid heightening the conflict and worsening its outcome.

Practicing Personal Renewal

Raising an ADHD child places huge demands on the mind and body, the heart and spirit. To replenish yourself emotionally, feel more in control of your life, and better equip yourself to handle unexpected stressful events, consider the following suggestions. You've heard many of them before, but there's bound to be something new as well. You deserve to take as good care of yourself as you do your ADHD child, and that means setting aside some time for yourself. If you're tempted to protest that you have no time, see the suggestions in the sidebar.

1. Take a Long Weekend Away

Sometimes the only way to renew your energies is to get away. Don't hesitate to do this. Go by yourself and have your spouse look after your ADHD child. Visit a friend, go to a spa, loll on the beach with a good book, or do something that appeals uniquely to you. Recharging your emotional batteries and catching up on your sleep are well worth the trouble of arranging this getaway. If there's someone you trust to care for your child, try to get away with your spouse now and then as well—marriages need renewal too.

2. Find a Hobby or Social Activity

The last thing that a child with ADHD needs is a martyr for a parent—someone who has sacrificed all of his or her personal pleasures and time for the sake of

One Key to Survival: Time Management

Time management does not come naturally to most people because it is not really time management at all. Time cannot be manipulated or managed. Time management is self-management, a skill to be acquired. It takes practice and effort, but its rewards can be enormous, especially for ADHD parents, who have so many demands on them.

There are many excellent books at libraries and in bookstores that can give full details on how to manage your time effectively. Most of them begin by explaining that your first step must be to set specific, well-defined, reasonable goals for both the long and short terms. When you do this you end up with a plan for each day, each week, each month—a plan that you can follow realistically, giving you the sense of satisfaction that you have achieved what you set out to do. ADHD children, by nature disorganized and disruptive, can make you feel as if your life has no order whatsoever, so getting this sense of accomplishment is particularly important to you.

Experts on time management divide time use into five categories: important and urgent, important but not urgent, urgent but not important, busy work, and wasted time. Knowing the difference can help you identify where your work usually falls and perhaps show you how to alter the nature of your current home or job activities to achieve your goals.

1. *Important and urgent.* Tasks that must be done immediately or in the very near future. Because they are urgent and important, they often get done. Usually this is not where time gets wasted.

2. *Important but not urgent.* It is here that the effective parent can be readily distinguished from the ineffective. These are tasks that you or others consider important for you to do, but they are not urgent. Most of the time you simply never get around to doing them. Time management can help elevate these personal priorities to a more urgent status so you do get them done.

3. *Urgent but not important.* Often minor or trivial stuff that others make urgent with their deadlines but that, if thought about, are only of modest importance. Yet because they are urgent you may give more attention to these than your more important but less urgent goals.

4. *Busy work.* Tasks of marginal importance such as housework, returning telephone calls, running errands. You may do them before the important ones because they are brief and diversionary and give you a feeling of productivity, but they rarely contribute to your real goals for yourself or your child with ADHD.

5. *Wasted time.* Whether it's watching lousy TV shows, sitting through a bad movie, or attending an unnecessary committee meeting, this type

(cont.)

> ### One Key to Survival: Time Management (*cont.*)
>
> of activity usually makes you feel you could have spent the time better doing something else. Most people think this is the cause of their poor time management, but usually, experts say, the real cause is allocating too much time to categories 3 and 4 and not enough to category 2. Take a look at how you spend your time. Could this be true of you?
>
> Watch out for the real time wasters too: indecision, blaming others for your lack of time, pursuing perfection instead of excellence, getting off track because of distracting stimuli, and letting those little tidbits of time spent waiting go unfilled.

spending it with the child. That parent will be weary, exhausted, stressed, and often ill-tempered or irritable. You owe it to yourself and to your child to find something that will provide a sense of personal gratification and fulfillment on a regular basis.

One parent I know was an amateur winemaker who formed a small club of fellow enthusiasts who met periodically to make new wines, study winemaking, and travel to wine tastings. Others have joined bowling leagues, church or barbershop choirs, quilting groups, running clubs, instrumental music groups, book clubs, or sports teams. There are also informal get-togethers like coffee klatches and potluck suppers. Then there are the private hobbies like woodworking, fly tying, model building, antique collecting, painting, sewing, reading . . . the list is endless. The point is that as long as you enjoy it, pursuing a personal interest can give you the same sense of renewal as going on a short trip.

3. Become Active in a Support Group

Maybe the last thing you want to do when you need to be reinvigorated is meet with a group of people who have the same problems you do, but attending these support group meetings regularly has multiple benefits. True, parent groups are a great source of information and advice, but they also provide the release of commiseration, and many parents end up making real friends there. Some groups even have babysitting cooperatives; see if your local chapter is willing to support one.

4. Seek the Comfort of Friends

Don't forget to renew your friendships with those you've been close to for years. Most of us let these relationships get away from us when we're busy, but we all need the "sure refuge" that Aristotle called true friends. Unburdening yourself to a close friend has tremendous therapeutic value; someone who knows and cares for you well can provide not only a shoulder to lean on but also a new perspective on your problems.

5. Practice Shared Parenting

If taking any of these suggestions sounds like pampering yourself and you think you have no time for that, you may need to talk to your spouse about redistributing some of the load of parenting your ADHD child. Often a disproportionate share falls to the mother, and even if this isn't the case in your home, you can probably benefit from agreeing that each of you will take full responsibility for the child every other day (or if one or both works away from home, every other evening). This gives you predictable times for pursuing personal interests as well as just giving you time to take a deep breath and have a little time off.

6. Practice Becoming Aware of Moments

Many of the world's great religious teachers and philosophers have advised us to focus our mind on the natural beauty, joy, peace, and wonder in the world around us at any point in time. Yet we become so wrapped up in preparing for upcoming events that we often miss the wonder of this very moment. My colleague Dr. Jon Kabat-Zinn has written a book that I highly recommend, *Wherever You Go, There You Are,* in which a principal theme is that concentrating on the moment, its sensory richness and textures and its scope, both broad and minute, repays our investment of time a hundredfold in the renewal of our personal energy, mental perspective, and emotional balance and control. It can greatly diminish the sense of stress, time, and urgency that those with ADHD children feel daily.

7. Identify and Alter Stressful Thinking Patterns

Emotionally at least, in large part, you are what you think. You've probably noticed that while you feel and act humiliated by, say, the tantrums your ADHD child throws in stores, other parents seem to go about managing their children's similar misbehavior matter-of-factly, without alarm or distress. Well, you may reason, maybe they can be calm because their children don't act this way every time they go into a store, while yours does.

Not necessarily. Many years ago the famous psychologist Albert Ellis, Ph.D., developed a theory that we determine how we will feel in a given situation by *what we are thinking* about those events or people. When we think negative, distressing, and self-critical thoughts, we fan the flames of our negative emotions. But if we identify these negative thought patterns and change them to constructive, positive, self-empowering ones, we can actually diminish or even eliminate the negative emotional reactions.

So when your child throws a tantrum in a store, you might think:

How can my child embarrass me like this? Everyone must be watching. What are they thinking of me? They must think I'm a terrible parent because I can't manage my child properly. I knew I should have stayed home. How dare this child humiliate me like this? Now I can never come back here again. Why am I such a lousy parent?

The other parents you've seen behaving so calmly in the same situation may be thinking:

I am not going to give in to my child's attempt at extortion. He knows the rules, and I told him before we got here that we were not buying any toys or candy on this trip. I am this child's teacher, and he may have to learn the hard way that I will not be intimidated by these tantrums. In a few minutes he will calm down. It's unfortunate that he has to embarrass himself like this and disturb other people's shopping. I've seen many parents have to discipline their children for these kinds of outbursts. In fact many children occasionally act this way in stores. But to give in to him now would teach him the wrong lesson.

You can learn to identify negative thought patterns by keeping a small notebook with you and writing in it what you were saying or thinking to yourself when an event that triggered a stressful or emotionally upsetting reaction occurred. Once you've begun to identify your negative or distressing thought patterns, try substituting more positive, upbeat, constructive, and forgiving ones the next time you sense stress coming on.

8. Exercise Regularly

OK, we've all heard this advice before, but where stressful lives are concerned it's important to heed it, so it's worth saying again: regular exercise lessens stress, builds stamina, and makes you generally more able to meet the demands of the day. If you don't think you can spare the time, try combining it with another self-renewal activity: ask a friend to become a cycling partner, put together a regular foursome for golf, or plan a hiking weekend with old friends (and see the sidebar on time management). But keep in mind that you'll benefit, say the fitness experts, from as little as 20 to 30 minutes of light exercise 3 times a week.

9. Avoid Chemical Substances

Again, you've heard it before: Alcohol, caffeine, and nicotine can take a lot more out of you than they give back. We all know the hazards of smoking by now, but alcohol and caffeine consumption seem to be more matters of quantity. Quite simply, moderation is essential if you're to preserve your energies. Alcohol, a sedative, when used chronically to excess, can result in fatigue, irritability, low frustration tolerance, and a withdrawal from responsibilities. Nicotine and caffeine, both stimulants, increase heart rate, blood pressure, breathing rate, brain activity, muscle tension, restlessness, and perceived stress or nervousness in a situation. The last thing you need is to overreact, I'm sure you'll agree. So take a minute to evaluate your habits and whether they're serving you well.

PART III

Managing Life with ADHD: How to Cope at Home and at School

CHAPTER 11

Eight Steps
to Better Behavior

With an ADHD child in residence, many families find their home is more battlefield than haven. The child violates household rules, neglects chores, resists homework, and generally disturbs the peace. There is no cure for ADHD, but there are some sound principles by which you can work with your child to improve behavior, social relationships, and general adjustment at home. This chapter presents the management principles that we teach at the ADHD clinic at the University of Massachusetts Medical Center. More than 70% of the families who come to our clinic find the principles help them significantly improve their ADHD child's behavior and their overall relationship with the child.

The tactics described here are designed expressly to reduce stubborn, defiant, or oppositional behavior while they increase the child's cooperativeness. The result in the great majority of cases is that the child becomes more successful at meeting daily demands for working and living within the larger family unit and acquires a wide range of positive behaviors that contribute to success in school, in the community, and in society at large.

Here's what you can expect to achieve by diligently applying these principles:

1. To strengthen the parent–child relationship through mutual respect, cooperation, and appreciation; to make that relationship more loving and friendly.
2. To reduce the daily conflict, hassles, arguments, and even temper outbursts—yours as well as your child's—that may now permeate your daily interactions.
3. To improve your child's range of appropriate and socially acceptable behaviors while you decrease his or her reliance on antisocial and unacceptable social behaviors.

4. To prepare your child to be socialized. The variety of child behavior problems for which this treatment program can be applied extends well beyond the home to all situations where parents must expect their children to behave in prosocial (effective and socially supportive) ways, trust them to carry out family and social responsibilities, and foster positive and cooperative social interactions between this child and other children and adults.

When young children learn to comply with parental requests and rules, they are acquiring a basic attitude of social cooperation and an openness to learning from adults that is absolutely critical to continuing social development and later adult social adjustment. And you will have fulfilled one of the most fundamental roles of a parent in society, the preparation of a child to be socialized within that family's larger social community. Make no mistake about the importance of this parental responsibility. The psychological research is crystal clear on this point: The young child who learns that disobedience, resistance to parental requests, stubbornness, tantrums, and aggressive behavior are successful means of escaping from adult requests and the imposition of social responsibilities is at high risk for later antisocial and criminal activity, school failure, peer and community rejection, and early substance abuse. This program is designed to address that risk directly and to improve your child's openness to be socialized by you and other important adults and to cooperate with you, peers, and the larger social community. This spirit of social cooperation and openness to the rules and wisdom of society is critical to the eventual adult adjustment of any child.

Is This Program for You?

This program can help you manage the behavior of an ADHD child who:

- Is between 2 and 10 years old
- Has generally normal language development
- Is not seriously oppositional or defiant (see sidebar)
- Is not likely to try to assault you or become seriously destructive when you try to set limits on the child's behavior

Do not attempt this program if:

- Your child's language development is below that of the average 2-year-old or
- Your child is age 13 or older (the program described in Chapter 14 may be more appropriate)

Try this program only with professional assistance if your child:

- Has been diagnosed as autistic, psychotic, schizophrenic, or severely depressed or has a pervasive developmental disorder or
- Is seriously defiant (see sidebar)

How Defiant Is Your Child?

Circle any of the following items that you believe your child displays *to a degree that is excessive or inappropriate for his or her age group* and that has been present for at least six months.

1. Often loses temper
2. Often argues with adults
3. Often actively defies or refuses adults' requests or rules
4. Often deliberately does things that annoy other people
5. Often blames others for his or her own mistakes or misbehavior
6. Often touchy or easily annoyed by others
7. Often angry and resentful
8. Often spiteful or vindictive

If you circled at least four of these items, your child has a significant degree of defiant or oppositional behavior and might have oppositional defiant disorder. You may want to consider having a mental health professional assist you with this program. Certainly if you circled six or more, you will probably run into a great deal of resistance from your child and should not attempt this program without professional help.

Whether your child has more or fewer than four of the behavior problems listed above, circle any of the following items that your child has shown during the past 12 months. (This list, of course, applies to children up to age 18 years or older.)

1. Often bullies, threatens, or intimidates others
2. Often initiates physical fights with others (not including fights with siblings)
3. Uses a weapon that can cause serious physical harm to others (e.g., a bat, brick, broken bottle, knife, gun)
4. Is physically cruel to people (e.g., ties up and abandons a victim, systematically cuts or burns a victim)
5. Steals with confrontation with a victim (e.g., mugging, purse snatching, extortion, or armed robbery)
6. Forces someone into sexual activity
7. Often lies or breaks promises to obtain goods or favors or to avoid debts or obligations (i.e., "cons" others)
8. Steals items of nontrivial value without confrontation with the victim (e.g., shoplifting, burglary, or forgery)
9. Often stays out after dark without permission, beginning before 13 years of age
10. Is physically cruel to animals

(cont.)

How Defiant Is Your Child? *(cont.)*

11. Deliberately destroys others' property (other than by firesetting)
12. Deliberately engages in firesetting with the intention of causing serious damage
13. Runs away from home overnight at least twice while living in parental or parental surrogate home (or once without returning for a lengthy period)
14. Is often truant from school, beginning before 16 years of age
15. Breaks into someone else's house, building, or car

If your child has shown three or more of these problems within the past year, seek the assistance of a professional with this program. Your child may have conduct disorder, a serious pattern of antisocial behavior and violation of the rights of others. Families with children who show such behavior problems are in need of more professional help than can be provided by this book.

To find professional help, ask a mental health or medical professional you are already working with if he or she is familiar with *behavioral parent training or child management programs.* If not, ask for a referral to a professional who teaches such behavioral child management programs. Or contact your local ADHD parent support association or school psychologist for the names of professionals whom they know employ such training programs in their practice. Ideally, you should find someone who has used this particular program. The full program as it should be conducted by a professional is detailed in my textbook *Defiant Children: A Clinician's Manual for Parent Training* (1987) published by The Guilford Press.

A final word of caution: If you are not ready to change your own behavior to help your child, this program is not for you. For some parents the principles demand significant changes in parent–child interaction, and if you're not prepared to comply fully with the program, it is bound to fail.

How to Use This Program

This program will take the average parent about eight weeks to complete. Plan on spending at least a week at each step before moving on. Do not go on to the next step until you feel comfortable with the step you have practiced that week. Your child has taken months—even years—to develop the current behavior pattern with you, so don't expect it to change quickly. Each step of this program builds on the previous one, so you must apply them in the order given. And *never* skip over the first three steps and go straight to the methods that involve discipline or punishment. To be effective, these later steps on discipline *must* be preceded by the earlier steps. Remember the rule you learned in Chapter 9: *rewards before punishment.*

Step 1: Learn to Pay Positive Attention to Your Child

Purpose and Goals

The attention you give a child is a very powerful reward or consequence. This is why your children seek you out, strive to get your attention, and bask in the glow of any positive attention you give them. This attention need not be positive, however, to be desirable to the child. In the absence of positive attention, negative attention—reprimands, criticism, or yelling—may seem worth seeking out, because any attention is better than none. A child who gets scolded for interrupting a phone call may obey our commands to stop that time but will surely be more likely to interrupt the next time.

Even our positive attention is often flawed. When we combine praise and criticism in backhanded compliments such as "You did a nice job cleaning up your room, but why can't you do that every day without being told?" we greatly reduce the power of our attention to reinforce our children's positive behavior.

Learning *when* to give your child your attention and when to withhold it are important goals of this program. Also important is *how* you pay attention to your child when you do so, the subject of this first step of the program. We will come back to this in the second step as well.

If you don't believe that how and when you pay attention to your child has a powerful influence on the child's compliance and other aspects of behavior, do the exercise in the sidebar. The goal of this step of the program is to help you become a parent with the characteristics of the best job supervisor you've ever had. The purpose is to change *your* behavior. Changes in your child should follow slowly, naturally, and eventually from changing yourself.

Step 1: Learn to pay positive attention to your child.
Step 2: Use your powerful attention to gain compliance.
Step 3: Give more effective commands.
Step 4: Teach your child not to interrupt your activities.
Step 5: Set up a home token system.
Step 6: Learn to punish misbehavior constructively.
Step 7: Expand your use of time-out.
Step 8: Learn to manage your child in public places.

Are You the Best or Worst Supervisor You Can Imagine?

1. Divide a sheet of paper into two columns and write "Worst Supervisor" over the left and "Best Supervisor" over the right.

2. Now recall the worst person you've ever worked for and think about how that person treated you. What did he or she say or do that made you dislike that style of management or interaction? This is a person you would not like to work for again if you could avoid doing so. Why? List in the left column at least five different negative characteristics. Parents usually give statements such as "Doesn't appreciate what I do," "Doesn't seem to listen to my point of view," "Dishonest," "Too bossy or overcontrolling," "Interrupts my work without apologizing," "Acts like I am his slave," "A real dictator," "Hot-tempered," "Very critical of others."

3. Next, think of the best person you've ever worked for—someone you'd enjoy working for again. If that person had asked you to do some extra work beyond the call of duty, you would have gladly volunteered to help out. Why? List in the right column five positive characteristics. Parents often give me answers such as "Honest," "Appreciated my work, even the little things," "Took an interest in me and my opinions," "Encouraged my efforts to improve my work," "Respected my time and my work," "Very positive and upbeat about herself and our work together."

4. Now look at the information in the two columns and honestly decide in which column your child would place you.

More than 90% of the parents I work with in our clinic are shocked to find that they are more likely to be acting like the "Worst Supervisor" with their children than the "Best Supervisor." *The way you give attention to your children when you supervise them can create the same feelings in them as it has in you.*

Instructions

This step of the program involves learning how to pay attention to your child's desirable behavior during playtime. If your child is below nine years of age, select a 20-minute period each day as your "special time" with your child—after other children are off to school in the morning if you have a preschool child or after school or dinner for schoolchildren. No other children are to be involved! If your child is nine years or older, you don't have to choose a standard time but instead choose a time each day as it arises when your child seems to be enjoying a play activity alone. Then stop what you're doing and begin to join in the child's play following the instructions given here.

If you've set up a standard time, simply say then, "It's now our special time to play together. What would you like to do?" The child chooses the play activity, within reason (television, a nonactivity, is out). If you have not set up a standard time, simply ask if you can join in.

In either case, don't take control of the play or direct it. Relax and casually watch what your child is doing for a few minutes before joining in. Obviously, you should not try to have this special playtime when you're upset, very busy, or planning to leave the house soon for some errand or trip. Your mind will be preoccupied by these matters, and the quality of your attention will be quite poor.

After watching your child's play, begin to describe out loud what your child is doing to show your interest. In other words, occasionally narrate your child's play. Try to keep what you say exciting and action oriented, not dull and in a monotone. Young children really enjoy this. With older children, you should still comment, but less so.

Ask no questions and give no commands! This is critical. Questioning is disruptive and should be limited to trying to clarify when you're uncertain of what your child is doing. Remember that this is your child's special time to relax and enjoy your company, not a time to teach or take over the child's play.

Occasionally, provide your child with statements of praise, approval, or positive feedback. Be accurate and honest, not excessively flattering. For instance, "I like it when we play quietly like this," "I really enjoy our special time together," and "Look at how nicely you have made that" are all positive, appropriate comments. If you find yourself at a loss for words, try some of these responses:

Nonverbal signs of approval
Hug
Pat on the head or shoulder
Affectionate rubbing of hair
Placing arm around the child
Smiling
A light kiss
Giving a thumbs-up sign
A wink

Verbal signs of approval
I like it when you . . .
It's nice when you . . .
You sure are a big boy/girl for . . .
That was terrific the way you . . .
Great job!
Nice going!
Terrific!
Super!
Fantastic!
My, you sure act grown up when you . . .
You know, six months ago you couldn't do that as well as you can now—
    you're really growing up fast!

Beautiful!

Wow!

Wait until I tell Mom/Dad [other parent] how nicely you . . .

What a nice thing to do . . .

You did that all by yourself—way to go!

Just for behaving so well, you and I will . . .

I am very proud of you when you . . .

I always enjoy it when we . . . like this.

If your child begins to misbehave, simply turn away and look elsewhere for a few moments. If the misbehavior continues, tell your child the special play-time is over and leave the room. Tell your child you will play later when he or she can behave nicely. If the child becomes extremely disruptive or abusive during play, discipline the child as you might normally do.

Each parent is to spend 20 minutes with the child in this special playtime. During the first week, try to do this every day or at least five times. After the first week, continue this special playtime indefinitely at least three to four times a week.

Don't worry if you give too many commands and questions or make too few positive comments at first. Just try harder to improve your attending skills the next time. You may want to spend this kind of special playtime with the other children in your family once you have improved your skills with the problem child.

If your practicing with your child goes reasonably well, you will probably find that your child enjoys your company. Your child may even ask you to stay and play longer after your "special time" is up. On rare occasions you may even find that your child starts to compliment you for the things that you do well or do for the child.

If you still don't feel comfortable acting this way with your child, spend another week practicing your new attending skills before going on to step 2. You're ready to move on to the next step when you find you can observe and play with your child while commenting on his or her activities without taking control of the play and directing it and asking lots of unnecessary questions. You should also find it relatively easy to give praise and positive feedback to your child for the good things you notice about his or her play and interactions with you. If you spend most of the playtime not saying anything to your child, then you need to practice this week's exercises for another week or so. For steps 1 to 4, you will know that you are ready by how your own behavior is changing, not by how well your child is improving. You should not expect much change for your child during these four steps.

Hints

1. Always show your approval immediately. *Don't wait!*
2. Always be specific about what you like.
3. Never give a backhanded compliment.

Step 2: Use Your Powerful Attention to Gain Compliance

Purpose and Goals

You are now going to take the style of paying attention you practiced during play and extend it to when your child is obeying you or complying with your instructions. It's the same style, just a different focus of your attention. Your goal is to improve the manner in which you supervise work in the hope that it will increase your child's willingness to work for you (obey) and improve how hard he or she works.

Instructions

When you give a command, give the child immediate feedback for how well he or she is doing. Don't just walk away; stay and pay attention and comment positively on your child's compliance (see the list of verbal signs of approval above).

Don't give any more commands or ask any questions while your child is working or obeying. Too often parents give multiple commands or ask unnecessary questions, which distracts the child from the task assigned.

Once you have noted your child's compliance, you can leave for a few moments if you must, but be sure to return frequently to pay attention and praise your child's compliance.

Should you find that your child has done a job or chore without being told to do so, provide especially positive praise, perhaps even a small privilege to help your child remember and follow household rules and jobs without always being told to do so. Even children with ADHD, despite their disability, can improve in their ability to recall and follow rules and instructions, and one way to help them is to reward them when they do so spontaneously.

This week, begin to use positive attention to your child for virtually every command you give. In addition, choose two or three commands your child follows inconsistently and make a special effort to praise and attend to your child whenever he or she begins to comply with these particular commands. In short, "Catch 'em being good!"

Setting Up Compliance Training Periods

It is very important during the next one or two weeks that you take a few minutes now and then to train compliance in your child. Select a time when your child is not very busy and ask him or her to do very brief favors for you, such as "Hand me a pencil" or "Can you reach that towel for me?" We call these *fetch* commands, and they should require only a very brief and simple effort from your child. Give about five or six of these, but only one at a time during these few minutes. As your child follows each one, be sure to provide specific praise, such as "I like it when you listen to me" or "It is really nice when you do as I ask" or "Thanks for doing what I asked." Then let your child go on to do something else.

Try to do this several times a day. Because the requests are very simple and brief, most children (even behavior problem children) will do them. This provides an excellent opportunity to catch your child being good and to praise his or her compliance. If your child does not obey one of the commands, skip it and make another brief request. Your goal at this point is not to confront or discipline noncompliance but to catch, attend to, and reward compliance. By doing so, you increase the likelihood that your child will comply with your other, necessary instructions.

You will know that you're ready to move on to the next step when you feel comfortable pointing out the small things that your child is doing well for you and when your child is complying with most or all of your requests during your compliance training periods, and you find it quite easy to praise compliance with each one.

After a week of practicing this, many parents tell me they begin to see a noticeable though not dramatic difference in their children's behavior toward them.

Step 3: Give More Effective Commands

Purpose and Goals

The purpose of this step is to improve the manner in which you ask your child to do work for you or obey your instructions. In my work with behavior problem children, I've noticed that if parents simply change the way they give commands to their child, they can often achieve significant improvements in the child's compliance.

Instructions

When you're about to give a command or instruction to your child, be sure to do the following.

Make Sure You Mean It!

Never give a command that you don't intend to follow through on. Plan on backing up any request with appropriate consequences to show that you mean what you say. It's better to focus on a few commands that you mean than to spew out hundreds and follow up on only half of them.

Do Not Present the Command as a Question or Favor

State the command simply, directly, and in a businesslike tone of voice. Don't say, "Why don't we pick up the toys now?" or "It's time for dinner. Wash your hands, OK?" These are command–questions or command–favors. The inflection at the end of the statement asks for your child's assent, which is far less effective than a more direct statement, such as "Pick up the toys now" or "It's dinnertime; wash your hands." You don't have to yell or scream; just be firm and direct.

Don't Give Too Many Commands at Once

Most children are able to follow only one or two instructions at a time. For now, try giving only one specific instruction at a time. If a task you want your child to do is complicated, break it down into smaller steps and give only one step at a time.

Make Sure Your Child Is Paying Attention to You

Be sure to make eye contact with your child. If necessary, gently turn the child's face toward yours to ensure that he or she is listening and watching.

Reduce All Distractions before Giving the Command

A very common mistake that parents make is to try to give instructions while a television, stereo, or video game is on. Parents cannot expect children to attend to them when something more entertaining is going on. Either turn off these distractions yourself or tell the child to turn them off before giving the command.

Ask the Child to Repeat the Command

Do this when you're not sure your child has heard or understood the command. Also, repeating a command seems to increase the likelihood that a child with a short attention span will follow through.

Make Up Chore Cards

If your child is old enough to have chores and to read, you may find it useful to make up a chore card for each job. Simply list on a three-by-five file card the steps involved in correctly doing that chore. Then, when you want your child to do the chore, simply hand the child the card and state that this is what you want done. These cards can greatly reduce arguing over whether a child has done a job properly.

Set Deadlines

You might also indicate on the cards how much time the chore should take and then set your kitchen timer so the child knows exactly when it is to be done. Whether you use the chore cards or not, give your child a specific deadline in the immediate future. Don't say "Sometime today you will have to take out the trash" or "Before noon you must clean up your room." Instead, wait until the time for the work to be done and then say "It is now time to take out the trash. You have 10 minutes to get the job done. I am setting the stove timer for 10 minutes. See if you can beat the clock."

Practice giving effective commands for the next week, continuing to do the exercises from the previous two steps as well. You will have a sense that you're ready to move on when you give most of your work requests or commands in a neutral, imperative form rather than as a favor or question. You should also notice that your commands are simpler in form. Ask yourself before moving on to the next step if you've reviewed your child's routine chores to see if a chore card with an assigned time limit was necessary to help with any of them. Also, do you now set a time limit with most tasks assigned? Giving explicit commands, keeping them relatively simple, and setting time limits for completion are three main indications that you're ready to go on to the next step.

Step 4: Teach Your Child
Not to Interrupt Your Activities

Purpose and Goals

Many parents of behavior problem children complain that they are unable to talk on the phone, cook dinner, or visit with a neighbor without the child interrupting. The following steps will help you teach your child to play independently of you when you are occupied. Many parents provide a lot of attention to a child who is interrupting and almost no attention when the child stays away, plays independently, and does not interrupt. No wonder kids interrupt parents so much!

Instructions

When you're about to become occupied with some activity, such as a phone call, give your child a direct two-part command, one part that tells the child what to do while you're busy and another that specifically tells the child not to interrupt or bother you. For instance, you can say "Mom has to talk on the telephone, so I want you to stay in this room and watch television. Don't bother me." The task you give a child should *not* be a chore, but some interesting activity such as coloring, playing with a toy, watching television, or cutting out pictures. Then stop what you're doing after a moment, go to your child, and praise him or her for staying away and not interrupting. Remind the child to stay with the assigned task and not to bother you, then return to what you were doing.

Wait a few moments longer before returning to your child and again praising him or her for not bothering you. Return to your activity, wait a little longer, and again praise your child.

Over time you will gradually be able to reduce how often you praise your child while increasing the length of time you can stay at your own task. Initially you'll have to interrupt yourself to praise your child very frequently, say every minute to two. After a few times like this, wait three minutes before praising your child. Then wait five minutes, and so on. Each time, return to what you're working on for a slightly longer time before going back to praise your child.

The same approach applies to teaching anything new to your child: Start with very frequent attention and praise and then gradually reduce how often you compliment the new behavior.

If it sounds as if your child is about to leave the activity and come to bother you, immediately stop what you're doing, go to your child, praise him or her for not interrupting, and redirect the child to stay with the task.

As soon as you finish what you're doing, give the child special praise for letting you complete your task. You may even periodically give your child a small privilege or reward for having left you alone while you worked on your project.

This week, choose one or two activities—preparing a meal, talking to an adult, writing a letter, accomplishing any special project, using the telephone, reading or watching television, doing paperwork, talking at the dinner table, visiting others' homes, housecleaning—with which to practice. If you choose talking on the phone, you might want to have someone call you once or twice a day simply as practice. That way, when important calls do come in, you have already trained your child so you can handle these calls with less interruption.

After a week of practice, ask yourself how easy you now find it to stop what you're doing to praise your child for leaving you alone and how often you remember to give your child something to do when you don't want to be interrupted. If these practices are becoming part of your typical interactions with your child, you are ready to move on.

Step 5: Set Up a Home Token System

Purpose and Goals

Children with behavioral problems often need a more powerful program than praise to motivate them to do chores, follow rules, or obey commands. One way to pair compliance with powerful rewards is the home poker chip program (for children four to eight years old) or the home point system (for nine-year-old and older children). Although you'll probably see quick results, the positive changes in your child's behavior are not likely to last if you stop using the program too soon, so plan on sticking with this program for about two months.

Instructions for a Chip Program

Find a set of plastic poker chips, then sit down with your child and start your reward program with a very positive tone: Say that you feel your child has not been rewarded enough for doing nice things at home, and you want to set up a program so he or she can earn privileges for behaving properly. For four- and five-year-olds, explain that each chip, regardless of color, is worth one chip. For six- to eight-year-olds, assign different denominations to the colors—white = 1 chip, blue = 5 chips, and red = 10 chips—then tape a chip of each color to a small piece of cardboard, label them with their points, and post the card where your child can easily refer to it.

You and your child should then make a bank—a shoe box, coffee can (with a dull rim), plastic jar, and others—for storing the chips earned. Have some fun decorating it with your child.

Now compile a list of the privileges the child will earn with the poker chips. These should include not only occasional special privileges (going to movies, roller-skating, buying a toy) but also the everyday privileges your child takes for grant-ed (television, video games, special toys already in the home, riding a bike, go-ing over to a friend's home, etc.). Be sure to list at least 10, preferably 15. They don't have to cost money; you can include any activity around the house that your child seems to enjoy.

Now make up a list of the jobs and chores you often ask your child to do—setting the table for a meal, clearing the table after a meal, cleaning a bedroom, making a bed, emptying wastebaskets, and other typical household chores. Also list self-help tasks that cause conflict, like getting dressed for school, getting ready for bed, washing and bathing, and brushing teeth.

Next, decide how much each job or chore is worth in chips. For four- to six-year-olds, assign from one to three chips for most tasks and perhaps five for really big jobs. For six- to eight-year-olds, use a range of 1 to 10 chips and perhaps give a larger amount for big jobs. Remember, the harder the job, the more chips you will pay.

Now calculate how many chips you think your child will earn in a typical day if he or she does most of the tasks you usually assign; write this number on a scratch pad. We generally suggest that two-thirds of the child's daily chips be spent on common privileges and one-third be saved toward the purchase of spe-cial rewards. If your child can earn about 30 chips a day for doing daily work, for example, 20 should be spent on everyday privileges. The easiest way to do this is to start assigning a price to each daily privilege and then add them up to see if they total about two-thirds of the child's daily earnings. If the total is higher, go back and reduce the price of the privileges until they do add up to about two-thirds. Don't worry about exact numbers; just use your judgment and be fair.

Now go back and assign a price to the special privileges. Ask yourself how often you think your child should have access to these, then multiply the num-ber of days you feel your child should wait to have each long-term privilege by the number of chips saved (one-third of the daily income). If your child earns 30 chips a day, and you wish your child to be able to rent a video game every two weeks, the price of that privilege should be 14 days times 10 chips or 140 chips. Do this for each long-term privilege, again not worrying about precise amounts. An example of a home chip program is provided in Table 4.

TABLE 4. Sample of a Home Chip Program Job and Privilege List for a Six- to Eight-Year-Old

Job	Payment	Reward	Cost
Get dressed	5	Watch television (30 minutes)	4
Wash hands/face	2	Play videogames (30 minutes)	5
Bursh teeth	2	Play outside in yard	2
Make bed	5	Ride my bike	2
Put dirty clothes away	2	Use a special toy	4
Pick up toys	3	Go out for fast food	200
Take dirty dishes to sink after eating	1	Rent a video game or movie	300
Homework (per 15 minutes)	5	Go bowling/miniature golf or	
Give dog fresh water	1	roller/ice skating	400
Take bath/shower	5	Stay up past bedtime (30 minutes)	50
Hang up coat	1	Have a friend play over	40
No fights with sibling		Have a friend sleep over	150
Breakfast to lunch	3	Go to a video arcade	300
Lunch to dinner	3	Get my allowance ($1.00/wk)	100
Dinner to bedtime	3	Choose a special dessert	20
Uses nice voice with mom when		Go play at a friend's home	50
asking for something	1		
Get pajamas on	3		
Come when called	2		
Tell the truth when asked about			
a problem	3		
Positive attitude	Bonus		

Note. I estimated that this child would earn about 50 chips each day for doing just the daily routine tasks on a typical school day. I then made sure that about 30 of these chips would be needed to buy the daily privileges of television (1.5 hours), videogames (1 hour), playing outside, riding a bike, and playing with a special toy that Mom and Dad control access to, such as a remote control car, a racecar set and track, a train set, an army battle station with troops, a doll with clothes and accessories, a personal tape player or CD player, roller blades, skateboard. The remaining privileges were priced by determining how often the child should have access to that reward, that is, how many days of waiting and saving.

Be sure to tell your child that he or she will have a chance to earn bonus chips when chores are done with a good attitude. That is, if the chore is done promptly and pleasantly, you will give your child extra chips and say that you like his or her positive work attitude. You should not give these chips all the time.

Be sure to tell the child that chips will be given only for jobs done on the first request. If you have to repeat a command, the child will not receive any chips.

Finally, be sure to go out of your way this week to give chips away for any small appropriate behavior. Remember, you can reward a child even for good behaviors that are not on the list of jobs. Be alert for opportunities to reward the child.

Do not take chips away this week for misbehavior!

Once your child has earned the chips, he or she has the right to spend them. There will, of course, be times such as bedtime when it just is not reasonable or convenient for your child to have that privilege at that time, but the child should be able to ask you when he or she can have this reward so you can schedule it at the next convenient time.

Instructions for a Home Point System

Set up a notebook like a checkbook with five columns, one each for the date, the item, deposits, withdrawals, and the running balance. When your child is rewarded with points, write in the job under "item" and enter the amount as a "deposit." Add it to the child's balance. When your child buys a privilege, note the privilege under "item," place this amount in the withdrawal column, and deduct this amount from the "balance." Only parents are to write in the notebook. The child may look at the book anytime but may not make entries.

The program works just like the chip system except that you record points in the book instead of giving poker chips and use larger numbers for the value of each job. We generally use a range of 5 to 25 points for most daily jobs and up to 200 points for very big jobs. A good rule of thumb is to give about 25 points for every 15 minutes of effort that a job might require.

Hints

1. Review the list of rewards and jobs every few weeks or so and add new ones as you deem necessary. Check with your child for new rewards he or she may want on the list.
2. You can reward your child with chips or points for almost any form of good behavior. They can even be used in conjunction with step 4 to reward your child for not interrupting your work.
3. Do not give the chips or points away before the child has done what he or she was told to do, but be as quick as possible in rewarding the child for compliance. Don't wait to reward!
4. Both parents should use the chip or point system to make it as effective as possible.
5. When you give points or chips for good behavior, smile and tell the child what you like that he or she has done.

Try this program for at least one week before moving on to the next step. You'll know that you're ready to move on when your child is doing most of the assigned jobs or chores, your child seems to be enjoying the program, and you find it fairly easy to remember to give out the chips/points. Do not move on to the next step until you believe this program has become routine. Some parents find that this takes two weeks.

Step 6: Learn to Punish Misbehavior Constructively

Purpose and Goals

This step is the most critical part of the program. Using this method of discipline with children when they misbehave or fail to comply with a command requires great skill. The goal is to decrease your child's defiant behavior, refusals to obey, or other misbehavior.

"If ADHD is causing my child to disobey," you may ask, "how can any method of discipline help?" ADHD does *not* directly cause children to refuse or defy your requests. It does, however, cause them problems with complying if the task assigned is lengthy, boring, repetitive, or otherwise tedious. It also causes them to be distracted more during the task. Refusing to obey initially with a request is not ADHD behavior. It is defiant behavior and can be greatly reduced by using this program.

Why do ADHD children become defiant in the first place? Partly because of all the criticism they receive for their lack of persistence; they learn to balk in circumstances where they fear they'll fail. Some adults unwittingly train the child to be oppositional by relying solely on excessive criticism and negative consequences. This is one reason this program emphasizes incentive programs before punishment. Parents also train ADHD children to become defiant when their response to an initial emotional display teaches the child that resistance, defiance, and negativity are an effective means of avoiding work. Also keep in mind that research on social cooperation, sharing, altruism, and concern for others shows that such behaviors develop when a person expects to interact with people again in the future. A child who has a restricted sense of future, as in ADHD, is less concerned about and motivated to cooperate with others.

It is the manner in which you respond to these initial gambits at resistance that determines how excessive and severe they will become. Consequently, by responding to defiance in the manner prescribed here, you can greatly reduce such behaviors in a child with ADHD.

Instructions for Fining Your Child

After you have been using the chip or point system for one to two weeks, you can begin to use it occasionally and selectively as a form of discipline. Just tell your child that whenever he or she is asked to perform a chore or an instruction, he or she can be fined for not listening to you or following through. From then on, if you give a command and your child does not respond or obey, follow up with "If you do not do as I said on the count of three, you will lose _____ chips [or points]." Count to three. If the child still has not begun to comply, deduct from the bank or point book the amount you would have paid for completing the work. If the job is not on the chore list, choose a fine that seems reasonable for the severity of the misbehavior.

You can use fines for any form of misbehavior from this week onward. However, be very careful not to fine excessively or too frequently, or you will wipe out your child's bank account quickly, and the program will no longer work. In general, use the three-to-one rule—for every three times you reward, you can fine the child once. If you find yourself fining your child too frequently and the program has lost its appeal or its ability to motivate your child, stop the program for a month or so. When you start anew, be sure not to fine your child so much.

Instructions for Using Time-Out

Time-out is a frequently used form of punishment for more serious misbehavior that involves removing the child to a quiet, isolated location to serve a penalty period. Use time-out with only one or two forms of misbehavior during the next week. Choose a type of misbehavior that is not responding very well to the token system you set up last week.

Never give a command that you do not intend to back up with consequences to see that the job gets done. *Always* give your first command to a child in a firm but neutral or pleasant voice. *Do not* yell it at the child, but also do not ask it as a favor. You may add "please" to your request or directive, but do not pose it as a favor or question.

After you have given the command, count to five. You may count out loud, but if you notice that your child gets used to this and waits until the very last count of five before obeying you, keep the counting to yourself.

If the child has not made a move to comply within these five seconds, make direct eye contact, raise your voice, adopt a firm posture or stance, and say "If you don't [do what I ask], then you are going to sit in that chair"! (Point to the chair in the corner.) Once you give this warning, count to five again. If the child has not started to comply within five seconds, take the child firmly by the wrist or upper arm and say "You did not do as I asked, so you must go to the chair!"

You should say this in a somewhat louder and even firmer tone of voice but not with anger. You are raising the volume of your voice to get the child's attention, not out of your own loss of emotional control. Then take the child to the time-out chair. The child is to go to the chair immediately, regardless of any promises he or she may make. If the child resists, use slight physical guidance if need be. For instance, grasp your child firmly by the upper arm or shoulder and escort the child to the chair. If necessary, take hold of the waist seam at the back of the trousers and at the back seam of the shirt collar to guide the child to the chair *without physical harm*. The child is not to go to the bathroom, get a drink, or stand and argue. The child is to be taken immediately to the time-out chair.

Place the child in the chair and say sternly, "You stay there until I tell you to get up!" You may tell the child that you are not coming back to the chair until he or she has become quiet, but don't say this more than once. Do not argue with the child or let anyone else talk to the child during this time. Instead, go back to your work, but be sure to keep an eye on what the child is doing in the chair.

Your child should stay in time-out until three conditions are met:

1. The child must always serve a "minimum sentence" of one to two minutes for each year of age—one minute for mild to moderate misbehavior and two minutes for serious misbehavior.
2. Once the minimum sentence is over, wait until the child is quiet. This may take several minutes to an hour or longer the first time your child

is sent to time-out. You are not to go to the child until he or she has been quiet for about 30 seconds or so, even if it means the child remains in time-out for up to one or two hours because he or she is arguing, throwing a tantrum, screaming, or crying loudly.

3. Once the child has been quiet for a few moments, the child must agree to do what he or she was told to do. If it was a chore, the child must agree to do it. If it is something the child cannot correct, such as swearing or lying, the child is to promise not to do it again. If the child fails to agree to do as asked (says "No!"), instruct the child to sit in the chair until you give permission to leave. The child is then to serve another minimum sentence, become quiet, and agree to do what was asked. The child is not to leave the chair until he or she has agreed to obey the command originally given. When the child has complied, say in a neutral tone of voice, "I like it when you do as I say."

Watch for the next appropriate behavior by your child and praise the child for it. This ensures that the child always receives as much reward as punishment and shows that you are not angry at him or her but at what the child did.

What If the Child Leaves the Chair without Permission?

Many children will test their parents' authority when time-out is first used by trying to escape from the chair before the time is up. Generally, a child is considered to have left the chair if both buttocks leave the flat seat. The child does not have to face the wall. We also consider rocking the chair and tipping it over leaving. The child should be warned about this.

The first time the child leaves the chair, put him or her back in the chair and say, loudly and sternly, "If you get out of that chair again, I am going to fine you!" When the child leaves the chair again, take a large number of chips or points—one-fifth of the typical daily earnings—from the child's bank account. Return the child to the chair and say "Now you stay there until I say you can get up!"

Thereafter, fine the child each time he or she leaves the chair, even if the child is sent to time-out again for some other misbehavior. If the child leaves the chair without permission, *do not* give the warning again, but go straight to fining. Do not, however, fine your child more than twice during this episode for leaving the chair. Instead, consider using one of the following penalties for escape: (1) place your child in the chair and stand behind him or her, pushing down with just enough firmness on the shoulders to restrain the child but not cause physical pain or harm; or (2) send your child to his or her bedroom for the time-out period. Be sure to remove all toys, videogames, TVs, stereos, and other sources of entertainment or play from the room. If it is not possible to clear the room of all attractive play materials, be sure to restrict your child to sitting on the bed.

Some parents and professionals believe that using a child's bed as a place for time-out may result in later sleeping problems, but I am aware of no scientific evidence for this.

Where Should the Chair Be Placed?

The chair should be straight-backed and placed in a corner far enough away from the wall that the child cannot kick it. No play objects should be nearby, and the child should not be able to watch television. Most parents use a corner of a kitchen, a first-floor laundry room, a foyer, the middle or end of a long hallway, or a corner of a living room (not occupied by others). You should be able to observe the child while continuing your business. Do not use bathrooms, closets, or the child's bedroom (at first). Sometimes the child can be told to sit on the first step of a stairway going to the second floor. Do not use the steps going into a basement since many young children have a fear of basements.

What Can You Expect This Week?

Typically children become quite upset when first sent to time-out. They may become quite angry and vocal or cry because their feelings have been hurt. For many children, this tantrum only prolongs the first time-out; anywhere from 30 minutes to one or two hours may pass before they become quiet and agree to do what was asked of them before the first time-out. Gradually your child will begin to obey your first commands, or at least your warnings about time-out, so that the frequency of time-out eventually decreases. However, this may take several weeks. Try to remember during this first week that you are not harming your child but helping to teach him or her better self-control, respect for parental authority, and the ability to follow rules.

What If You Find Yourself Getting Upset?

Most parental anger comes from having to repeat unheeded requests many times over a long time. Few parents I know have found themselves getting upset using this program because little time elapses between the child's first failure to obey and the next move they are supposed to make. Should you find that you are getting emotionally upset, however, consider the following possible causes:

- Are you repeating your requests too frequently before imposing a consequence for noncompliance? Are you stringing this interaction out so long that you have plenty of time to build anger?
- Are you permitting a problem elsewhere in your life to spill over into your interactions with your child? If so, sit down and try to think of ways to deal directly with that problem. Letting it affect your relationship with your child is grossly unfair to your child and to you.
- Are you becoming persistently depressed or anxious? These emotional states can make your reactions more bitter, hostile, or irritable. Seek help from a qualified psychologist, psychiatrist, or other mental health specialist for evaluation and possible treatment.

Hints

1. The child is not to leave the time-out chair to use the bathroom, get a drink, or eat a meal (the child can eat in the chair if necessary). Make no effort to prepare the child a special snack later to compensate for a missed meal, because what makes time-out effective is what your child misses while in the chair.
2. If you want to use the time-out method for bedtime behavior problems, you will need to double the penalty period your child serves because children are not missing much at bedtime by sitting in the chair.
3. Do not use these punishment procedures out of the home for the next two weeks.
4. Be sure to continue the exercises from the previous steps, especially the token system, during the next week.

Step 7: Expand Your Use of Time-Out

Purpose and Goals

Just keep using the time-out and fining program. If the particular misbehavior you were targeting for time-out is now declining, target one or two new types of misbehavior this week. Remember, the goal is not to use punishment excessively. Do not extend the use of time-out to any new misbehavior if you're still using time-out fairly frequently (more than two to three times per week) for the last misbehavior.

You can move on to the next step when you have been using time-out for at least two or three weeks at home and find that the targeted misbehaviors are declining in frequency. You do not need to eliminate or reduce all behavior problems at home to move to the next step. If the child is not responsive, and conflicts are as bad as or worse than when you started, return to your mental health professional for advice or find one who is expert in child behavior management methods like those used here.

Step 8: Learn to Manage Your Child in Public Places

Purpose and Goals

Once you feel that you have your child's behavior under reasonable control at home, you can use these methods in stores, restaurants, church, others' homes, and other places. Your goal this week is to begin to reduce your child's misbehavior when you're away from home. You can do this fairly easily by using the methods learned up to this point: (1) positive attention and praise for good behavior; (2) praise for complying with directions; (3) effective delivery of commands; (4) tokens or points for good behavior; and (5) fines and time-out for misbehavior.

Instructions

The key to managing children in public places is to establish a plan and make sure your child is aware of the plan *before* you go into the public place. This method was introduced in Chapter 9. Follow these three easy rules:

Rule 1: Set Up the Rules before Entering the Place

Just before you enter a public place, *stop* and review the important rules of conduct with your child. Give your child about three rules that he or she commonly violates in that particular place and tell the child to say them back to you. If your child refuses to repeat them, warn your child that he or she will be placed in time-out in the car. If the child still refuses, return to your car and place the child in time-out.

Rule 2: Set Up an Incentive for the Child's Compliance

While still standing in front of the place, tell your child what he or she will earn for adhering to the rules. Chips or points can be used as effective rewards for good behavior while out of the home or, for children under age four, take along a small bag of relatively healthy snack food (peanuts, raisins, pretzels, corn chips, etc.) or some juice to dispense periodically for good behavior throughout the trip. On occasion, you may wish to promise your child a purchase of some sort at the end of the trip, but this should be done only on rare occasions and for exceptionally good behavior so the child does not come to expect it.

A comment about using food rewards with children: Current folk wisdom and pop psychology have it that some children become obese adults because they or their parents used food as rewards for successes or accomplishments. I am aware of no scientific research that supports such conditioning. Nevertheless, use snacks or treats only if other, more social or symbolic rewards, such as praise, tokens, or points, are not effective.

Rule 3: Set Up Your Punishment for Noncompliance

While still outside the place, tell your child what the punishment will be for not following the rules or for misbehavior. In most cases this will be the loss of points or chips for minor rule violations and the use of time-out for moderate to major misbehavior or noncompliance. Don't be afraid to use the time-out method in a public place—it's the most effective method away from home. As soon as you enter the public place, look for a convenient time-out location and attend to and praise your child for following the rules.

Give chips or points to your child periodically throughout the trip rather than waiting until the end. In addition, give frequent praise and attention to the child for obeying the rules.

If your child starts to misbehave, *immediately* take away chips or points or place the child in time-out. Do not repeat commands or warnings.

The minimum sentence for time-out in a public place should be only half of what it is at home. If the child leaves time-out without permission, use your at-home fining method.

Whenever you are out with your child, act quickly so that misbehavior does not escalate into a loud confrontation or a temper tantrum. Also, be sure to give frequent praise and rewards throughout the trip to reinforce good behavior.

Time-Out Spots in Public Places

In Department Stores: (1) Place the child facing a dull side of an uncrowded display counter or a corner. (2) Take the child to the coats section and have him or her face the coat rack. (3) Use the gift wrap or credit department area where there is a dull corner. (4) Use a dull corner of a rest room. (5) Use a changing or dressing room if nearby. (6) Use a maternity section (it is not very busy, and there are sympathetic moms there).

In Grocery Stores: (1) Have the child face the side of a frozen foods counter. (2) Take the child to the farthest corner of the store. (3) Find the greeting card display and have the child face the dull side of the counter while you look at cards. Most grocery stores are difficult, so you may have to use one of the alternatives to time-out listed on page 172.

In Places of Worship: (1) Take the child to the "crying room" found in most churches and synagogues. (2) Use the foyer or entryway. (3) Use a rest room off the lobby.

In a Restaurant: Use the rest rooms or one of the alternatives listed in the text.

In Another's Home: Explain that you are using a new child management method and may need to place your child in a chair or in a dull corner if misbehavior develops. If this cannot be done, use one of the alternatives listed in the text.

During a Long Car Trip: Review the rules with the child and set up your incentive before the child enters the car. Be sure to take along games or activities for the child to do. Explain that chips can be earned or lost. If you need to punish the child, take away chips or points. If this fails, pull off the road to a safe stopping area and have the child serve the time-out seated on the ground beside the car, with you standing nearby. Never leave the child in or beside the car unattended.

When Time-Out Is Impractical.   There are always a few places where put-ting your child in a corner for misbehavior is not possible. Here are some alter-natives, but use them *only where you cannot find a time-out area:*

1. Take the child outside the building and have him or her face the wall.
2. Take the child back to your car and have the child sit on the back seat. Stay in the front seat or beside the car.
3. Take along a small spiral notepad. Before entering the public place, tell the child that you will write down any episode of misbehavior and the child will have to go to time-out as soon as you get home. You will find it helpful to take a picture of the child when he or she is in time-out at home and keep this with your notepad. Show this picture to the child in front of the public place and explain that misbehavior will put the child in time-out when you return home.
4. Take along a pen. Tell the child in front of the public place that if he or she misbehaves, you will lightly place a hash mark in ink on the back of the child's hand. The child will then serve a minimum sentence in time-out at home for each ink mark on the hand.

When Future Behavior Problems Occur

At this point you should find your interactions with your child more positive, particularly in work-related situations, and your child more cooperative with your requests. If you have found no change in your child and the level of conflict is still distressingly high, by all means return to your mental health professional or someone expert in assisting parents with child behavior management problems.

However, even if you've been successful with these eight steps, remember that all children occasionally develop behavior problems. Fortunately you now have the skills to deal with these problems. Here are some steps to follow if a new problem develops or an old problem returns.

1. Take out a notebook and begin recording the behavior problem. Try to be specific about what your child is doing wrong. Record the rule that is being broken, exactly what the child is doing wrong, and what you are now doing to manage it.

2. Keep this record for a week or so. Then examine it to see what clues it may give you about how to deal with the problem. Many parents find that at least part of the problem is caused by their return to old, ineffective ways of deal-ing with the child. Always review your own behavior as well as your child's. Are you:

- Repeating commands too often?
- Using ineffective methods for commands?

- Providing insufficient attention, praise, or reward to the child for following the rule correctly? (Have you stopped your poker chip or points system too early?)
- Not providing discipline immediately for the rule violation?
- Stopping your special playtime with the child?

If you find yourself slipping back to these old habits, correct them. Go back and review the steps from this program to make sure you're using the methods properly.

3. If you need to, set up a special program for managing the problem. Explain to your child exactly what you expect to be done in the problem situation. Set up a poker chip or point system to reward the child for following the rules. Immediately impose mild fines each time the problem behavior occurs.

If the fines don't work, try using a time-out immediately upon the occurrence of the misconduct or defiance. If your notes indicate that the problem seems to be occurring in one particular place or situation, follow the steps for managing your child for public places: (a) anticipate the problem, (b) review the rules just before the problem develops, (c) review the incentives for good behavior, and (d) review the punishment for misbehavior.

The methods described in this chapter should be used immediately and frequently, with little talk or discussion. They should be applied consistently and fairly and, above all, with the principles from Chapter 9 firmly in mind. Never become so emotionally or personally invested in the program that you cannot maintain a sense of perspective on your child's disability and a sense of humor about your role as parent of a child with ADHD. Most important, don't personalize your child's behavior problems. Practice daily forgiveness of your child's transgressions and your own mistakes.

You stand to reap substantial rewards. Parents who follow this eight-step program find their child's behavior more socially appropriate, cooperative, and friendly. They instill in their child a sense of responsibility and an openness to learning from adults through compliance with their advice, rules, and instructions. The ADHD child's interactions with siblings also become more positive and cooperative. Some parents even find that their ability to manage other children in the family is greatly improved, as is their marital relationship now that the ADHD child's behavioral problems have been diminished. Certainly most parents undertaking this program report a renewed sense of self-confidence and competence in their roles as parents, teachers, and friends to their ADHD children. I hope that you find this program does the same for you.

CHAPTER 12

Taking Charge at Home: The Art of Problem Solving

The principles in Chapter 11—and in the rest of the book—should prepare you for many different situations, but they cannot cover every possible eventuality. Undoubtedly there will be times when you're not sure how to handle a new problem. When that happens, try some of the following methods, recommended by Dr. Charles Cunningham at McMaster University Medical Center in Hamilton, Canada.

A System for Solving New Problems

Many of us are already adept at problem solving, but we use this ability somewhat automatically and would not find it easy to call it forth on command. The following seven steps systematize the process so that you can tap this natural resource even when the stress of the situation is clouding your mind. Most of the time they will reveal a plan of action that you might not have thought of otherwise. This process works even better if you go through it with a spouse or close family friend. Two heads, as they say, are better than one.

Step 1: Define the Problem

Before you can solve a problem, you must define it clearly. For instance, the problem may be that your child does not pick up toys or do homework when asked. Either of these descriptions is a better way of stating the problem than "My child won't listen to me" or "Why won't my child do as I ask?" The first approach uses clear and specific terms to define the problem; the second is vague and does not convey what the child is or is not doing or what, precisely, you expect of the child.

Write down on a sheet of paper exactly what behavior problem you wish to solve.

Step 2: Rephrase It as Positive Behavior

Now rephrase the problem as the behavior you desire from the child instead. "My child does not pick up his toys," for example, could become "My child will learn to pick up his toys when asked to do so." This makes the objective of your behavior management plan very clear.

Let's take a slightly more complicated example. Suppose you stated the problem as "My child lies." This is not a bad first attempt but could be more specific: "My child lies to me when I confront her about something wrong she has done." This makes it clear that your child does not lie all the time but only when confronted about some possible misdeed. Then you could rephrase it as "My child will learn to be honest and tell me the truth when I ask her about something she may have done wrong."

This is how educational plans are written for children in special education programs. Rephrasing problems as objectives guides school staff to help the child by stating more clearly and usefully what they wish to achieve with the child. Doing this has a way of making the means of accomplishing your goal more obvious. When you know what behavior you want to encourage, it's often easier to remember that reinforcing that behavior should be your goal. So the solution could be "I will reward my child when she tells me honestly what she has done" or "I will test my child's honesty periodically throughout the day by asking her what she has been doing. If she gives me an accurate answer, I will reward her for it."

Write down the word *Goal* on your sheet of paper and underline it. Next to this word write down the positive alternative behavior to the problem behavior you just recorded. You now have two statements on your sheet: the problem, stated specifically, and the goal, the desired alternative to the problem.

Step 3: List Your Options

Here's where you let your creativity flow. Your job now is to brainstorm as many possible options as you can think of to handle the problem behavior and achieve your goal. This sounds easier than it actually is because many people start to list a possible solution and immediately become critical of their own ideas. When you criticize yourself too quickly, you stop your creative juices from flowing. Leave the criticism until later. For now, your task is to be inventive. Let your mind be free to wonder about anything you like related to your objective and to wander across the subject. Think about how other parents seemed to handle this problem. Think about what you may have seen on television or in the movies or what you may have read in books about this problem. How would your own parents have handled it? How would your best friends handle it? What do you think a physician or psychologist might tell you?

On your sheet of paper, write down the word *Options* and underline it. Below this, start to write down all possible options or alternatives, no matter how silly they seem. Write down any solution you think others might propose, even if you think you would not handle it their way. Your job right now is to get as many options or solutions on paper as possible.

Step 4: Constructively Evaluate Your Options

Now return to the first option on your list and think about how it will work. What will likely happen if you try this? Do you foresee any problems? Could those problems be handled easily? Be reasonable and fair in your evaluation. Don't discard an option just because it might take a little effort to implement. It could turn out to be the most effective option on your list.

After you evaluate each option this way, place a number from 1 to 10 next to it, with 1 representing the lowest or most negative evaluation and 10 your most positive evaluation.

Step 5: Select the Best Option

Most of the time this is pretty easy. The numbers next to each item naturally guide your attention to those with the most desirable ratings. Focus on these for a moment. Perhaps you ranked several as equally useful. Reconsider them. Which do you feel is most likely to work for you or to be responded to by your child? If you cannot decide, just pick one at random to try first. You're simply going to test this idea, as you'd test a hypothesis in a scientific experiment. If it doesn't work, you can return to your list to try the other positive options. If it works, you can continue trying it. The point is that we are not expecting you to pick the right answer. None of us knows beforehand which is going to be right for our child. If you expect to predict accurately, you're asking for much disappointment. Testing the ideas that you believe have merit with an open mind is what we call scientific parenting—surely a more realistic, practical, and forgiving approach than striving to be right all the time.

Circle the option you've chosen. If necessary, write it out in more detail so you know exactly what to expect of yourself. Put the solution into practice for a week and, if it seems to be working, continue it for as long as seems necessary. If it does not work very well, look at other possibilities on your list and put another likely solution into effect for a week. Continue this way until you feel you've solved the problem.

Step 6: Compromise on Disagreements

If you've been working at problem solving with another adult, such as your spouse, you may disagree on the choice of options. Try not to be too wedded to your own choice in that case. Ask your partner to explain his or her reasoning in more detail and listen carefully. Then briefly explain your own choice. One of you may find yourself convinced.

If you're still deadlocked, give in to your partner—yes, give in! Remember, you are experimenting for a week or so, not changing your family routine for life. You can afford to go along with your partner's preference for a week. That means being fair too; avoid any temptation to sabotage your partner's choice. If it fails on its own merits, you can go back to your list and try out the one you had chosen.

Step 7: Carry Out Your Plan and Evaluate Its Success

Now that you have a plan, stick to it. Child behavior problems are not likely to resolve in just a few days. Don't be thrown off the track by failure to see results at the start or by the objections of others—especially those of your child. I have worked with parents who set up a behavior contract with a child to do homework and then withdrawn it just because the child expressed some initial displeasure. If this happens to you, stay with your plan. Your child's protests may mean that you're right on target—that the child has recognized the need to change behavior to succeed under this new plan, which is exactly what you want. You would not avoid having your child inoculated against disease just because your child dislikes shots; neither should you drop efforts that you know will improve your child's behavior in the long run.

After a week or so of consistently following your plan, you can take time to evaluate its success. If it does not seem to be working, go back to your list and select another option. But don't criticize yourself because the first plan did not work. Remember, you are experimenting, and that means there are no guarantees.

Preparing Your Child for Transitions

Knowing that ADHD children live in the moment and have trouble anticipating and preparing for the future, you probably are not too surprised when your child has trouble adapting quickly to a new activity. All children get frustrated by adults' control over their use of time, but for children with ADHD, making the transitions that even a regular schedule imposes can be a struggle. Typically ADHD children have difficulty switching from a fun, rewarding activity such as play to one they perceive as boring such as homework or chores, from TV time to dinnertime or bedtime. But they also have trouble switching gears, from active outdoor play, for example, to an inactive long drive in the car. Your child might also find switching abruptly to a new set of rules problematic: being quiet when a phone call interrupts time spent with a parent or being courteous and staying in one room when a visitor arrives in the middle of the child's playing freely at home. A non-ADHD child may learn to anticipate transitions from, say, TV time to homework time because that activity transition occurs at about the same time each school day. To the ADHD child, however, the switch may seem far more intrusive because the child does not learn to anticipate as well.

As suggested in Chapter 11 for managing your child in a public place, the best approach is to help your child prepare:

1. A few minutes *before* the transition to the new activity must take place, give your child advance notice, such as "Dinner will be ready in just a few minutes. At that time I will ask you to turn off the TV, wash your hands, and come to the table." These statements help to prepare your child for the upcoming transition and set the occasion for you to come back in a few minutes and give a firmer command about coming to dinner.

2. Politely ask your child to repeat this warning back to you so you know that the child heard what you said. This is especially important when your child is mentally absorbed in another activity, such as TV or a video game. Simply saying, "Did you hear what I said?" may elicit a "Yes" just so the child isn't scolded for not listening.

3. When the transition time arrives, give the instruction to obey as a direct but neutral, businesslike command: "Tommy, as I told you a few minutes ago, it's now time for dinner. Turn off the TV and wash your hands." Ignore any protests and don't argue. Simply restate the command if necessary, then ensure that it is followed even if that means turning off the TV yourself. Reward your child for following through on the instruction. If your child does not listen, follow the steps given in Chapter 11 for fines, loss of privilege, or time-out.

Using When/Then Strategies

Just as children with ADHD don't anticipate transitions, they are unlikely to anticipate the future consequences of their present actions or associate these later consequences with what they are now about to do. So spelling out the consequences is very helpful to them. You can also take this a step further: Rearrange events so that how your child behaves now does lead to something more rewarding to do a little later.

Making artificial arrangements between a child's current behavior and later rewards has been called the *Premack principle*, after Dr. David Premack. According to the Premack principle any activity or behavior that occurs frequently can be used as a reward for one that occurs less often. (Some people have also called this *Grandma's rule*.) Dr. Cunningham calls it a *when/then strategy*, and it involves denying the child access to a fun activity until some nonfun but necessary work is done—"*When* you do your homework, *then* you can watch TV." This is a very inexpensive way of rewarding children because it transforms activities that are already usually available to the child into privileges to be earned. Because the child is used to having free access to these privileges, however, sticking to your guns may require some extra diligence.

The strategies presented in this chapter all require you to plan ahead to reduce hassles when a problem develops. They can actually be fun to use, can become a natural part of your parenting behavior, and can help your child be happier and more socially cooperative in your family and with others.

CHAPTER 13

How to Help Your Child with Peer Problems

"Andrea called me the other day and said that she didn't want us to bring Bobby to her house for the holidays this year. In fact, he's not welcome at family dinners at all—unless he can learn to 'behave.' I was devastated—this is my own sister!"

"We were really hoping that Brownies would be a positive experience for Sammy, and we tried to explain to the troop leader what she might expect from our daughter. So when she told us Sammy was too disruptive to remain in the troop, all we could think was 'Why couldn't we have worked together on this?'"

"Last week our next-door neighbor arrived at our door with our son in tow and a litany of Tommy's infractions. Each one, of course, was just another way of saying 'Why can't you control this kid?' And I knew then that Tommy would never be invited back. What am I going to do with him after school every day? He's alienated everyone on the block."

"We've tried to keep her from finding out about these things, but kids can be cruel. What do you say to your daughter when she comes to you with tears in her eyes and wants to know why she's the only one in her kindergarten class who wasn't invited to the birthday party—*again?*"

My colleagues and I hear stories like these every day at our ADHD clinic. You're probably familiar with this kind of treatment too. If so, you know that peer relationship problems can be the most upsetting of all the problems that ADHD children face. As adults you know full well the lifelong value of friendship, yet you also know that you cannot make other children like and befriend your ADHD child. Watching your child be rejected over and over by peers can be emotionally devastating. You see the impact that it has on your child's self-esteem and the loneliness it creates. Even though you can work with the child to solve problems at home and have the staff do the same at school, in the social arena you often must stand by helplessly.

I am reminded of the "Dennis the Menace" cartoon in which his mother is kneeling and holding a crying Dennis in her arms as he says that he came home early from school because he needed someone to be on his side. No other picture I have seen captures so well the feeling that parents of ADHD children can have that they are the only ones, at times, who are on their children's side.

Many children with ADHD have serious problems getting along with other children. The overactivity and impulsivity of the ADHD child is often aversive to other children, especially if the other children are trying to work or play a game together. Other children will also not like the bluntness or frankness of the ADHD child, especially if the child makes cruel remarks about them. Certainly other children are threatened by how easily and suddenly the ADHD child becomes upset, frustrated, or aggressive. When the ADHD child is verbally or physically aggressive, defiant, oppositional, or hostile, problems getting along with other children are particularly acute. The end result is a bad reputation for the ADHD child among neighborhood peers or classmates.

Trying to help an ADHD child with social problems can be a major challenge for a parent and may not always be fruitful. It's not just that the child doesn't know how to behave with other children. Typically the child fails to use appropriate skills when called for, to inhibit impulsive urges to say or do something inappropriate, and to take the other child's perspective. Parents normally can't be there during their child's interactions with peers, so they can't prompt their child to inhibit impulsive urges or to stop and think about how to behave. For these and other reasons, parents are not likely to have a great deal of influence over their children's social skills or peer relations. Nevertheless, they can have some influence.

"Our son has no friends. What can we do so that other children will like him?"

Experts on ADHD children's social interaction problems, such as David Guevremont, Ph.D., recommend that parents try (1) practicing good social skills, (2) arranging for positive peer contacts at home, (3) setting up positive peer contacts in the community, and (4) recruiting help with peer problems from the school.

Practicing Good Social Skills

Although it may not carry over into social interactions with other children out-side the home, working on social skills within the home or family certainly can-not hurt your child's social relationships. Try doing the following:

1. Establish a home reward program, such as the token or chip program described in Chapter 11, focusing on one or two social behaviors you would like to see increased in your child's daily behavior toward other children. These could be sharing, taking turns, keeping hands to self, speaking quietly, staying seated, not being bossy, or even asking other children what they want to play or how they want to play something. Don't choose too many of these to work on all at once, or it will be too cumbersome for you and unlikely to succeed.

2. Write the one or two behaviors down on a chart and post them in a place where you and your child can see them, such as on a refrigerator door or the side of a cabinet. Don't make them too obvious a display, especially if you or your child is having company that day, because this could embarrass your child and create another social problem with other kids. This chart should simply re-mind both you and your child of what you are trying to work on over the next week or two.

3. Whenever you have a chance to observe your child playing with other children, take the opportunity to stop what you are doing and call your child over to you. Quietly review the two social behaviors you and the child are trying to work on this week. Remind your child that he or she can earn points or tokens for trying out these new skills and can lose points for unacceptable behavior. This procedure is similar to the strategies discussed in Chapter 12 for preparing for transitions except that the rules you are reviewing with the child deal with how to interact with other children.

4. Now start monitoring your child's behavior during play with others more frequently than you otherwise do. Whenever you notice your child using the new skills (or otherwise behaving well with the other child), take a moment to praise your child for this and even award a point or token. In other words, "catch 'em being good." Make sure you wait for a natural break in the action, however. I have found that children are less likely to be embarrassed if you call them away from the play group and reward them out of earshot of the others.

5. Several times each week, set aside a few minutes to review with your child the new social skill that you wish to work on that week. During these few minutes you should (a) explain the skill you would like the child to try to use, (b) role-play a situation where you pretend to be a child and model the new skill, (c) have your child try it now with you pretending to be a child, and (d) then en-courage the child to try this new skill when he or she is playing next with another child. As Dr. Guevremont says, act as if you are a social skills "coach" similar to a sports coach in rehearsing the new skill. After this teaching session, be sure to use steps 1 through 4 to observe your child, remind the child to use the skill

just before going off to play with others, watch for your child to use the skill, and then reward its occurrence.

6. Try videotaping your child's play interactions with siblings or other neighborhood children. It is probably wise not to say why you are videotaping or at least not to call too much attention to it since you want to capture typical behavior. Videotapes offer a concrete visual display of behavior that can be very useful to ADHD children since they are often unaware of how they act toward others. If they are to be an effective teaching tool, however, you must make your review of them positive and constructive, even fun, not preachy or punitive. First point out what you found positive about your child's play with other kids. Make an effort to find several positive things and dwell on these, giving your child lots of positive feedback. Then pick out just one or two inappropriate things your child did. Follow step 5 to teach your child what to do instead. After the review, reward your child with points or a small privilege for taking this time. Once again, follow steps 1 through 4 for monitoring your child to catch the child being good.

7. Another step you can take to increase your child's positive social skills is to identify another child familiar to you both who seems naturally to use good social skills. Point out what this child is doing that is positive and that your child might want to try when playing with others. But be careful; you can create resentment, especially if your child has had problems with the child you're using as a role model. Also don't use a sibling for this. The last thing most children want is to be compared unfavorably to a brother or sister.

Whichever of these approaches you try, pay attention to the following areas of social skills that may be a problem for your child: (1) beginning an interaction with another child or group; (2) starting and maintaining a conversation with another child (this includes listening to the other child, asking about the other child's ideas or feelings, taking turns in the conversation, and generally showing interest); (3) resolving conflicts; and (4) sharing things with others.

Setting Up Positive Peer Contacts at Home

Your child does not have to be the most popular kid in the peer group to have satisfying social contacts or friendships, Dr. Guevremont says. Popularity really refers to social status and is not as important as having friendships. Many children with ADHD are not very popular in that sense, and you will find it difficult to change your child's social status. A better goal for a parent is to encourage friendships. How can you do this?

1. Encourage your child to invite classmates to your home after school or on weekends. If your child has serious social skill problems, do not leave this playtime unstructured. Plan things for the children to do—going to the movies, renting a video to view at home together while having special snacks available,

playing video games with your supervision, doing crafts or models together with your assistance, or anything else you think the other child might enjoy but that has a clear structure and purpose and, above all, your close supervision. These structured peer contacts, as Dr. Guevremont notes, can be an initial building block toward more positive peer contacts that may foster friendships.

2. When your child has other children over to play, monitor the activities more closely and watch for signs that the interactions may be getting out of control—increasing silliness, horse play, or roughhousing or simply louder-than-normal conversations. Of course you should also watch for signs of escalating frustration or hostility. In either case, interrupt the play and have the children take a short break for a snack or a more structured and calmer activity. You could ask the children to tell you things so their attention is focused on you, not each other, or you could even shift the location of their play.

3. Make every effort to avoid setting examples of aggressive behavior at home, especially if your ADHD child already has problems with aggression. Watch your own behavior and that of family members to see if you're modeling such behavior unintentionally, whether it's yelling, name-calling, or throwing things. You should also more closely monitor your child's TV and movie viewing habits. While exposure to the violence that seems endemic in so many children's programs, including cartoons, usually doesn't increase the aggressiveness of normal children, it can do so for children already prone to aggressive and impulsive behavior, such as your ADHD child. If you can't limit TV watching, consider occasionally watching TV with your child and pointing out what is inappropriate aggressiveness that would not be liked by other children.

4. Eliminate aggressive playmates that your child may have drifted into playing with lately. The last thing an ADHD child needs is the reinforcement of an aggressive peer who may also be experiencing social rejection. Encourage your child to associate with and invite over to your home children who are positive role models for peer relations. Don't be concerned if your child plays with either younger or older children since many ADHD children seem to do this. Such children may be more tolerant of your child's social immaturities. Just be sure that these children are positive influences and generally well behaved.

Creating Positive Peer Contacts in the Community

This will not be as easy to do as the preceding recommendations, but you can still make some efforts that may help your child establish more positive peer relationships. Try the following ideas:

1. Enroll your child in organized community activities for his or her age group—Scouts, clubs, sports, hobby groups, or church social groups. Summer camps or day activity programs run by a parks or recreation department can also be useful. The advantage to these is that they offer structured activities under adult

supervision, which can limit the likelihood of behaviors escalating out of control for your ADHD child. These activities seem to be best if they involve relatively small groups of children, such as a Cub Scout den. ADHD children often have more trouble in large group settings, which can backfire and lead to social failure.

2. Try to avoid peer group activities that involve a great deal of coordinated effort with other children or complex rules for success, since these can be overwhelming to your ADHD child. Also steer clear of activities that involve a lot of passive or sitting time, because your child will find this demand hard to meet. For instance, if your ADHD child plays Little League, an infield position will be better than outfield because the greater action in the infield will help keep the child's attention on the game. Many an ADHD outfielder has become bored and distracted by butterflies or bugs nearby, things happening off the field nearby, or just his own thoughts, only to miss the ball that was hit out to him.

3. Activities that involve more structure (organization) and adult supervision are better than unstructured ones or those with little or no supervision.

4. Dr. Guevremont believes that ADHD children have more favorable experiences when their peer contacts do not involve a lot of competition. These can trigger emotional overarousal, increased disorganized behavior, and frustration. The exception is where your child has a clear talent in the area of the activity and can be successful despite its competitive nature.

5. Try arranging for some cooperative learning tasks even if you have to volunteer to organize them yourself. These involve having a small group of children complete a task as a team working toward a common goal—building a model together, building a camp or tree fort in the backyard, solving practical problems, running simple science experiments, or engaging in a craft or hobby together. Each child is given a particular assignment within the group that is necessary to achieve the goal. All group members share in the positive consequences of completing the task. Usually children participating in these types of activities display positive feelings toward and an increased liking of each other.

Getting Help from Your Child's School

The peer problems that children have at home and at school can be quite different. School settings involve much larger groups of children. Structured class time is interspersed with free play or unstructured periods (recess), and schools have a different set of expectations for social behavior. For all of these reasons and others, your ADHD child may have greater problems with peer relations at school than at home. Consider trying the following recommendations.

1. Attempt to develop better classroom behavior in your child through meetings with the child's teacher or the other methods recommended in Chapter 16. Disruptive and inappropriate classroom behavior is strongly associated with peer

rejection of ADHD children. All of your other attempts to help your child socially may be for nothing if they are reversed by disruptive behavior at school.

2. If necessary, consider whether your child should be placed on one of the medications discussed in Chapter 18. The stimulant medications have been found to increase positive peer relationships and status, probably by decreasing the ADHD child's excessive and disruptive behavior.

3. Do not be overly concerned if your child is receiving some type of special education assistance. Children do not reject others just because they receive some sort of special help at school. It is the negative comments or attention of teachers, the greater use of discipline, and more generally the singling out of the ADHD child at school for criticism that can create problems with other children. Encourage your child's teacher to try some of the behavior change methods in Chapter 16 for developing positive behaviors.

4. Ask your child's teacher to assign special responsibilities to your child in the presence of other children. Dr. Guevremont believes that this permits other children to observe your child in a positive light and enhance your child's feelings of acceptance within the classroom.

5. With your child's teacher, develop a behavior rating card that contains two or three social skills you would both like to see your child using more often at school with classmates. List these two or three behaviors on the left side of the card or sheet of paper. Across the top, create five to seven columns that represent the number of times each day the teacher can evaluate the child for performance of these social skills. The columns can reflect the end of specific subject periods that provide natural breakaway points for the teacher to provide an evaluation. Or they can represent the different free play or group activity situations that occur each day that may be a problem for your ADHD child, such as arrival at school, recesses, lunch period, in-class play periods, large group activities, or small group cooperative tasks.

Once you have designed this rating form, make a number of copies so that you can use a new one each day. Have the teacher evaluate your child's behavior in the two or three areas listed on the form at the end of each period of time represented by each column. Your child should expect to be evaluated on interacting with others five to seven times each day. The evaluation can simply involve placing a number from 1 to 5 on the form (1 = excellent, 2 = good, 3 = fair, 4 = below average, 5 = poor). The teacher can also write additional comments on the bottom or back of the form. The teacher can dispense rewards at school geared to how well the child is succeeding in these areas. This form is to go home so that you can reward your child as well. You can do this by assigning a certain number of points, tokens, or chips to each number. For instance, 1 = 15 points, 2 = 10 points, 3 = 5 points, 4 = −10 points, and 5 = −15 points. Add up all the positive points, subtract the negative or penalty points, and the balance can be used by your child to buy rewards and privileges from a reward list like the kind described in Chapter 11.

6. If your school guidance counselor, psychologist, or social worker provides a social skills training group within the school day, consider having your child

enrolled in this group. Such training groups are likely to be more successful than those run by clinics or other agencies outside of school because they involve your child's natural peer group.

Helping an ADHD child with peer relationship problems can be a difficult task. Be realistic about your expectations for change in this area and what you can reasonably accomplish. As a parent, you don't see your child for a good part of each school day. Look for any opportunities to arrange for situations in which your child can have a good chance of positive peer contacts. Avoid situations that are likely to lead to social failure. Your efforts should eventually build toward more positive peer contacts and maybe even closer friendships for your ADHD child.

CHAPTER 14

Getting Through Adolescence with an ADHD Child

with Arthur L. Robin, Ph.D.

Strong adults dissolve into Jell-O when they contemplate the prospect of raising an ADHD adolescent. The tremendous physical, emotional, and mental changes undergone by teenagers can bring on endless parent–child arguments, demonstrations of disrespect, rebellion against authority, and other behavior that strikes terror in the hearts of adults worldwide. As your child passes puberty, he or she is faced with a new world of opportunities—alcohol, drugs, and sexual activity among them—and must make smart choices to prevent such opportunities from becoming hazards.

These are just the *normal* challenges of adolescence, and they can be magnified dramatically for teenagers with ADHD. ADHD may hamper your teen's mastery of the developmental tasks facing this age group. Your ADHD teen may encounter academic failure, social isolation, depression, and low self-esteem and may also become embroiled in many unpleasant conflicts with other family members. These often escalating problems can put your family into a state of acute crisis—in which case you may need immediate help from a mental health professional—or at the very least can transform the following areas (and others) into issues of constant conflict:

- Completing schoolwork and homework in a timely and organized manner
- Performing routine chores around the home
- Choosing appropriate friends and suitable places to socialize
- Respecting the rights and privacy of other family members
- Conducting themselves responsibly while away from home

- Returning home at established curfew times
- Using alcohol and tobacco, engaging in sexual activity, and using the family car (for older teens)

The central conflict is, of course, often the one that is at the core of all parent–teenager strife: the adolescent's natural desire to make his or her own decisions versus the parents' desire to retain decision-making authority. Handling these conflicts with as little damage to your relationship as possible while still adequately preparing your teen to eventually move to independence from you in young adulthood is the major challenge of getting through this developmental period.

Golden Rules for Survival

Several golden rules can help you improve the quality of life for you and your adolescent:

1. Understand adolescent development and the impact of ADHD on it.
2. Develop a coping attitude and reasonable expectations.
3. Establish clear-cut house and street rules.
4. Monitor and enforce house and street rules, working as a team.
5. Communicate positively and effectively.
6. Problem-solve disagreements mutually.
7. Use professional help wisely.
8. Maintain your sense of humor and regularly take vacations from your teenager.

Adolescent Development and ADHD: A Crash Course

It may not be obvious from a parent's point of view, but teenagers have a lot of work to do. During these years they are supposed to go from the complete dependence of childhood to equality with their parents as adults. In the course of becoming independent, they are supposed to figure out who they are and what they stand for (i.e., identity and values), how to make deep friendships and form lifelong relationships, how to tame their sometimes overwhelming sexual urges, and what they want to do with their lives (education and career goals). Adolescents are supposed to accomplish all of these tasks while being successful in school and getting along with their families.

Imagine a nation establishing its independence, changing from a dictatorship to a democracy. Often there is a bloody revolution. Why should we expect a family to make it through the independence seeking of its children without a disturbance of the peace? A certain amount of conflict is inevitable, especially at age 12 to 14, as adolescents push away from their parents yet quickly return when the cruel world mistreats them.

Meanwhile, the tremendous physical changes, particularly rapid physical growth and sexual maturation, are bringing with them increased moodiness, sensitivity to criticism, and fragile self-esteem. Teenagers may have a need to feel omnipotent to insulate themselves against the rapid changes they experience and to establish that they can be independent. To admit they might have any faults may seem catastrophic to them.

ADHD adolescents undergo the same metamorphosis in physical maturity and face the same challenges as all other teenagers. Yet they may not necessarily be more socially or emotionally mature than they were as children. Consequently, the teen with ADHD may seem even more volatile than the "normal" adolescent, reacting defensively to even the slightest criticism or perhaps anything perceived as criticism. The ADHD teen may be less ready to assume the responsibilities of independence, but he or she desires independence as much as any other teenager.

The truth is that as long as this teen remains at home under your care and responsibility, he or she is likely to require greater assistance and intervention from you than non-ADHD teens do, even if you have been working diligently on the child management skills and problem-solving steps discussed in earlier chapters. Remember that the goal of these methods (and the ones in this chapter) is not to cure your child but to lessen conflict and chaos. Ideally your child will eventually learn those skills and the better forms of social behavior they create and will come to use them spontaneously as called for in social situations. But you should never expect to stop using these methods entirely.

It's important to understand that while biological maturity will bring some quantitative improvement in inattentiveness, impulsiveness, hyperactivity, and lack of self-control, your ADHD child will lag behind other children in developing that increasingly complex and sophisticated set of mental abilities that assists them with self-control and organization, frees them from control by momentary circumstances, and directs their behavior ever farther into the future. The sense of hindsight, forethought, planning, and goal-oriented behavior of non-ADHD children is ever increasing and coming to play a greater role in their lives, but these abilities will be less mature and slower to emerge in your child. It is deficiencies in these newly developing skills that will be your greatest concern during adolescence because, combined with the existing inattentiveness and hyperactivity, they will create a whole new complicated matrix of family conflicts:

- Many teens can't seem to stick to agreements made with parents. Is this a manifestation of the disability in attentiveness or true defiance? Often the answer is "both."
- Impulsiveness can make the ADHD teen moody and unable to tolerate frustration or consider consequences, which can lead to explosive outbursts,

frequent arguments, speedy escalation of conflicts, and even physical confrontations with parents.

- The hyperactivity that persists into adolescence in 30 to 40% of ADHD children, when manifested as fidgeting or looking bored during discussions with parents, can easily be misinterpreted as signs of disrespect, setting in motion an escalating chain of angry and hostile communication.

Coping Attitudes and Reasonable Expectations

These conflicts often converge in the conclusion by parents that the ADHD teenager has "an attitude problem." The fact is that parents can also have an attitude problem. If you want your teenager to change his or her attitude, you must first adjust your own thinking.

Expectations versus Demands

It is helpful to expect your ADHD teen to achieve satisfactory grades and complete homework without a tremendous hassle. It is helpful to expect your ADHD teen to follow basic rules for living in a family and to treat other members of the family with respect. It is helpful to expect your teen to learn to communicate with you positively and try to resolve conflicts without violence or excessive temper outbursts. It is helpful to expect that you and your youngster's school will need to provide more structure to accomplish these tasks than is necessary for non-ADHD youngsters.

These are *expectations*, not *demands*. Do not expect perfection or total obedience. Do not expect flawless academic performance or compliance with a smile. If you have unrealistic expectations, you will undoubtedly be disappointed, disheartened, and angry much of the time. Your disappointment and anger will prevent you from dealing with your adolescent's problem behaviors in an effective, rational manner. You can easily lose control and impulsively do things you will later regret if you adhere rigidly to unrealistic expectations for perfection and obedience.

Anticipating Ruination

Parents often come to fear that an adolescent who makes too many mistakes will *ruin* his or her future and that one who has too much freedom will be ruined by failure to handle the freedom responsibly. Will failure to complete homework or clean up his room make your son an aimless, unemployed welfare case? Will being allowed to stay out late or go places without supervision lead your daughter to drug abuse? Many such fears are exaggerated. The problem with exaggerated beliefs is that they can become self-fulfilling prophecies: Your adolescent picks up on your lack of trust and reasons that he may as well do the very things you fear the most.

Making Malicious Attributions

If your adolescent fails to take out the trash or make his bed, you may conclude that he is purposely trying to annoy you. ADHD adolescents do things for a variety of reasons, some unpredictable, but most of the time not designed to upset parents. If you interpret many of your adolescents' actions as malicious, you will stay angry and have a difficult time dealing appropriately with the child.

Are you guilty of unreasonable expectations? Table 5 will help both you and your teenager evaluate your tendency to operate under unreasonable expectations and distorted beliefs.

Changing Your Expectations

If you are having trouble developing reasonable expectations, try the following exercises:

Imagine How You Would Feel . . .

Close your eyes and imagine that your teen has come home two hours past curfew; have your child do the same thing. Now think of how disrespectful and unappreciative it was for the teen to disregard a rule that already was stretched to the limit to give the teenager as much freedom as you can tolerate. Ask your adolescent to imagine how unfair and embarrassing it was to have to leave a party early and how much parental rules are ruining his or her social life. Now, what do you feel at that moment? It's likely that very strong anger and frustration will emerge. Ask yourself about the potential outcome of a family discussion when everyone is so emotionally aroused. Family members we know usually agree that a "bloodbath" rather than a logical discussion would probably ensue.

This exercise demonstrates that an event (A) gave each of you an extreme thought (B), which made each of you angry (C). Professionals call this the *ABC model of emotions*. It shows that your feelings are really created as much (or more) by yourself and your thoughts as by the event or what someone else did. Consider changing your beliefs about the other person's (your child's) behavior. You can control how upset the behavior makes you by evaluating and altering your beliefs to be more flexible and reasonable.

The Worst-Case Scenario

What is the worst that could happen if you gave in and compromised with the other person on a point of disagreement? For example, if your teenager is failing to complete his homework, you might think, "If Bill doesn't get his math homework done, he will fail math, fail ninth grade, fail to graduate, get a lousy job, and end up an unhappy adult." Or you could think, "So he gets an F on one of his math homework assignments. It is only one assignment out of many. What's the worst thing that can happen? He could get a lower grade. Didn't I ever fail

TABLE 5. Common Unreasonable Beliefs

Parents

I. Ruination: "If I give my teen too much freedom, he (she) will ruin his (her) life, make bad judgments, and get in serious trouble."
    Examples: 1. Room incompletely cleaned: "He will grow up to be a slovenly, unemployed, aimless, worthless welfare case."
                  2. Home late: "She could get hurt out late. She could get pregnant, addicted to drugs, and become an alcoholic."
                  3. Homework incomplete: "He will never graduate from high school, will never get into a good college, will not get a good job, and won't be able to support himself. He will be a drain on us forever."

II. Malicious intent: "My teen misbehaves purposely to hurt me."
    Examples: 1. Forgetting to turn the lights off: "She's trying to make me go broke."
                  2. Talking disrespectfully: "He's talking that way to get even with me."
                  3. Playing stereo too loud: "She's blasting that stereo just to get on my nerves."

III. Obedience/perfectionism: "My teen should always obey me and behave like a saint."
    Examples: 1. Doesn't follow directions: "He can't even take out the trash without me bugging him 10 times. What disrespect/disobedience! If I did this to my dad, I would have been dead meat."
                  2. Acting hyper around relatives: "At her age she should be able to sit still and act mature."

IV. Appreciation/love: "My teenager should spontaneously show love and appreciation for the great sacrifices I make."
    Examples: 1. "Look what I got after all I've done for you. You don't care about me. You're selfish."
                  2. "What do you mean you want more allowance? After all the money I give you and all the things I buy, you should be perfectly happy."

Adolescents

I. Unfairness/ruination: "My parents' rules are totally unfair. I'll never have a good time or any friends. My parents are ruining my life with their unfair rules."
    Examples: 1. Curfew: "Why should I have to come earlier than my friends? That's unfair. I'll never have any friends."
                  2. School: "Mrs. Jones is unfair. She always gives me a hard time. She has it in for me. She's the reason I'm failing math."

II. Autonomy: "My parents have no right to tell me what to do."
    Examples: 1. Smoking: "It's my body. I can do whatever I want with it. You have no right to interfere."
                  2. Chores: "I don't need any reminders. I can get it all done by myself."

III. Appreciation/love: "My parents would let me do whatever I want if they really cared about me."
    Examples: 1. "If my parents really loved me, they would let me use the car and go to the concert."
                  2. "Sally's mother buys her all those designer clothes. Her parents really love her. Mine hate me and want me to look ugly."

to get my homework done? I survived, and he will too." The latter is reasonable and flexible, the former unreasonable and illogical.

Remember to be flexible and forgiving with yourself too. Even if you start to think differently, you can slip back into your old rigid or distorted ideas about your teen. You may need to practice a lot at catching distorted beliefs before you will be good at preventing them from influencing the way you react to your teenager.

Consider a father who is very angry because his son shows no appreciation for all of the money that has been spent on books, school clothes, supplies, computers, tutoring, and therapy to help him succeed in school and because of the "disrespect and disobedience" his son shows by acting restless and bored whenever the topic is brought up, usually in a lecture. This parent might begin to change his own rigidity by pinpointing the extreme belief: Adolescents should always express deep appreciation for their parents' sacrifices, and it is a sign of extreme disobedience and disrespect when an ADHD teen with a biological handicap in self-control who has never sat still for more than 10 minutes fidgets while his dad lectures to him for a half-hour about his lack of caring. Now he might ask himself how much appreciation his son's friends are likely to express to their parents or even how much he appreciated his parents when he was a teen. He could talk to other parents about their children and read a book on normal adolescent development. All of this could lead him to the alternative belief that even though adolescents love and appreciate their parents, they rarely express it.

These strategies are well worth the effort. Ask yourself this question: What is worse, losing a compromise to your teen for a week or losing your relationship with your teen? Successfully parenting the ADHD adolescent is like riding a roller coaster. There may be a thrill a minute, but there are also many bumps and bruises. Try not to overreact to each little bump but to go with the flow, deciding which issues are high priority for immediate action and which are trivial and best ignored. Keep in mind your adolescent's relentless quest for independence and the impact of ADHD on this process as you try to develop reasonable expectations and accurate interpretations of your teenager's actions.

Establishing House Rules and Street Rules

With young children, parents often resolve conflicts through the use of power, making their positions stick through forceful administration of rewards and punishments. Because of the independence seeking and increased strength of adolescents, simple use of power will not work; your teen will develop the skills to circumvent that kind of parental control. When parents discover that they cannot simply dictate to their teens, they sometimes throw up their hands in desperation and say, "I can't deal with this; do whatever you want and suffer the consequences." Such a laissez-faire approach doesn't work either, because ADHD teens will do whatever they want, which *won't* usually include schoolwork and *will* often include dangerous, if not illegal, activities. When authorities contact the parents about the adolescents' problem behavior, they may again crack down in an authoritarian manner. Over time, the parents may alternate between over-control and undercontrol, and the ADHD teen quickly learns to recognize the cycle and to wait out the tight rules and wear down the parents, because freedom is around the corner.

> "My teenager does as he pleases. He comes and goes
> at all hours of the day and night. He doesn't do anything
> around the house to help. How can we get him to listen to us?"

Research has found that a more democratic approach, involving the adolescent in the decision making when possible, generally works better than a strict dictatorial approach. Negotiating solutions that everyone can live with seems to foster responsible adolescent conduct, perhaps because the teen sees the reasons for the decisions and takes part in them. Most important, the teenager can take this process for solving disagreements outside the home for later use in life.

If your instinctive reaction is that ADHD teens are too manipulative, defiant, and aggressive to be given any input, understand that there is an important distinction between issues that can be handled democratically and those that are nonnegotiable. Each family has a set of bottom-line rules for living together, which are a function of the parents' values and generalized tenets for civilized living. Before proceeding further, make a list of these rules. Keep it short and simple and divide it into (1) house rules, which apply at home, and (2) street rules, which govern conduct everywhere else. Examples of house rules might be: (1) no violence or cursing; (2) no smoking, drugs, or alcohol; (3) you can express anger, but treat people with respect; (4) respect family members' privacy; (5) ask before you take another person's property; and (6) no friends in the house without a parent present. Street rules might include (1) use violence only to defend yourself and only after trying everything else; (2) no smoking, drugs, or alcohol; (3) attend school as scheduled; (4) tell your parents where you are going, and call them if your plans change; and (5) come home by a designated curfew time.

Post the list on the refrigerator. Go over it often with your adolescent. Clarify any ambiguities. Discuss the reasons such rules are necessary and, if need be, ask the adolescent to imagine what life would be like if people didn't follow basic rules for living together. Remind your adolescent of the street rules before he or she goes out with friends.

Monitoring and Enforcing Rules

Enforcement of rules only gets more difficult as ADHD children get older, so consistency and teamwork remain essential. In any family where parents have inadvertently shown their children that the decisions of one parent can be overruled by appealing to a second parent, a teenager will learn numerous creative ways to divide and conquer. Because parents of ADHD teens may need to set more than the customary limits, however, the ADHD home is fertile ground for adolescent experimentation with such tactics. So communication between parents to erect an unbreachable united front is paramount. Single parents have a particularly tough job and should enlist the aid of anyone they can count on for *consistent* support.

The first step in enforcement is monitoring—keeping track of your teen's compliance with house and street rules, checking up on his or her general whereabouts, and keeping track of the teen's progress toward completion of any structured task within time parameters. Monitoring is really just another facet of the structuring that is central to dealing with any individual who has ADHD. ADHD teens need closer, more frequent monitoring than other adolescents; you should always know where your teen is. When your teen goes out with peers during free time, you should require an accounting of the child's destination, including notifying you of any changes in plans. You also need to be awake and waiting at curfew time to keep teens honest; stay in the house during homework time too.

Just as parents are sometimes prone to undercontrol or overcontrol of their ADHD child, they run the risk of being disengaged at one extreme or overinvolved at the other. It's wise neither to leave the adolescent at home alone for a weekend nor to show up at a party to check up on your adolescent. Disengagement promotes dangerous behaviors and failure to complete tasks, whereas overinvolvement stifles achievement of independence. Striking a balance that respects your adolescent's privacy yet reminds the teen that there is always accountability is, of course, not easy. Here are some suggestions:

Continue Using Positive and Negative Consequences

You can and should adapt many of the techniques described in Chapter 11 for setting up a point system that establishes positive consequences for compliance and negative consequences for noncompliance with house and street rules. The main difference is that the consequences will reflect the age of the child: Besides TV privileges and assigning of work around the house, consequences for an adolescent may revolve around use of the family car and the telephone, for example.

Project Authority

Parents must project a no-nonsense, controlled but strong-willed tone to get results. Teens need to know from a parents' voice tone and mannerisms that the parent means business about the nonnegotiables. Be prepared to "go to the wall" in consistently backing each other up and following through on unpleasant consequences with very angry teens. This is especially important when your teen is accustomed to getting his way. Your new united front will evoke much anger and frustration from the teen, and you'll have to stand firm in the face of such reactions.

When Parents Unite: A Success Story

Fourteen-year-old Andrew Nordon was having impulsive temper tantrums four or five times a week, often set off by minor provocations at home. When his father refused to take him to the store to purchase a Halloween costume, Andrew squirted a bottle of mustard on his father's $400 suit, ruining it. When his mother refused to give him his favorite dessert, he threw a bottle of pop at her, making a hole in the wall. He terrorized his sister constantly, randomly punching her, pulling her hair, and stealing her money and possessions. Mr. and Mrs. Nordon disagreed vehemently with each other about how to handle their son. Mr. Nordon favored physical punishment ("the belt"), while his wife was afraid that Andrew and his dad would hurt each other. She tried to "reason" with her son and in fact stood between her husband and son to prevent physical confrontations. Aside from reasoning, she did nothing in response to the tantrums.

With the help of a therapist, the Nordons agreed that the "bottom line" would be to call the police and press charges in the event of assaultive behavior and to require financial restitution in the case of destruction of property. They had great difficulty, though, agreeing on how to respond at the time of each impulsive episode. Mr. Nordon insisted on the necessity for corporal punishment, and his wife insisted on doing nothing but having a quiet discussion with her son at a later time. Each parent rigidly accused the other of perpetuating Andrew's tantrums. Andrew downplayed the intensity of his tantrums, claimed he could control them at any time, and objected to his parents' "stupid" rules, perceiving his destructive behavior as "getting even."

The therapist pushed the parents to reach a number of agreements for controlling Andrew's tantrums. The father agreed to refrain from physical violence toward his son if his wife would be more assertive in telling Andrew to control himself or go to his room for 30 minutes until he calmed down. For a month Mrs. Nordon either "forgot" to be assertive or responded to her son in a "mousy manner." Mr. Nordon would at first exercise restraint, but by the third time his wife refused to assert herself, he resorted to physical punishment. Only when her husband actually stood by and coached her every statement was Mrs. Nordon able to begin to respond to her son assertively. An episode when Andrew hit and taunted his sister so intensely that she huddled in the corner sucking her thumb and crying hysterically was the turning point for Mrs. Nordon. She "realized" how much of a tyrant her son was and began to crack down. Mr. Nordon could not believe she could do it, but he strongly supported his wife. Within three more weeks, the tantrums had diminished from four or five to one or two per week. Andrew claimed the change in his behavior was due to his own "willpower," a fantasy that the therapist did not challenge.

Be Prepared to Seek Help

There are times when you may not be able to exert appropriate control over your adolescent and effectively enforce house and street rules. You may need the assistance of a therapist or, in extreme cases, external authorities such as the juvenile court and the police. Try not to shrink from this recourse if you've tried everything else.

Communicating Effectively

It is very easy for you and your adolescent to develop bad communication habits. With ADHD compounding the normal conflicts of adolescents, it's no surprise that many parents "lose it" when talking to their teenagers. Families find that their "discussions" constantly involve putdowns, accusations, defensive remarks, or sarcasm. Parents give endless lectures, and teens respond by tuning them out, giving them the silent treatment, or cursing them out. Negative modes of communication can so enrage both of you that you act based on hot emotion rather than cool logic and end up with nothing to show for the encounter but regrets.

Take a moment to review Table 6, which lists common negative communication habits and some more constructive alternatives. Try to think about recent events in which these habits came into play. How angry did your teen's negative communication make you? How angry did your teen get, and what happened?

Discuss with your teen how negative communication styles can hurt: how they can offend the other person, even eliciting a counterattack or retaliation. Start by stating some of your own bad communication habits and how you will try to change them the next time you discuss a problem with your teen. Beginning by saying you want to review the child's bad habits will make your teen immediately defensive.

Next, point out the more positive alternatives, using the examples in Table 6 but also asking your teen to give you examples. Try role-playing these new communication styles. Take care to emphasize that you are not urging your teen to suppress his or her feelings and hide anger. Instead you are trying to get the child to express legitimate feelings without offending or hurting someone else's feelings in the process. Don't forget to include nonverbal communication such as eye contact and good posture.

Make a contract with your adolescent to work on one or two of these communication skills at a time. Then give each other feedback throughout the day about the selected communication habit and try to replay the scene using the more positive behavior. Sometimes tape-recording conversations such as at the dinner table and then reviewing the tapes can be helpful. When your teen tries out new communication skills, be liberal in praising his or her efforts.

For example, one mother and her ADHD 16-year-old decided to focus on impulsive interruptions. They often interrupted each other in midsentence, leading

TABLE 6. Negative Communication Habits

Check if your family does this:	More positive way to do it:
1. __ Call each other names.	Express anger without hurtful words.
2. __ Put each other down.	"I am angry that you did _____."
3. __ Interrupt each other.	Take turns; keep it short.
4. __ Criticize all the time.	Point out the good and bad.
5. __ Get defensive when attacked.	Listen carefully and check out what you heard—then calmly disagree.
6. __ Give a lecture/big words.	Tell it straight and short.
7. __ Look away, not at speaker.	Make good eye contact.
8. __ Slouch or slide to floor.	Sit up and look attentive.
9. __ Talk in sarcastic tone.	Talk in normal tone.
10. __ Get off the topic.	Finish one topic, then go on.
11. __ Think the worst.	Keep an open mind. Don't jump to conclusions.
12. __ Dredge up the past.	Stick to the present.
13. __ Read each other's mind.	Ask the other's opinion.
14. __ Command, order.	Ask nicely.
15. __ Give the silent treatment.	Say it if you feel it.
16. __ Throw a tantrum, "lose it."	Count to 10; take a hike; do relaxation; leave room.
17. __ Make light of something serious.	Take it seriously, even if it is minor to you.
18. __ Deny you did it.	Admit you did it, but say you were accused.
19. __ Nag about small mistakes.	Admit no one is perfect; overlook small things.

Your "Zap score" (total no. of checks) ____

Note. From A. L. Robin (1990), "Training families with ADHD adolescents." In R. A. Barkley, *Attention-deficit hyperactivity disorder: A handbook for diagnosis and treatment* (pp. 462–497). New York: Guilford Press. Copyright 1990 by The Guilford Press. Reprinted by permission.

to rapid flashes of anger and immediate arguments. They both agreed to try to let the other person finish no matter how much each wanted to get her own say in. They also agreed to keep their statements short. If one interrupted, the other agreed to say, "You're interrupting. Let's start over." It took several weeks to change this pattern, but as they succeeded, they noticed that they had many fewer arguments.

Problem-Solving Conflicts with Your Teen

As you begin to practice new ways of communicating with your teenager, you're ready to put your communication skills to use in resolving conflicts and disagreements. The first area to try to improve on is the steps you follow in discussing a problem. Do you skip around to a number of problems in the same conversation without resolving any of them? Are your discussions more for ventilating anger than for arriving at real solutions? Whatever kind of trouble you have with problem solving, consider following the steps for problem solving in Chapter 12. Start with a couple of sheets of paper and review the problem-solving steps listed in Table 7. Before you begin, be sure both parents and the teenager agree on the following approach:

TABLE 7. Problem-Solving Outline

I. Define the problem.
   A. Tell the others what they do that bothers you and why. "I get very angry when you come home 2 hours after the 11 P.M. curfew we agreed upon."
   B. Start your definition with an "I"; be brief, be clear, and don't accuse or put down the other person.
   C. Did you get your point across? Ask the others to paraphrase your problem definition to check whether they understood you. If they understood you, go on. If not, repeat your definition.

II. Generate a variety of alternative solutions.
   A. Take turns listing solutions.
   B. Follow three rules for listing solutions.
      1. List as many ideas as possible.
      2. Don't evaluate the ideas.
      3. Be creative; anything goes, since you will not have to do everything you list.
   C. One person writes down the ideas on a worksheet (see Table 8).

III. Evaluate the ideas and decide upon the best one.
   A. Take turns evaluating each idea.
      1. Say what you think would happen if the family followed the idea.
      2. Vote "plus" or "minus" for the idea and record your vote on the worksheet next to the idea.
   B. Select the best idea.
      1. Look for ideas rated "plus" by everyone.
      2. Select one of these ideas.
      3. Combine several of these ideas.
   C. If none are rated "plus" by everyone, negotiate a compromise.
      1. Select an idea rated "plus" by one parent and the teen.
      2. List as many compromises as possible.
      3. Evaluate the compromises as described in steps III-A and III-B.
      4. Reach a mutually acceptable solution.
      5. If you still cannot reach an agreement, wait for the next therapy session.

IV. Plan to implement the selected solution.
   A. Decide who will do what, where, how, and when.
   B. Decide who will monitor the solution implementation.
   C. Decide upon the consequences for compliance or noncompliance with the solution.
      1. Rewards for compliance: Privileges, money, activities, praise.
      2. Punishments for noncompliance: Loss of privileges, groundings, work detail.

Note. From A. L. Robin (1990), "Training families with ADHD adolescents." In R. A. Barkley, *Attention-deficit hyperactivity disorder: A handbook for diagnosis and treatment* (pp. 462–497). New York: Guilford Press. Copyright 1990 by The Guilford Press. Reprinted by permission.

1. As parents you will remain calm and businesslike throughout the discussion and take an interest in the teen's view.
2. These discussions will feature a mutual give-and-take in which each side is out not to win but to set up a reasonable plan that both sides can live with.
3. Each party will show a willingness to listen to what the other parties have to say.

4. Start with a topic of disagreement that does not seem to have intense anger or "heat" associated with it.

5. Do not try to resolve all of your disagreements in one meeting. Try working on only one or, at most, two problem areas in one session with your teen. Then wait at least a week to discuss any more problems until you have had a chance to put your last plan into action and to evaluate how well it has been working. Only when that area of conflict seems to have been resolved should you proceed further down your list of issues to problem-solve the next one or two.

6. Assign one family member to be the secretary, who will record the information from the discussion. We find it helpful to alternate this responsibility between you and your teen from one discussion to the next.

Step 1: Define the Problem

Each family member defines the problem by making a clear, short statement that pinpoints his or her view of the problem. As each person gives a definition, the other should check out his own understanding of the definition by saying it back to the speaker in the speaker's own words. For instance, in a discussion about curfew you might say to your teenager, "I hear you saying that you would like more time out of the house on weekend nights" or "It sounds to me like you think the curfew is too strict."

Restating the definitions sometimes reveals that several different problems are being brought up at once. For instance, during the discussion about curfew, you might raise the fact that your teen brings the car back with an empty gas tank, that the child is spending too much money when out with friends, or that you have detected the smell of alcohol or tobacco smoke on the teen's breath when he or she returns. These are actually separate problems. Write them down on a sheet of paper in a list of problems to be discussed at another time.

Use the second sheet as a worksheet that focuses on the curfew problem only. Set the worksheet up something like the completed one shown in Table 8, and record on it everyone's statement of the problem.

Step 2: Generate Possible Solutions

Now the family members take turns generating a variety of alternative solutions to the problem. Follow these rules for brainstorming: (1) List as many ideas as possible; quantity breeds quality. (2) Don't evaluate the ideas since criticism stifles creativity. (3) Be creative, knowing that just because you say it doesn't mean you will have to do it.

Usually parents and adolescents begin by suggesting their original positions as solutions. Gradually new ideas emerge. If the atmosphere is very tense or the family runs out of ideas, try to suggest some outlandish ideas just to lighten the atmosphere with a little humor and spur creativity. Try writing down the most extreme solutions first so you can see that your own ideas are actually less ex-

TABLE 8. Example of a Completed Problem-Solving Worksheet

Name of Family: The Johnsons

Topic: Household chores

Definitions of the problem:

Mom: I get upset when I have to tell Allen 10 times to take out the trash and clean up his room.

Dad: It bothers me to come home and find all the trash still in the house and Allen's records and books all over his room, with my wife screaming at him.

Allen: My parents tell me to take out the trash during my favorite TV show. They make me clean up my room when all my friends are having fun.

Solutions and Evaluations:	Mom	Dad	Allen
1. Do chores the first time asked	+	+	−
2. Don't have any chores	−	−	+
3. Grounded for 1 month if not done	−	+	−
4. Hire a maid	+	−	+
5. Earn allowance for chores	+	+	+
6. Room cleaned once by 9 P.M.	+	+	+
7. Parents clean the room	−	−	+
8. Close the door to room	+	−	−
9. Better timing when asking Allen	+	+	+
10. One reminder to do chores	+	+	+

Agreement: Nos. 5, 6, 9, 10.

Implementation Plan: By 9 P.M. each evening Allen agrees to clean up his room, meaning books and papers neatly stacked and clothes in hamper or drawers. Doesn't have to pass "white glove test." Will earn extra $1.00 per day on allowance if complies with no reminders or one reminder. By 8 P.M. on Tuesdays, Allen agrees to have trash collected and out by curb. Will earn $2.00 extra if complies.

Punishment for noncompliance: Grounding for the next day after school. Dad to monitor trash; Mom to monitor room.

Note. From A. L. Robin (1990), "Training families with ADHD adolescents." In R. A. Barkley, *Attention-deficit hyperactivity disorder: A handbook for diagnosis and treatment* (pp. 462–497). New York: Guilford Press. Copyright 1990 by The Guilford Press. Reprinted by permission.

treme than you might think. For the curfew problem, you could write down "Stays out all night" and "Does not go out at all on weekend nights." The extremeness of these options helps to suggest that there are degrees of solutions that fall in between that could be useful. When you see that there are at least one or two "workable" ideas—ideas that may achieve mutual acceptance—on the list, move on.

Step 3: Evaluate the Alternatives

Now each family member evaluates the ideas and decides on the best one. First think about the consequences of using each solution, and then rate it as one you could live with (+ on the worksheet) or do not like (− on the worksheet). Focus only on the person's feelings about the options, avoiding digressions, and continue to restate those feelings to be sure everyone understands.

When the ideas have all been rated, review the worksheet to determine whether a consensus was reached. You may be surprised to find that a consensus can be reached about 80% of the time. Then select one of the ideas rated positively by everyone or combine several such ideas into the solution.

If a consensus was not reached, you are going to have to negotiate a compromise. Look for the idea on which members came closest to agreement. Use this idea as a starting point for coming up with variations that might be more acceptable to everyone. Look closely at those parts of the option that seem to be creating the disagreement with your teen. Try to work on suggesting substitutes for these parts that might bring you both closer together. Be attuned to the possible role of distorted expectations and be willing to compromise or give in. You can always discuss the problem again next week and try another option.

Step 4: Implement the Solution

Circle or underline the chosen solution, if necessary rewriting it at the bottom of the worksheet. You also must decide who will do what, when, where, and with what supervision to make the solution work. With ADHD adolescents in particular, establishing clear-cut consequences for compliance or noncompliance is very important, as is reminding your teen during the next week to remember to do the things involved in the solution. Whatever consequences you decide on, be sure that they are also written at the bottom of the worksheet so everyone knows what to expect. Then have everyone sign the bottom of the worksheet so it becomes a contract.

Try the solution for at least one to two weeks before deciding whether or not it is working. If necessary, you can always come back and renegotiate the contract if it seems unfair or unworkable.

Try this problem-solving approach for several weeks by sitting down once each week to discuss just one or two of the problem areas on your list of disagreements. You may wish to schedule regular family meetings at which you and your adolescent apply problem solving to any disagreements that have accumulated in the past week.

Using Professional Help Wisely

We subscribe to the "dental checkup" model of professional help for adolescent ADHD. By following a preventive regimen, you catch problems before they get too serious, so we advocate establishing a relationship with a professional—psychologist, physician, or social worker—with whom you meet periodically to review your adolescent's progress. If a problem arises in school or at home, the professional may suggest a more intensive intervention until the problem is resolved; afterward, you may return to the checkup mode of follow-up care. Or if you're applying the "golden rules" in this chapter without success, it may be time to check in with a professional and enroll in some therapeutic intervention. Many of the ideas in this chapter require the assistance of a person outside the family to implement initially if you and your adolescent have a history of conflict.

ADHD and Problem-Solving Skills

Experience has taught us that ADHD brings special concerns into problem solving. To apply the four-step method successfully, pay attention to these matters:

1. The adolescent may have trouble paying attention during crucial moments of each discussion. Keep your comments brief and to the point, bring the adolescent into the discussion whenever possible, and talk in an animated and enthusiastic manner with a constructive or positive tone. You can even reward your teen for having the discussion with you the first few times you try it. If your adolescent takes medication, hold the discussions while the medication is active.

2. Some younger ADHD teens, say those 12 to 14 years old, are not always fully able to understand the concepts of problem solving or may not be ready emotionally or developmentally to assume responsibility for coming up with options and negotiating solutions. In such cases you may have to set up behavioral contracts on your own and then discuss them with your teen. Or you could simplify the steps of problem solving so they are manageable by an immature adolescent. For example, generate a list of alternative solutions, and, through evaluation, boil them down to three options, which you then present to the adolescent for a vote.

3. If either of the parents also has ADHD, volatile discussions may be unavoidable. In that case, consult a professional to assist you in carrying out these discussions.

4. ADHD adolescents can be so impulsive and distractible that you may feel the need to correct everything they do or say. This can create an endless series of issues and negative communication patterns. You need to learn to pick your issues wisely, deciding what to take a stand on and what to ignore. Some families have also dealt with disruptive behavior during the discussions by using a point system to reward positive communication skills.

Taking Vacations and Keeping Your Sense of Humor

This last golden rule may well be the most important: Maintain your sense of humor, and take vacations from your ADHD adolescent. It can be very difficult to try to see the humor in many parenting situations with ADHD adolescents, but if you try, you will get through your child's adolescence much more easily. And at least several times per year, you and your adolescent need a vacation from each other. Use camps, teen travel, grandparents, friends—whatever it takes—to get away from each other every once in a while. Vacations always help parents recharge their batteries and look at problems with a fresh perspective.

If you wish to read further about the ideas in this chapter, you might consult:

Negotiating Parent–Adolescent Conflict by Arthur L. Robin and Sharon L. Foster (1986). New York: Guilford Press.

Parents and Adolescents Living Together by Marion Forgatch and Gerald Patterson (1989). Eugene, OR: Castalia.

CHAPTER 15

Off to School on the Right Foot: Managing Your Child's Education

with Linda J. Pfiffner, Ph.D.

I f you're among the many parents who first learn of their child's behavior problems through a teacher, you already know that children with ADHD have some of their greatest difficulties in adjusting to the demands of school. Roughly a third of all ADHD children will be held back in school in at least one grade during their educational career, up to 35% may never complete high school, and their academic grades and achievement scores are often significantly below those of their classmates. Between 40 and 50% of ADHD children will eventually wind up receiving some degree of formal services through special education programs, such as resource rooms, and up to 10% may spend their entire school day in such programs (known as *self-containing programs*). Complicating this picture is the fact that more than half of all hyperactive children also have serious problems with oppositional behavior. This helps explain why between 15 and 25% of ADHD children will be suspended and even expelled from school because of their conduct problems.

Teachers frequently respond to the challenging problems exhibited by children with ADHD by becoming more controlling and directive. Over time, their frustrations with these difficult children may make them more negative in their interactions as well. While we are not sure how a negative child–teacher relationship affects the long-term adjustment of ADHD children, experience tells us that it can certainly worsen the already poor academic and social achievement of these children, reduce the motivation to learn and participate in school, and lower self-esteem. All of this could ultimately result in school failure and dropping out.

A positive teacher–student relationship, to the contrary, may improve academic and social adjustment not only in the short term but also in the long term. Adults who had been hyperactive as children have reported that a teacher's caring attitude, extra attention, and guidance were "turning points" in helping them overcome their childhood problems.

The fact is that the single most important ingredient in your ADHD child's success at school is your child's teacher. It is not the name of the school program your child is in, the school location, whether it is private or public, whether or not it is relatively wealthy, or even the size of the class. It is first and foremost your child's teacher, the teacher's experience with ADHD, and his or her willingness to provide the extra effort and understanding your child will require to have a happy and successful school year. The difference that this important individual can make is illustrated in a 15-year-old's poignant account of his school history in the sidebar in this chapter. So you should not wait until August to find out who will be your child's teacher for the coming school year. Nor should you allow some computer or school bureaucrat to make a random selection. You should start negotiating with the principal for the best possible teacher for the next academic year as early as March or April.

The main focus of this chapter, therefore, is how to find the best teacher and, should the available teachers be unfamiliar with the methods that help ADHD children succeed in school, how to help them gain that knowledge to serve your child best. The rest of the chapter addresses secondary matters that are nonetheless commonly of concern to parents—what to look for in a school, classroom structure, and curriculum, what type of placement is best for children with ADHD, and whether retention, especially in kindergarten, is likely to serve the child's interests.

What to Look for in a School

A first step in helping an ADHD child achieve educational success is to choose the right school. In the real world, many of us don't have such a choice. Either economics rule out private school or the community is not large enough to provide a variety of options. In these cases you select the options that are available to you, which often comes down again to getting the best possible teacher. Still, more and more parents today—whether their children have ADHD or not—are basing their housing decisions on the local school system, so if your child has ADHD you may want to know what to look for in a school.

1. Speak with principals about their awareness of ADHD as an educational disability, how much inservice training the teachers have had on the disorder, and how receptive the school is to taking in such children.

Attention Deficit through the Eyes of a Child, by Alan Brown, age 15

I often wondered why I wasn't in group time in kindergarten. The teacher sent me in the corner to play with a toy by myself. Because of being singled out I didn't have many friends. I was different, but I didn't know why or what it was. Toward the middle half of first grade the teacher called my Mom in for a conference. She was telling my Mom, "I'm always having to call on Alan. 'Alan, be still, please. Yes, you can sharpen your pencil for the third time. You have to go to the bathroom again?'" That evening my teacher educated my Mom. She told my Mom about attention deficit disorder (ADD). My teacher suggested taking me to the doctor and letting him run some tests. Mom and I went to see the doctor. After some testing the doctor put me on Ritalin. Within about two weeks the teacher said I was completing my homework, making good grades, and feeling good about myself. Although we (my Mom and I) thought our battle was won, we had no idea what adventures were waiting for us.

Second grade went by. I was doing OK in school. My teacher would usually write on my report card, "Alan worked hard this six weeks. Encourage him to read at home." I hated to read; it was so hard to understand what I had read. I loved to play outside, run in the field, and ride on my bicycle. A free spirit.

By the time I got to third grade things were getting off track. I felt like nothing I did was right. I would try to do good work. My teacher would write on my papers, "Needs to concentrate more on answers," "Needs to turn in all work," "Needs to follow directions." I really didn't think my teacher liked me. She was very stern, never seemed to smile, and was always watching me.

Fourth grade was the year everything in my world fell apart! Before school started, my mom took me to see the doctor the way we did every year. The doctor prescribed the same dose as I had taken the year before. He didn't want to raise my dosage unless he really had to.

First six weeks passed. I didn't do very well, but the doctor said it might be the new school year or getting settled in and used to a new teacher. My Mom told the teacher the doctor was considering raising my Ritalin dosage. The teacher said something had to be done because my grades were low. I wasn't always prepared for class, was slow getting my books out, and always needed to go to my locker because I had forgotten something. My doctor did raise my medication to one pill in the morning and one pill at lunch. Everyone in the room would say, "Dummy has to go take his pill."

(cont.)

ADD through the Eyes of a Child (*cont.*)

My teacher wanted to make me concentrate better, so one day she put my desk in the far corner, separated from the rest of the class. A few days had passed. I still wasn't finishing my work on time, but I was trying to do the work correctly. The teacher didn't care; it wasn't finished. She then put a refrigerator box around my desk so I couldn't see anyone in class. I could hear as other kids in class would make fun of me. It really hurt; I was ashamed of myself and mad at my teacher. I couldn't tell my Mom because I might get in trouble. I hated school, didn't like my teacher, and started not liking myself. Imagine a nine-year-old going through this day after day. It was hard to face the next day. A week had passed, and I poked holes in the cardboard so I could see who was making fun of me. I started peeping through the holes, making the other kids laugh. The teacher would get so annoyed. So I became the class clown. I was expelled for two days. When my Mom found out what was going on, boy, did she get angry.

She was mad that the teacher would do this and mad that the principal allowed it, and no one could see what this was doing to me.

Mom called my doctor, explained what was going on, asked him to recommend a specialist. We needed some help! I remember my Mom cried over the phone. It scared me. I thought I was really in trouble, but instead, she put me in her lap, kissed my cheek, gave me a hug, and said, "You're special to me, and I love you. Together we are going to get through this." It made me feel good because Moms can always fix everything.

The next day Mom explained that we were going to meet someone special, someone I could talk to. I was kind of nervous. This person was a licensed clinical social worker. She was nice. I played games while we talked. After a while I felt like she was a friend. It was time to meet with the principal to return to school. Mom and I went to the office. The principal wanted to give my place to a more deserving student, a higher academic achiever. It would make the school look better. At that point Mom asked about my rights as a handicapped student. She didn't like the thought that no one seemed to care what they had done to me, and she said so. At that point the principal made a phone call to one of his friends, also a principal. It had something to do with Mom not going to the school board meeting to discuss this matter.

I was going to a new school, a school close to where my Mom worked, thanks to that phone call.

On the way home that day Mom explained to me that what they had done to me wasn't right, and they should be ashamed. She said that

(cont.)

ADD through the Eyes of a Child (*cont.*)

there were a lot of smart, successful in people this world who were not happy with themselves. She said, "It's more important in life to be happy and know within yourself that no matter what comes your way you can survive. Academics are important, but self-worth is too."

The new school was a more positive atmosphere; my grades came up. The doctor changed my medication to a slow-release pill so I didn't have to leave class to take it anymore.

Fifth grade came along. It was great! I had the best teacher; she smiled a lot and was flexible yet had a structured day planned. One day I remember she asked me to go to the closet and get the book *Charlotte's Web*. I went to the closet and found the most wonderful book, *King of the Wind*, a story about a horse. I hid the book *Charlotte's Web* and told the teacher I couldn't find it but that this horse book was there, and I really liked horses. All along the teacher knew those books were in that closet. She thought if *King of the Wind* looked that interesting to me, maybe it would be worth doing instead of *Charlotte's Web*. After reading the book, I wrote a report about the story. The teacher was so impressed. She posted the book report in front of the class and made a comment on my report card. I was so proud—proud of myself. I was on track again; life was great. My parents were going to be so proud.

Sixth grade came, and I did fairly well. I had to change classes. It was hard to adjust to better organization skills. I color-coded folders for classes and kept a schedule of where and when classes were.

Seventh grade was a little rocky, but I made it. There were more students. I kind of got lost in the shuffle. By eighth grade it was a struggle every day. More peer pressure to fit in, and I was going through a lot of changes, puberty. I would find myself daydreaming a lot, wanting to be with my grandfather. In the summer I got to spend a lot of time with him. Grandfather owned his own business, and he taught me a lot. Learning was fun that way. It was hands-on learning. Anyway, that year my report card read, "Needs to finish work. Didn't turn in all papers. Needs to show more effort." I dreaded every day. Sometimes I even cried when I was by myself. How could I get these people to understand me? I went to automatic shut-off; everything seemed negative with school.

Summer came. I needed a break; I worked with Grandfather. That summer my family spent a lot of time preparing me for high school.

High school! What a big step! I was growing up. More things were going to be expected of me. I wanted to fit in and not be a jerk or dork. My parents warned me about wrong crowds and told me high school grades

(*cont.*)

ADD through the Eyes of a Child (*cont.*)

were really important to my future. What pressure! My mom talked to the guidance counselor about my having ADD. The counselor assured her I would do just fine.

I was really nervous the first day, but guess what? All freshmen are. The first six weeks went by. Not all of my teachers had taken the time to read my school records. They didn't realize I had ADD. Boy, did things get out of hand.

Later that year, when Mom went in for a conference, one of my teachers said, "I would never have guessed Alan was ADD." Mom looked surprised. The teacher said, "He dresses so nice, has a clean haircut, and shows respect for teachers, not a smart aleck. He doesn't get into trouble." Mom rolled her eyes but didn't say anything until we got into the car. "Alan, that teacher doesn't understand about ADD. It's no respecter of persons. Anyone can get it. It's not a shame to have ADD. At least we know what we are dealing with. Remember, build on your strengths rather than magnify your weaknesses. Ignore that teacher's comment. She needs to be better educated in this field. School isn't just for ABCs anymore!"

I wanted to belong. I acted tough, even started to tell lies. I told stories that made me look big in people's eyes, but everyone knew they were lies. I just made things worse. In high school you are with a lot of people every day. You meet lots of teachers. Some teachers are there just to earn a paycheck, and there are a few who really care about the students they have. I have such a teacher. She took time for me, time to try to understand me better. When I needed someone to stand up for me, this teacher did.

Once, a teacher asked everyone to write a story as if they were in a make-believe world. She asked me about my ideas. I replied, "I deal in the real world." This really puzzled the teacher. I am fifteen now. I have to deal in the real world. Dreaming is nice. Being an ADD student takes all my energy to meet the goals I have set for myself.

Through my years in school so far, I've been through a lot. My Mom says I have a good heart; I care about those in need. I'm not dumb. You can't always measure smartness by tests. I feel I'm doing better in school. The school psychologist has become an important tool for me. I can talk to him when I get a teacher who doesn't understand, if I disagree with something, or if I'm just having problems. It helps to talk to someone who understands. What I'm trying to say is: No matter what comes my way, I can survive.

I have those who really care, and from that I draw my strength.

2. If the school accepts such children, inquire about class sizes. They should be as small as possible (12 to 15 is ideal, and 30 to 40 is absurd). Also, what extra assistance is available to help a teacher? Does the school have psychiatrists, psychologists, and special educators who consult with them about problem children? Are there master teachers within the school who have extra training in dealing with ADHD, learning-disordered, or behavior-disordered children who can serve as advisers or mentors on classroom management?

3. What is the school's attitude toward behavior-modifying drugs used with ADHD children? Some schools believe that medication is neither necessary nor beneficial. These schools are clearly out of touch with the scientific literature and should be avoided. Even if your child is not currently taking any medicine, if at some point he or she needs it, you will want a school that is knowledgeable and cooperative.

What mechanisms does the school have in place for the administration and monitoring of medication? Most schools have formal policies about such matters. Many schools require, for example, a signed statement from the physician about the type and dosage of medication and the timing of its administration. Public schools also often require the physician to submit a separate approval form to the state Department of Education before they will permit medicines to be given at school.

4. Does the school have formal procedures for disciplinary actions and appeals of those decisions? If so, get a copy of the written policies to see what rights your child may have should behavior problems necessitate discipline for misconduct. Then determine how comfortable you are with these policies. Be sure they are not just punitive but also stress the efforts the school is likely to take to help the child avoid repeating the offenses.

5. Does the principal encourage open and frequent home–school communication? Will you be welcome to drop by the school periodically to see how your child is doing? Can you request parent–teacher conferences without a lot of red tape? Is the input of parents valued by the school? Some schools provide daily journals that the children take back and forth between home and school each day. They indicate what was studied in each major subject and what the homework in that subject is each day. The children are often the ones to complete this information after each subject period, and the teacher then adds brief comments. These are great for keeping you informed about your child's performance each day.

6. If you feel it necessary, is the school staff open to having an outside professional or expert visit the school with you to discuss your child's educational program and, perhaps, make further recommendations to improve it? If the school principal or teacher seems defensive about such outside advice, find another school.

7. How many other children entering your child's grade or class also have behavioral, learning, or emotional problems? Most teachers can handle only a few such children in any regular classroom with other normally functioning children. If there are more than two or three per class, ask for a different classroom or find another school.

Choosing a Teacher for Your ADHD Child

In making the best possible choice for your ADHD child, you need to evaluate teachers on the basis of two factors: knowledge and attitude.

How Well Informed Is the Teacher?

Unfortunately, many teachers are uninformed about ADHD or are out of date in their knowledge of the disorder and its management. We have found that some teachers have a poor grasp of the nature, course, outcome, and causes of this disorder. They also may have misperceptions about which treatments are helpful and which are not. Where this is the case, little positive change will be made from attempting to establish behavior management programs within that classroom. Just as the first step in helping your child was for you to become educated about ADHD, the initial step of school intervention is the education of teachers about the disorder. Armed with the information in this book, you should be able to determine from interviews with the principal and teachers whether a particular teacher is informed on ADHD. If not, you can do a lot to help.

By understanding the methods presented here and in Chapter 16, you become equipped to pass along recommendations to your child's teacher for possible implementation. You can also raise these techniques as suggestions at school conferences about your child's school performance or even request, where appropriate, that some of them become a formal part of your child's written Individual Education Plan (IEP) if your child is going to be receiving special educational services.

You can also help educate the teacher by providing brief reading materials similar to those mentioned throughout this book and in "Suggested Reading" at the back of this book or even by sharing this book. We also have made two videotapes (*ADHD—What Do We Know?* and *ADHD in the Classroom*) that summarize the disorder and cover issues of classroom management; many teachers have found them more convenient than reading materials.

What Is the Teacher's Attitude toward ADHD and Behavior Modification Techniques?

Whether any individual teacher can and will adopt the behavioral programs advocated in this book is greatly influenced by the teacher's educational training and philosophy as well as personal experience and beliefs about the educational process. In some cases, intensive training of your child's teacher by a school or clinical psychologist expert in these behavioral programs may be required. Even then "booster" visits by the professional to the school following training may be necessary to maintain the teacher's use of the procedures.

Teachers who use a permissive approach to education are often unlikely to use behavior modification out of misplaced concern that these methods are too mechanical and do not adequately foster a child's natural development and motivation to learn. This is certainly not true. In some cases these beliefs may be altered through the success of a consultation with a professional trained in behavioral programs. In other cases such beliefs will not change. Then they may greatly interfere with the effective use of behavioral programs in your child's classrooms. In that case a transfer to an alternative teacher with a philosophy more consistent with using behavioral programs may be beneficial.

In cases of poor teacher motivation or a conflicting philosophy, be assertive. Press the school administrators for either greater teacher accountability or a transfer of your child to another classroom or school rather than waste a year of your child's education. Where this is not possible, you may have to supplement your child's education outside of school through additional tutoring, summer school review programs, and your extra involvement at home in reviewing schoolwork.

Some teachers resist behavioral techniques not because of a conflicting teaching philosophy but because they believe the problems of the ADHD child are emotional, stemming from conflicts or chaos at home, or that medication is the only solution because ADHD has a biological basis. Other teachers may resent altering their teaching style if they believe this suggests their own behavior is causing the child's problems.

> *"Her teacher doesn't believe in ADHD. She says that too many children are being labeled and given excuses for their misconduct. How can I deal with her?"*

Another important thing to consider is how well adjusted your child's teacher is and whether other parents have filed complaints against this teacher for "malpractice" or ineffective teaching. You certainly cannot request that each of your child's teachers undergo a psychological evaluation, but you can seek information from the principal or other school staff about that teacher's reputation in dealing with children with behavior problems. You can also ask for the names of parents whose children are currently in that teacher's care so you can call those parents to get a clearer view of that teacher's competence.

What You Can Do to Help

Overall, the importance of a close collaboration among you, your child's teacher, and any professional behavioral experts on the treatment team cannot be stressed enough. However, successful collaboration can easily be hindered by attitude—not just the teacher's but yours as well. Are your efforts being hampered by an attitude formed by a long history of conflicts with school personnel? Or are your expectations unrealistic? Are you waiting for the school to cure your child's problems? If your child is having few difficulties at home, have you persuaded yourself that poor teaching or management at school is causing your child's difficulties in the classroom? Be sure to reexamine your attitudes periodically to see if they're hindering the collaborative process.

If antagonism has arisen between you and the teacher, it is quite likely to undermine any intervention. In that case you may want to ask a professional consulting with you to the school to help mediate.

Also be aware that in many cases the behavioral programs suggested here will need to be combined with medication to treat an ADHD child's school problems. Recent research shows that the combination of behavioral programs and medication produces improvements that are superior to either treatment used by itself. Therefore, if your child is having serious problems with school adjustment, you should give thoughtful consideration to using medication (see Chapters 18 and 19).

Finally, when you find a good, sensitive teacher for your ADHD child, be supportive and praising, assist the teacher in any way you can, be open to the teacher's suggestions of what you can do to help, and convey your approval and admiration not only to the teacher but also to the school principal. This can greatly strengthen your relationship with such teachers, increase their desire to tailor their classroom programs to your child's special needs and abilities, assist you in finding future teachers of similar thinking as your child progresses through that school, and encourage them to come to your defense and your child's when decisions about educational programming must be made by school administrators. Positive attention to your child's teachers builds a stronger relationship with them just as it does with your children.

Some Advice about Classroom Structure and Curriculum

A variety of factors related to the structure of the classroom environment, classroom rules, and the nature of work assignments are important to consider if you are to help your child at school. In the past, professionals told parents and teachers to reduce the amount of stimulation in the classroom because it could lead to excessive distractibility in ADHD children. Research evaluating such measures found, however, that they did not improve classroom behavior or academic performance in ADHD children. Similarly, suggestions that traditional classrooms are too restrictive and that classrooms affording greater freedom and flexibility are best have not been supported by research.

There are several features of the classroom, however, that may need some adjustments when a teacher is working with your ADHD child. Keep these things in mind when you are shopping for next year's classroom and teacher for your child. Remember them as well when you meet with that teacher to plan the approach to the school year. Believe it or not, one important point is the seating arrangement in the classroom. Recent research shows that a traditional desk arrangement in rows facing the front of the classroom is far better for ADHD children than modular arrangements where several or more children share a larger table, especially if they face each other while working. Such arrangements seem to provide too much stimulation for social interaction with other children that distracts the ADHD child from attending to the teacher or class work.

You can also ask that your child be moved closer to the teacher's desk or wherever the teacher spends most of her time while instructing the class. This not only discourages classmates from giving your child attention for disruptive behavior but also makes it easier for the teacher to monitor your child and dispense rewards and fines quickly and easily. Altering seating arrangements is sometimes as effective as a reward program in increasing appropriate classroom behavior.

Classrooms that are physically enclosed (with four walls and a door) are usually much better for your ADHD child than the so-called open classrooms. Open classrooms are usually noisier and contain more visual distractions. Research shows that noisy environments are associated with less attention to work and higher levels of disruptive behavior in ADHD children.

A well-organized and predictable classroom routine is also helpful. The posting of a daily schedule and classroom rules can add to this sense of structure. Use of feedback charts at the front of the class that display how children are doing in following rules, behaving, and working may also help your ADHD child.

In some cases "nag tapes" are particularly helpful. While this is not really a factor in classroom structure, it is an example of the type of measure the school should be open to using. Before doing work at his or her desk, the child takes out a small, portable tape recorder, puts on an earpiece so the tape does not distract other students, and turns on the tape player. The child then proceeds to do the work while the tape is reminding him or her—usually using the father's voice since we know ADHD children tend to listen better to their fathers than their mothers—to remain on task, not bug others, and the like. The effectiveness of these tapes will depend greatly on their being combined with consistent methods for enforcing rules and the use of rewards and punishments for working and proper conduct.

The following additional changes to classroom structure and curriculum are likely to be helpful:

1. As with all children, academic tasks should be well matched to the child's abilities. In the case of ADHD children, increasing the novelty and interest level of the tasks through use of increased stimulation (e.g., color, shape, texture) seems to reduce disruptive behavior, enhance attention, and improve overall performance.

2. The teacher should change the style of presenting lectures and task materials to children to help maintain the children's interest and motivation. When low-interest or passive tasks are assigned, they should be interspersed with high-interest or active tasks to optimize the child's attention or concentration. Tasks requiring an active as opposed to a passive response may also allow ADHD children to better channel their disruptive behaviors into constructive responses. In other words, give the ADHD child something to do as part of the class lecture, work assignment, or activity, and the child will be less of a problem.

3. Academic assignments should be brief to fit with the child's attention span. A good rule of thumb is to assign the amount of work that would be appropriate for a child 30% younger. Feedback regarding accuracy of assignments should be

given immediately, and time limits for getting work done should be short. This can be aided by the use of timers such as clocks or cooking timers.

4. A child's attention during group lessons may be enhanced by delivering the lesson in an enthusiastic yet task-focused style, keeping it brief and allowing frequent and active child participation. A teacher who pretends to be more like an actor, who is vibrant, enthused, and emotionally charged, will get much more attention than one who drones on about some dry subject.

5. Mixing classroom lectures up with brief moments of physical exercise may also be helpful. This reduces the sense of fatigue and monotony the children may experience from extended academic work periods. Try jumping jacks by the desk, a quick trip outside the classroom for a brisk two-minute run or walk, forming a line and walking about the classroom in "conga line" fashion, or other such brief physical activities. These can rejuvenate the child's attention span.

6. Schedule the difficult academic subjects in the morning. Leave the more active, nonacademic subjects and lunch to the afternoon periods. It is well known that the ADHD child's ability to concentrate and to inhibit behavior greatly decreases over the school day (see Chapter 4).

7. Whenever possible, augment classroom lectures with direct-instruction materials—drills of important academic skills or, even better, computers with software that does the same thing.

What Placement Is Best for an ADHD Child?

In many cases the measures described so far and the programs presented in Chapter 16 are sufficient, especially for children with mild to moderate ADHD symptoms or for children whose attentional and behavioral problems are controlled with medication. However, in other cases, especially those with severe ADHD symptoms and accompanying problems of opposition, aggression, or learning disabilities, alternative educational placements—for example, special education, private school—may be necessary. Ideally, these placements should include classes with a small student–teacher ratio, and the classes should be taught by teachers with expertise in behavior modification.

Special Educational Services

Obtaining special educational services for ADHD children is often a difficult process. Many ADHD children did not previously qualify for special educational services according to the guidelines specified in the Public Law 94-142, now known as the Individuals with Disabilities Education Act. Now they do! If your ADHD child is failing, he or she may be eligible for formal special education services under this law under the category known as "Other Health Impaired." Ask your school district to explain this law and your child's rights. Keep in mind, however, that your child must be experiencing a significant impairment in school performance because of ADHD to get special education services; a diagnosis alone is insufficient.

Unfortunately, the ADHD child without associated problems is likely to be eligible for little special education in most states. When associated problems do exist, the child will probably be assigned to classes focusing on those problems, such as learning disabilities or classes for the emotionally disturbed when the ADHD child is particularly aggressive and defiant. Certainly, ADHD children with significant speech and language or motor development problems are likely to receive speech, occupational, and physical therapy, or even adaptive physical education, provided that these developmental problems are sufficient to interfere with academic performance.

Although the situation is changing at the moment, you may need to bring pressure on your school district to abide by the existing laws. Efforts are now under way by national parent support associations to force states to follow the recommendations of the federal government to improve services for ADHD children, but any change is likely to come only after much debate and may hinge on the need to limit any costs that would escalate for school districts that opened their special educational programs to another handicapped population.

In the meantime, it is essential that you become familiar with federal, state, and local district guidelines. You can get all of this information from your school district. Other information of help to you can be found in three recent excellent paperback books:

CHADD Educators Manual by Mary Fowler (1992). Contact CHADD's national headquarters in Plantation, FL, at 305-587-3700 to order this manual.
ADD and the Law by Peter and Patricia Latham, attorneys (1993). To order, call Stonebridge Seminars at 508-836-5570 or the ADD Warehouse at 305-792-8944.
Turning the Tide by Karen Richards and John Lester, M.D. (1993). Milgard Press, 4050 Pennsylvania Ave., Suite 310, Kansas City, MO 64111.

In addition, you should become acquainted with the director of special education within your school district. You are only as good as your Rolodex in dealing with the educational problems of your ADHD child. A good Rolodex file can go a long way toward locating resources within the private sector, such as private schools, formal and informal tutoring programs, and special summer camps. Also contact your local CHADD or ADDA parent support association for advice on resources in your area for school problems. These organizations can sometimes even send a professionally trained advocate with you to school meetings. In some cases you may need to get a "second opinion" on your child's problems because you disagree with the school staff over the nature and extent of your child's problems and the child's eligibility for services.

It is also important to understand the concept of the "least restrictive environment" as it applies to decisions regarding special educational placement. Public Law 94-142 makes it clear that special services are to be provided such that handicapped children are not unreasonably precluded from interactions with nonhandicapped peers. School districts are therefore likely to err in the direction of placing ADHD children in the least restrictive environment necessary to manage the academic and behavioral problems. That is, they may put the children in the program that provides the greatest contact with normally functioning students. Some teachers are not always in agreement with this. They prefer that even the child with mild ADHD be removed to special educational settings rather than have to adjust their classroom curriculum and behavior management style to accommodate the needs of these children. Parents may be equally biased toward special education, believing that the smaller class sizes, better-trained teachers, and greater teacher attention they provide are preferable. School districts are likely to resist these pressures so as not to violate the rights of the child to the least restrictive environment or risk legal action for doing so. Parents may find this frustrating but must understand the philosophy behind this placement bias and its basis in law.

Should You Retain Your ADHD Kindergarten Child?

Anywhere from 23 to 35% of children with ADHD will be retained at least once before reaching high school, most in the early elementary years. Therefore many parents will have to determine whether retention is the solution to their own child's difficulties. Terri Shelton, Ph.D., who worked at the ADHD clinic at the University of Massachusetts Medical Center, believes that it probably is *not* the best measure for most children. Here is what she has to say (somewhat paraphrased):

It's understandable that retention would be recommended in so many cases since the ADHD child often displays the characteristics of a child who is immature for his or her age. Many teachers might reasonably recommend "another year to grow up." Yet several studies have failed to identify any significant advantages in achievement as a result of delaying school entry. Perhaps this is because when the observed difficulties are related to ADHD and not just developmental immaturity, repeating the same approach for a second year is not likely to help. It does not, after all, address the specific problems of ADHD. And, in fact, a child who repeats kindergarten or first grade may be bored when reviewing the old material and thus be doomed to fail. Taken to its extreme, this solution could result in what one mother said was "having him repeating every single grade. At that rate, he would graduate at 30!"

Questions/Options to Consider

So when is it wise to consider retention?

Academic Status

Although it is true that children with ADHD are likely to do better in one-on-one situations than in the classroom, individual testing, coupled with a classroom observation and rating scales/interview from the teacher, can be helpful in determining the child's mental capabilities separately from his or her ability to perform in the regular classroom environment. Just be sure that the professional uses tests that are appropriate for the young child, such as the Woodcock–Johnson Psychoeducational Battery, the Kaufman Assessment Battery for Children, or the Stanford–Binet (fourth edition), among others, which provide a broad range of tasks above and below the five- to six-year range. In general, if the child is mentally capable of completing the work, a different type of academic environment (e.g., greater reinforcement, smaller class), not retention, is needed.

If delays are identified, the child's overall academic ability should be assessed. If there is a global delay, retention is recommended. If not, the child should be promoted, and supportive educational services can be provided in the delayed areas.

Physical Size and Age

Parents and children have commented on the social problems of retention when the child's size did not fit in with that of classmates. So retention might seem wiser when the kindergartener is small in stature and/or has a birthday near the school district's cutoff for first grade.

Emotional Maturity

The impulsivity and low frustration tolerance, among other characteristics, that mark the ADHD child's emotional immaturity are not likely to be cured by another year in kindergarten. Instead, some type of intervention, such as a program of social skills training within the school setting, might be helpful. We use the social skills training program called *Skillstreaming* by Dr. Arnold Goldstein and published by Research Press. It has been used successfully by regular classroom preschool and elementary teachers within the typical academic curriculum.

In fact many of the child's difficulties can be addressed through remedial services provided in the regular classroom as an alternative to retention. Occupational therapy can be used and recommendations given by the therapist for the regular classroom teacher to use in the classroom. Speech and language therapy may also be beneficial, especially when they focus on communication, in which case such therapy becomes an effective social skills program.

Style and Expectations of the First-Grade Teacher

As already discussed, teachers vary considerably both in what they expect their students to be able to do and in their attitude toward disorders like ADHD. A number of relatively simple behavioral strategies, discussed in Chapter 16, can be used in the regular classroom by a teacher who is open to that approach, eliminating the need for retention. So the choice of a first-grade teacher is a critical determinant in the decision about whether to retain a kindergartener.

Alternative Classroom Options/Curriculum

In addition to regular kindergarten or regular first grade, there are options that may be possible within the school district. These include a language-based kindergarten or first grade, which provides a supportive language-based curriculum and a smaller student–teacher ratio. You could also ask about a K–1 transitional program that is often used for children who are somewhat slow in development.

Because they provide a lot of feedback and do so immediately, computers can be very useful for young children with ADHD. Have you ever met a child with ADHD who didn't like Nintendo? Using computer games to enhance learning of academic skills can be a helpful aid to a regular classroom curriculum. A number of computer programs—Reader Rabbit and Math Blaster, for example—enhance reading and math readiness.

So, in general, even when retention is recommended and especially when it is not, considerable attention needs to be directed toward what type of teaching approach was provided last time and what can be done this time to make sure it is more effective.

CHAPTER 16

Enhancing Education at School and at Home: Methods for Success from Kindergarten through Grade 12

with Linda J. Pfiffner, Ph.D.

Now that you've found the best possible setting for your child's education, you can begin to look at specific techniques for maximizing school success on a day-to-day basis. Here is another area where you must become an expert; it may very well be up to you to help plan the intervention and train the teacher in the effective use of behavior management programs. It is certainly up to you to see that your child's education is enhanced by what goes on at home. This chapter goes into detail on general principles and specific methods for improving an ADHD child's success in school.

First, however, remember to try to involve your child in this process to increase the child's motivation to succeed. Include any child over age seven in some of your initial planning meetings with the teacher. This gives the child some input into setting goals and determining appropriate and valuable rewards and penalties for behavior. One important product of such meetings is behavioral contracts that outline the details of the programs and can be signed by parent, teacher, and child to help maintain the consistent use of the program over time and to clarify each person's role.

General Principles for School Management

Whether or not medication is used, a number of important principles are helpful to keep in mind in developing classroom management programs for your ADHD child. These stem from the theory presented in Chapter 2 that ADHD involves an impairment in your child's inhibition of behavior. They are also founded on the principles for managing your child at home given in Chapter 11.

1. Rules and instructions must be clear, brief, and, wherever possible, represented physically in the form of charts, lists, and other visual reminders. Relying on the child's memory and verbal reminders is often ineffective. Encourage the child to repeat instructions out loud and even to utter them softly to himself while following through on the instruction.

2. Rewards, punishments, and feedback used to manage the child's behavior must be delivered swiftly and immediately, and the entire approach to using consequences must be well organized, systematic, and planned.

3. Frequent feedback or consequences for following the rules are crucial to maintaining the ADHD child's compliance.

4. ADHD children are less sensitive to social praise and reprimands, so the consequences for good or bad behavior must be more powerful than those needed to manage the behavior of non-ADHD children.

5. Rewards and incentives must be put in place before punishment is used, or your child will come to see school as a place where he or she is more likely to be punished than rewarded. Make sure the teacher waits a week or two after setting up a reward program at school before starting to use punishment. Then make sure the teacher gives away two to three rewards for each punishment. When punishment fails, first determine whether the rewards are insufficient; when they are, punishment will not control your child's behavior.

6. Token reward systems can be kept effective over an entire school year with minimal loss of power provided that the rewards are changed frequently. ADHD children become bored with particular rewards faster than other children, and teachers who fail to recognize that fact often give up on the program too soon, believing it has stopped working.

7. Anticipation is the key with ADHD children, especially during times of transition. To ensure that your child is aware of an impending shift, ask the teacher to follow the strategies presented in Chapter 12: (a) review the rules *before* going into the new activity; (b) specify the rewards for good behavior in the next activity; (c) describe the punishment for misbehavior; and (d) follow through on this plan once the activity begins. *Think aloud, think ahead* is the important message to educators here.

You can also share the principles from Chapter 9 with your child's teachers: (1) strive for consistency; (2) do not personalize the child's problems; (3) maintain a disability perspective of the child; and (4) practice forgiveness. With these rules in mind, a creative teacher can easily devise an effective management program for your ADHD child.

Behavior Management Methods for the Classroom

Positive and negative consequences are the most effective tools for behavior management in the classroom, just as they are at home. Positive consequences usually include praise, tokens and tangible rewards, and special privileges. Punishments commonly are ignoring, verbal reprimands, fines or penalties in a token system, and time-out. The greatest improvement in classroom behavior and academic performance is likely to come only from a combination of strategies.

Using Positive Consequences

Positive Teacher Attention

Praise and other forms of positive teacher attention such as a smile, nod, or pat on the back are some of the most basic management tools teachers have at their disposal. Positive attention is valued by most children, including your ADHD child, though attention alone is rarely enough to manage all of the problems ADHD children may have at school.

> "The teacher asked me, 'Why should I give your child lots
> of rewards for behaving well when I don't do this for the children
> who behave normally? They'll resent it.' How can I respond?"

Giving praise and acknowledgment may seem simple, but the organized and systematic use of such attention requires great skill. The teacher must be specific about what he or she likes and must convey genuine warmth. Praise must be delivered quickly and must vary in wording to have the best strategic effect. Effective use of praise also requires increased monitoring or supervision so the teacher can catch the child being good more often and give the positive consequences earned. But this is easier said than done. The demands on a teacher's time and attention in the average classroom are considerable. Supervising your child more closely inevitably competes with monitoring all the other children and teaching the curriculum. Some teachers may even feel that your child does not deserve this extra attention and supervision—that the other children in the class do not get this kind of attention for behaving well, so it is not fair to give it to your ADHD child for misbehaving. If your teacher makes such remarks, share your knowledge as discussed in Chapter 15 so that the teacher understands ADHD is a disability, not simply naughtiness or laziness.

Using Cues to Provide Consequences. Several devices can be used to help a teacher remember to provide frequent feedback to an ADHD child:

1. Smiley face stickers can be placed about the classroom where the teacher may frequently glance, reminding him or her to check out what the ADHD student is doing and praise the child if it is at all positive.

2. A soft tone can be taped at random intervals (more frequently for the first week or two and then spaced out farther) on a 90-minute or 120-minute cassette to remind the teacher to check on the student and provide praise as appropriate. For students eight years old and up, the teacher can use this program to teach self-monitoring. The student gets a small white file card divided down the middle to form two columns with a plus sign (+) or smiley face over the left column and a minus sign (−) or frown face over the right column. Whenever the child hears the tone, he or she can record a point (hash mark) in the plus column for obeying instructions or one in the minus column for being off task. The teacher's job is to check quickly on the child's behavior when the tone sounds and make sure the student is recording accurately. Self-monitoring is enhanced when an easel at the front of the classroom lists five or so rules for each class period so the teacher can flip to the appropriate page throughout the day.

3. The teacher also can start a class period with about 10 bingo chips in, say, a left pocket, moving a chip to the right pocket whenever positive attention has been given to your ADHD child. The goal is to move all 10 chips to the right pocket by the end of that class period.

Tangible Reward and Token Programs. Despite the usefulness of praise and ignoring, these procedures are often not enough by themselves. A variety of more powerful rewards, often in the form of special privileges such as helping the teacher, earning extra recess, playing special games, having computer time, and doing art projects, can be given. It's important that a long list of choices be available to prevent boredom. Also, because frequent rewards are important to helping the ADHD child, some of these rewards should be possible to earn a few times a day. More valuable rewards, like a pizza party or special class outing, should be earned over longer periods of time, such as weekly.

Using token, point, or chip programs to earn rewards can also be very effective (see Chapter 11). Teachers may find it helpful to interview the ADHD child about the kinds of activities or other rewards the child would like to earn as well as selecting some based on observation of the child. If few powerful enough rewards are available at school, you may have to set up a home-based reward program, discussed later in this chapter. Or you could donate a favorite type of toy or piece of play equipment from home for the teacher to use with a classroom reward system.

One very powerful reward kids seem to like these days is a video game such as Nintendo. We have been successful in approaching local civic clubs for donations of such equipment or some funds to offset the expense of buying it by giving presentations on the seriousness of classroom behavioral problems and the critical need for such rewards in the management of disruptive children.

Token programs can also be used for a group of children, with all class members earning rewards based on the behavior of one or more of the classmates or of the entire group. Group programs can be particularly effective when peers are rewarding an ADHD child for disruptive behavior by laughing or joining in the inappropriate conduct. In some group programs, the performance of an ADHD student serves as the standard for determining how much reward is given to the entire class. In other cases, tokens or points are given to each child in the classroom, including the ADHD child, based on how the ADHD student has done. This has the advantage of motivating the other children in the class to help the ADHD student behave well, follow the rules, and get work done. A different form of this program involves breaking the class up into small teams, which earn or lose points depending on their behavior. The team with the greatest number of positive points or fewest negative points earns privileges for that entire team. The group approach has the advantage of not singling out the ADHD child, but that benefit must be weighed against the potential for the ADHD child to be vilified for causing the whole class to be penalized when the ADHD student does poorly.

Token programs can also be used to increase your child's academic productivity and work accuracy. In one program we set up, the token system involved children earning checks on an index card for each correct answer, with the checks redeemable for a large variety of backup rewards at school, such as candy, free time, school and art supplies, picnics in the park, and so forth, later in the day. This program sharply increased math and reading scores and reduced disruptive behavior to a level similar to that seen when the children had previously been on medication.

In another, very novel program, tokens were given for successful completion of four tasks: two that involved learning to read and using new vocabulary words in sentences and two that involved teaching these tasks to another student, called *peer tutoring*. When a token had been earned for completion of each of these four tasks, it was exchanged for 15 minutes of play on a pinball machine or electronic "pong" game in the classroom. Additional game time was earned whenever a child passed a subject's unit test, such as a chapter in the reading assignment. This token program dramatically increased both the completion of schoolwork and the accuracy of the work. It also improved the students' performance on the school district's weekly reading exams. This program was carried out by just a single teacher.

The types of goals selected for token programs are critical to their success. Giving rewards for outstanding performance works for other children, but many ADHD children need affirmation for lesser achievements. At the start, therefore, give rewards for smaller accomplishments, such as for completing a part of the work when the child has a long history of failing to complete work or for being quiet for part of the day when the child is often disruptive throughout the day.

Tokens also need to be adjusted for the age of the ADHD children involved. Tangible tokens, such as poker chips, are very important in managing four- to seven-year-olds, while points, numbers, or hash marks on a card can be used through high school. With preschool or kindergarten children, however, using plastic chips may actually serve as a distraction, so we have often used small fabric pockets pinned to the back of the child's clothing. When tokens are dispensed, the teacher reaches to the child, slips the token into the child's "knapsack," and gives a light affectionate squeeze to the child's shoulder. Several times each day, the pockets are removed and emptied and the children can exchange their tokens for various classroom privileges.

Using Negative Consequences

Ignoring

Ignoring is often used as one of the first treatments for mild misbehavior, especially when children's misbehavior seems to be encouraged by teacher attention. Unfortunately, it is not easy to distinguish the cases when an ADHD child is trying to get attention by misbehaving from those in which the child is not. Most misbehavior stems from your child's biological handicap in inhibiting behavior and sustaining attention.

Ignoring does not mean simply failure to monitor a child's behavior; it means *contingent withdrawal* of teacher attention when the misbehavior occurs. It works best in combination with praise—for example, praising the children who stay in their seats while withdrawing attention from an ADHD child who is wandering around the classroom. But even when a powerful reward program is used as well, ignoring may not be sufficient punishment to teach a child with ADHD to stop misbehaving. In these cases, additional negative consequences appear necessary. Ignoring is also not indicated in cases of aggression or destruction—acts of misconduct that deserve swift, certain punishment to reduce their repetition in the future.

Reprimands

The reprimand is probably the most frequently used negative consequence in the classroom, but its effectiveness can vary considerably. Brief, specific reprimands given swiftly, without much emotion (businesslike), and consistently backed up with other punishment if not heeded can be effective for your ADHD child. Reprimands that are vague, delayed, long-winded, emotional, and not backed up with other consequences are not helpful. Reprimands mixed with positive feedback also fail, as do inconsistently delivered reprimands. For example, children who are sometimes reprimanded for calling out but other times responded to as if they had raised their hands are apt to continue, if not increase, their calling out. Reprimands also appear to be more effective when delivered with eye contact and in close proximity (nearby) to the child. In addition, children respond better to teachers who deliver consistently strong reprimands at the outset of the school year than to teachers who gradually increase the severity of their discipline over time. In summary, reprimands, like praise, are not always sufficient to change your child's behavior. More powerful backup consequences may be necessary.

Behavior Penalties or Fines

Penalties, or what professionals call *response cost,* involve the loss or removal of a reward based on the display of some misbehavior. Lost rewards can include a wide range of privileges and activities or even tokens in a token system (fines). Fining can easily be adapted to a variety of behavior problems and situations; it is more effective than the use of reprimands alone and seems to increase the effectiveness of reward programs.

In one research study the teacher deducted one point every time she saw a child not working. Each lost point meant a loss of one minute of free time. A digital counter was placed at each child's desk to keep track of the child's point totals. One child's counter consisted of numbered cards that could be changed to a lesser number each time a point was lost. The teacher had an identical counter on her desk where she kept track of point losses. The child was instructed to match the number value on his counter with that of the teacher's frequently during the class. A second child had a battery-operated electronic "counter" with a number display. The teacher simply took away points for this on the display by using a remote transmitter like that used in an electronic garage-door opener.

Both of these methods increased the time the children paid attention to their work and their academic performance. The results were almost as good as when the children had been on stimulant medication. The swiftness with which the consequences were delivered in either procedure certainly helped to make the program work. In addition, these procedures were very easy to use, practical, and efficient for the teacher.

The electronic counter and transmitter used in this study, invented by Dr. Mark Rapport, has been mass-produced by Dr. Michael Gordon under the name the Attention Trainer and is available from Gordon Systems, DeWitt, NY.

As with other punishments, however, the use of fines or penalties has raised some concerns about possible negative effects. Ways to reduce these are discussed later in the chapter. We have found that giving lots of rewards in class and avoiding unreasonably strict standards can reduce the number of penalties that need to be used.

Time-Out

Time-out, discussed for use at home in Chapter 11, really means time out from positive reinforcement or rewards. It is frequently recommended for use at school with ADHD children who are particularly aggressive or disruptive. Time-out can be applied in several ways. One of these, often called *social isolation,* which involves placing the child in a chair in an empty room for a few minutes, has come under much criticism. Now professionals generally recommend just removing the child from the area of rewarding activities rather than from the classroom. This may involve having the child sit in a three-sided cubicle or sit facing a dull area (e.g., a blank wall) in the classroom. In other cases children may be required to put their work away (which eliminates the opportunity to earn rewards for academic performance) and to put their heads down (which reduces the opportunity for rewarding interaction with others) for brief periods of time.

Another time-out procedure uses a good-behavior clock. Rewards—penny trinkets, candy—are earned by a child and by the class based on that child's behaving appropriately for a specified period of time. A clock runs whenever the child is paying attention, working, or behaving appropriately. The clock is stopped for a short period of time when the child is disruptive or off task. Studies have found dramatic decreases in hyperactive and disruptive behavior as a result of this method.

Most time-out programs set specific rules that must be fulfilled before the child can be released from time-out. Typically, these rules involve the child being quiet and cooperative for a specified period during time-out. In some cases extremely disruptive or hyperactive children may fail to comply with the typical procedure. They may refuse to go to time-out or escape from the time-out area before finishing their penalty period. To reduce problems in these cases, children may earn time off their penalty period for good behavior or for complying with the procedure (i.e., the length of original time-out is reduced). Alternatively, when a child refuses to follow the time-out rules, the length of the original time-out may be increased for each rule infraction. In another approach, the child may be removed from the class to serve the time-out elsewhere (e.g., in another class or in the principal's office). Failure to comply with time-out may also be responded to with a penalty or fine in the class token system. For instance, activities, privileges, or tokens may be lost for uncooperative behavior in time-out. One strategy that may be particularly effective for reducing uncooperativeness with time-out involves having the children stay after school to serve their time-out when they are not cooperative in following time-out rules during school hours. The use of this procedure, however, depends on having staff available to supervise after school.

There are cases when a child's problem behavior typically increases during time-out. This requires the teacher to intervene or restrain the child to prevent harm to the child, to others, or to property. Alternative procedures to time-out may be needed. Most schools have some guidelines for the types of punishment they permit. Parents may want to ask for copies of these so they can be familiar with what limits the school district may place (or not place!) on these methods.

School Suspension

Suspension from school (usually from one to three days) is sometimes used as punishment for severe behavior problems, but it should be used with much caution. Many children may find staying at home or full-day day care more enjoyable than being in school. Suspension is also undesirable when the parents do not have the management skills needed to enforce the suspension or are overly punitive or abusive.

How to Limit the Negative Effects of Punishment

Despite the overall effectiveness of punishment, some unpleasant side effects may occur if it is used improperly. These unwanted effects include the escalation of the problem behavior, the child's dislike of the teacher, or in rare cases the avoidance of school altogether. Drs. Susan and Daniel O'Leary from the State University of New York at Stony Brook offer several guidelines to reduce possible adverse side effects:

1. Punishment should be used sparingly. Excessive criticism or other forms of punishment may also make the classroom unpleasant or aversive. Frequent harsh punishment may even increase a child's defiance. This is especially likely in cases where a teacher mistakenly serves as an aggressive model—that is, the teacher's use of punishment teaches the child to be aggressive like the teacher.

2. When negative consequences are used, children should be taught and rewarded for alternative appropriate behaviors that are not compatible with the inappropriate ones. This practice will help by teaching the child appropriate skills as well as by decreasing the potential for the occurrence of other problem behaviors.

3. Punishment involving the removal of a reward or privilege is to be preferred to punishment involving the use of an aversive event, such as isolation. The use of physical punishment is often limited in schools for ethical and legal reasons.

Getting Positive Results to Last and Carry Over to Other School Situations

Despite the substantial success of behavioral methods in school, there is little evidence that the gains made by a child under these programs last once the programs are stopped. Also, the improvements that may occur in one setting where the programs are used, say reading class, often do not carry over to settings where the programs are not being used, say math class or recess. This can be very disappointing to both parent and teacher.

One current solution is to use management programs wherever the child's behavior is a problem, but this approach has practical limits. Most programs won't be easy to carry out at recess, for example. Instead, withdrawing the management methods gradually—by reducing the frequency of feedback (fading from daily to weekly rewards) and substituting more natural rewards such as praise and regular activities for token rewards—may increase their endurance. One study found that the abrupt removal of punishment, even when a powerful token program was in use, led to a dramatic deterioration in class behavior, but when punishment was removed gradually, high levels of paying attention and hard work were maintained.

One particularly effective way to fade out a management program involves changing the places in school where the programs are in effect on any given day. The child is never quite sure when or where the programs will be used and learns that the best bet in these circumstances is to keep behaving well.

Even though research continues on these problems, the difficulties have not been resolved. Specially arranged treatment programs for ADHD children simply may be required across most school settings. For now we know these must be kept in place for long periods of time over the course of the child's education to be helpful. This observation may seem discouraging, but given our view that ADHD is a fairly chronic developmentally handicapping condition, it is no surprise.

Having Classmates Help with Behavior Management

The disruptive behavior of ADHD children often prompts their peers to respond in ways that promote or maintain the problem behavior. On the one hand, classmates may reward clowning and silliness by an ADHD child with smiles and giggles. On the other hand, they may also retaliate against teasing or intrusiveness by the ADHD child. Either way, the ADHD child gets a bad reputation among peers. As discussed previously, using group-based reward programs may be effective in counteracting peer attention for misbehavior by an ADHD child. However, some studies show that classmates can also intervene directly to produce good behavior in their ADHD classmates.

One of the most powerful ways classmates can help is by being encouraged to ignore the ADHD child's disruptive and inappropriate behavior. Peers can also increase their classmates' appropriate behavior by giving the ADHD child praise and positive attention for it. We see this in action during sporting events, when team members cheer and congratulate each other for successful plays, and it can be extended to praising one another for being a good sport, getting a high grade on an exam (or accepting a low grade without a tantrum), contributing to a class discussion, or helping another student. Token programs, in which classmates monitor the ADHD child's behavior and give or take away tokens for good or bad behavior, can also be successful as long as they are supervised by a teacher.

Of course these classmates should usually be rewarded for their own efforts. Otherwise, what's in it for them? In some cases praise is sufficient, but the teacher can also use tangible rewards or a token program. Rewarding these children not only reinforces their efforts but also ensures that the program is carried out well.

The use of classmates as "behavior sheriffs" has practical advantages—it provides an alternative to the teacher's having to observe everyone all the time and may require less time than traditional teacher-mediated programs—as well as serve to improve the behavior of the "sheriffs" and encouraging carryover into other situations. However, programs carried out by classmates are successful only to the extent that these classmates have the ability and interest to learn the methods and to carry them out accurately. The teacher should train and supervise classmates carefully and should not let them get involved in the punishment aspects of any program.

Home-Based Reward Programs

In a home-based reward program, the teacher sends home an evaluation of the ADHD child's behavior in school that day, and the parents use it to give or take away rewards available at home. This method has been effective in modifying a wide range of problems with ADHD children at school. Because of its ease of application and the fact that it involves both the teacher(s) and parents, it is often one of the first interventions you should try.

The teacher's reports can consist of either a note or a more formal report card. We recommend the use of a behavior report card. The card should show the "target" behavior(s) that are to be the focus of the program listed on the left side. Across the top should be numbered columns that correspond to each class period at school. The teacher gives a number rating reflecting how well the child did for each of these behaviors for each class period. An example is shown in Figure 2. Teacher reports are typically sent home daily. In some cases notes are sent home only when a child has met certain goals for behavior or academic work that day. In other cases a note can be sent home on both "good" and "bad" days. As the child's behavior improves, the daily reports can be reduced to twice weekly, twice monthly, or even monthly, and finally phased out altogether.

A variety of home-based programs may be developed and tailored for your child. Some of the behaviors targeted for the program may include both social conduct (sharing, playing well with peers, follows rules) and academic performance (completed math or reading assignments). Targeting low academic performance (poor production of work) may be especially effective. Some such home-based programs have resulted in improvements in both academics and social conduct. Examples of behaviors to target include completion of all (or a specified portion) of the work, staying in an assigned seat, following teacher directions, and playing cooperatively with others. Negative behaviors (e.g., aggression, destruction, calling out) may also be included as target behaviors to be reduced by the program. In addition to targeting class performance, homework may be included. ADHD children often have difficulty remembering to bring home work assignments. They may also complete their homework but forget to return the completed work to school the next day. Each of these areas may be targeted in a note-home program.

We suggest that you target only four or five behaviors to work on. Start out by focusing on just a few behaviors you wish to change to help maximize your child's success in the program. When these behaviors are going well, you can add a few more. The daily ratings of each behavior may be global and subjective (e.g., "poor," "fair," "good"). However, it helps to make them more specific and objective (e.g., frequency of each behavior or the number of points earned or lost for each behavior). We recommend including at least one or two positive behaviors that the child is currently doing well with so that the child will be able to earn some points during the beginning of the program.

DAILY STUDENT RATING CARD

NAME _____ DATE _____

Please rate this child in each of the areas listed below as to how he performed in school today using ratings of 1 to 5.   1 = excellent, 2 = good, 3 = fair, 4 = poor, 5 = terrible or did not work.

AREA	CLASS PERIODS / SUBJECTS					
	1	2	3	4	5	6
participation						
class work						
handed in homework						
interaction with other children						
teacher's initials						

Place comments on back if needed:

FIGURE 2. A daily school report card for controlling ADHD behavior at school, used with a home-based token reward system. From L. J. Pfiffner and R. A. Barkley (1990), "Educational placement and classroom management." In R. A. Barkley, *Attention-deficit hyperactivity disorder: A handbook for diagnosis and treatment* (pp. 498–539). New York: Guilford Press. Copyright 1990 by The Guilford Press. Reprinted by permission.

Typically children are monitored throughout the school day. However, to be successful with frequent problem behaviors, you may want to have the child rated for only a portion of the school day at first. As the child's behavior improves, the ratings may be increased gradually to include more periods/subjects. In cases where children attend several different classes taught by different teachers, the program may involve some or all of the teachers depending on the need for intervention in each class. When more than one teacher is included in the program, a single report card may include space for all teachers to sign. Different report cards may be used for each class and organized in a notebook for children to carry between classes. Again, the card shown in Figure 2 can be helpful because it has columns that can be used to rate the child by the same teacher at the end of each subject or by different teachers if more than one is involved.

The success of the program depends on a clear, consistent method for translating the teacher's reports into consequences at home. Some programs involve rewards alone; others use both positive and negative consequences. Some studies suggest that a combination of positive and negative consequences may be most effective. One advantage of home-based programs is that a wide variety of consequences can be used—praise and positive attention as well as tangible rewards, both daily and weekly.

Overall, home-based reward programs may be even more effective when combined with classroom-based programs, which give the parents frequent feedback, remind parents when to reward a child's behavior, and forewarn parents when behavior is becoming a problem at school. Furthermore, the type and quality of rewards available in the home are usually far more extensive than those available in the classroom, a factor that may be critical with ADHD children who need more powerful rewards. Aside from these benefits, note-home programs generally require much less time and effort from your child's teacher than do classroom-based programs. As a result, teachers who have been unable to start a classroom management program may be far more likely to cooperate with a note-home program.

Despite the impressive success of note-home programs, the effectiveness of the program depends on accurate evaluation of the child's behavior by the teacher. It also hinges on the fair and consistent use of consequences at home. In some cases children may attempt to undercut the system by failing to bring home a report. They may forge a teacher's signature or fail to get certain teacher signatures. To discourage these practices, missing notes or signatures should be treated the same way as a "bad" report (e.g., child fails to earn points or is fined by losing privileges or points). The child may even be grounded for the day (no privileges) for not bringing the note home.

Some Examples of Note-Home Programs

The card shown in Figure 2 contains four areas of potential problems with ADHD children. Columns are provided for up to six different teachers to rate the child in these areas or for one teacher to rate the child many times across the school day. We have found that the more frequent the ratings the more effective is the feedback to the children and the more informative is the program to you. The teacher initials the bottom of the column after rating the child's performance during that class period to ensure against forgery. Where getting the correct homework assignment home is a problem for some ADHD children, the teacher can require the child to copy the homework for that class period on the back of the card before completing the ratings for that period. In this way the teacher merely checks the back of the card for accuracy of copying the assignment and then completes the ratings on the front of the card. For particularly negative ratings, we also encourage teachers to provide a brief explanation. The teachers rate the children using a five-point system (1 = excellent, 2 = good, 3 = fair, 4 = poor, and 5 = terrible or very poor).

The child takes a new card to school each day. These can be kept at school and a new card given out each morning, or you can provide the card as your child leaves for school, whichever is most likely to be done consistently. Upon returning home, you should immediately inspect the card, discuss the positive ratings first with your child, and then proceed to a neutral, businesslike (not angry!) discussion with your child about any negative marks and the reason for them. Your child should then be asked to formulate a plan for how to avoid getting the negative mark tomorrow. You are to remind your child of this plan the next morning before your child departs for school. You should then award your child points for each rating on the card and deduct points for each negative mark. For instance, a young elementary-aged child may receive five chips for a 1, three chips for a 2, and one chip for a 3 while being fined three chips for a 4 and five chips for a 5 on the card. For older children, the scale might be 25, 15, 5, − 15, and − 25 points, respectively, for marks 1 to 5 on the card. The chips or points are then added up, the fines subtracted, and the child may then spend what is left on privileges from the home reward menu.

Another note-home card program was developed for an aggressive ADHD child who was having problems with getting along with others during school recess periods each day. This card, shown in Figure 3, was to be completed by the teacher on recess duty during each recess period. It was then inspected by the class teacher and sent home for use in a home point system. The class teacher was also instructed to use a "think aloud, think ahead" procedure with the child just prior to the child's going out for recess.

As these cards illustrate, virtually any child behavior can be the target for treatment.

Training ADHD Children to Think Aloud, Think Ahead

Many treatment programs for ADHD children have used methods that teach the children to talk to themselves out loud, give themselves instructions on what they should be doing, and reward themselves verbally for how they did. These methods are often called *cognitive behavior modification, self-instruction,* or *self-control programs.*

One such program involves teaching children a set of self-directed instructions to follow when doing their work. Self-instructions include (1) having the children say out loud to themselves what the task or problem is they have been assigned to do; (2) saying what plan of attack or strategy they will use to approach the problem; (3) keeping their attention on the task; (4) describing their plan as they follow it through to completion; and (5) telling themselves how they think they have done. This may also include giving themselves a reward, such as a point or token, for getting the problem correct. In the case of an incorrect answer, the children are taught to say something encouraging to themselves, such as "Next time I'll do better if I slow down."

At first an adult trainer typically shows the child how to do the self-instruction while performing the work. The child then performs the same task while the

Name _____   Date _____

Please evaluate this child in the following areas of behavior during free or unstructured school time, especially during *recess*. Using a rating of 1 = excellent, 2 = good, 3 = fair, 4 = poor, please place a number beside each behavior listed below for each recess or free-time period this child is observed each day.

Free Time/Recess

	#1	#2	#3	#4
1. Keeps hands to self; does not push, shove, pinch, or touch others wrongly	—	—	—	—
2. Does not fight with other children (hitting, kicking, biting) or try to provoke them by tripping them, shoving them, or taking their things	—	—	—	—
3. Follows rules	—	—	—	—
4. Tries to get along well with other children	—	—	—	—

Other comments:

FIGURE 3. A daily shool report card for controlling aggressive behavior at recess, used with a home-based reward system. From L. T. Pfiffner and R. A. Barkley (1990), "Educational placement and classroom management." In R. A. Barkley, *Attention-deficit hyperactivity disorder: A handbook for diagnosis and treatment* (pp. 498–539). New York: Guilford Press. Copyright 1990 by The Guilford Press. Reprinted by permission.

trainer provides the instructions. Next the child performs the task while giving himself the instructions aloud. This talking aloud is then faded to silent speech (or whispering). Rewards are typically provided to the child for following the procedure as well as for selecting the correct solutions. Children can use these methods for virtually any type of schoolwork or even on their homework.

Despite the apparent promise of these methods for ADHD children who are obviously impaired in self-control, many research studies have failed to show positive results. In general, the results of these programs do not seem to last once the program is stopped. The results also do not carry over into other classes, places, or situations where the methods are not being taught or where the children are not rewarded for their use.

For these reasons, we strongly recommend that this approach never be the only program used, that it not be the principal approach in the child's classroom, and that it be used in the classroom by the teacher, not taught by someone else outside the classroom, where it is not likely to carry over back into the classroom.

Managing Academic Problems with ADHD Adolescents

All of the recommendations made so far apply as much to adolescents with ADHD as to younger children. However, the changes that take place in high school—the greater number of teachers involved with the student, the shorter class periods, the increased emphasis on individual student responsibility, and the frequent changes in class schedules from day to day—are likely to result in a dramatic drop in educational performance in many ADHD children entering high school. This is compounded by the fact that there is little or no accountability of teachers for a particular student at this level of education. Only when the misbehavior of the teen becomes sufficiently serious to attract attention or academic deficiencies are grossly apparent will someone take notice. Usually the response of the school is punitive rather than constructive.

> "You say that my son needs more structure and supervision
> in high school, but the principal says this is just coddling him,
> that if we keep doing this he will never learn self-discipline or
> to manage himself. She says it is time for him to sink or swim,
> to experience the natural consequences of his mistakes
> and disorganization. Is that true?"

It is very easy for average ADHD adolescents to fall through the cracks at this stage unless they have been involved with the special educational system before entering high school. Those that have will have been "flagged" as in need of continuing special attention. But the others will likely be viewed merely as lazy and irresponsible. It is at this age level that educational performance becomes the most common reason ADHD adolescents are referred for professional help.

> "Our son won't go for the extra help from his teachers.
> He says he doesn't need it, that he can bring up his grades on his own.
> He refuses the medication you recommended, too. What can we do?"

Dealing with large schools at this age level can be frustrating for parent and ADHD teenager alike. Even the most interested teacher may have difficulties mustering sufficient motivation among her colleagues to be of help and keep the ADHD adolescent out of trouble at school. Here are a few ideas that may help:

1. If your teenager is failing or doing poorly and has never had special education, immediately request a special education evaluation if not done before or not within the past three years. Federal law (Individuals with Disabilities Education Act) requires a reevaluation every three years that a child is in special educa-

tion. Special educational services will not be forthcoming until this evaluation is completed, and this can take up to 90 days or longer in some districts. The sooner it is initiated, the better.

2. ADHD adolescents usually require counseling about the nature of their disability. Although many have already been told that they are "hyperactive" or have ADHD, a lot of them have not come to accept that they actually have a disability. Counseling can help these teenagers learn to accept their limitations and find ways to prevent their disability from creating significant problems. Such counseling is difficult, requiring a sensitivity to adolescents' desire to be independent and to form their own opinions of themselves and their world. It often takes more than a single session to succeed, but patience and persistence can pay off. Find a counselor or professional who knows about ADHD and ask him or her to spend a few sessions counseling your teen about the disorder. Your teen is more likely to listen to the professional than to you.

3. Counsel the adolescent on the advantages of returning to medication if it has been used successfully in the past. Medication can improve school performance and help the teen obtain those special privileges at home that may be granted as a result of such improved performance (use of the car, more privileges or allowance, etc.). Adolescents who are concerned about others learning that they are on medication should be reassured that only they, their parents, and the physician will be aware of this. Be prepared for resistance to the idea of medication and consider setting up a behavior contract by which the teen earns certain rewards (money, extra free time, etc.) for taking the medication daily.

4. Schedule a team meeting at the beginning of each academic year, and more often as needed, at the teenager's school. This meeting should be attended by the teachers, school psychologist, guidance counselor, principal, parents, *and ADHD adolescent*. Take with you a handout describing ADHD to give to each participant. If you think it is helpful, ask a professional to go along with you to give advice. Briefly review the nature of the adolescent's disorder and the need for close teamwork among the school, parents, and teen if the teen's academic performance is to be improved. Get the teachers to describe the current strengths and problems of the teen in their classes and make suggestions as to how they think they can help with the problem. Some of these might include being available after school a few days each week for extra assistance, reducing the length of written homework assignments, allowing the teen to provide oral means of demonstrating that knowledge has been acquired rather than relying on just written, timed test grades, and developing a subtle reminder system to alert the teen when he or she is not paying attention in class without drawing the whole class's attention to the fact.

At this conference the teen then publicly commits to what he or she will strive to do to improve school performance. The team should agree to meet again in one month to evaluate the success of the plans and troubleshoot any problem areas. Future meetings may need to be scheduled depending on the success of the program to date. Meetings should be scheduled at least twice a year to monitor progress and keep the school attentive to the needs of this teen. The adolescent always attends these meetings.

5. Introduce a daily home–school report card as described earlier. These are often more critical for teens than any other age group to provide daily feedback. Also, a home point system must be set up that includes a variety of desired privileges that the teen can purchase with the points earned at school. Points can also be set aside in a savings book to work toward longer-term rewards. Remember, however, that it is the daily, short-term privileges and not these longer-term rewards that give the program its motivational power. So don't overweight the reward menu with long-term rewards.

Once the adolescent is able to go for three weeks or so with no 4s or 5s (negative ratings) on the card, the card is cut back to once or twice a week. After a month of satisfactory ratings, the card can either be faded out or reduced to a monthly rating. The adolescent is then told that if word is received that grades are slipping, the card system will be reinstated.

6. Get the school to provide a second set of books to you, even it means putting up a small deposit, so that homework can be done even if the teen leaves the book at school. These books can also be helpful to any tutor you've hired.

7. Get one of the teen's teachers, homeroom teacher, guidance counselor, or even a learning disabilities teacher to serve as the "case manager." This person's role is to meet briefly with the teen three times a day for just a few minutes to help keep him or her organized. The teen can stop at this person's office at the start of school. At this time the manager checks to see that the teen has all the homework and books needed for the morning's classes. At lunch the teen checks in again with this manager to see if the teen has copied all necessary assignments from the morning classes, to help the teen select the books needed for the afternoon classes, and then to see that the student has the assignments that are to be turned in that day for these afternoon classes. At the end of school the teen checks in again with the manager to see that he or she has all assignments and books needed for homework. Each visit takes no more than three to five minutes, but, interspersed as they are throughout the school day, these visits can be of great assistance to organizing the teen's schoolwork.

8. If you feel you can't help with homework, consider a private tutor or have your teenager attend any extra help periods that the school requires the teachers to hold at the end of the school day. The student can go to one extra help period per week for each course.

9. Set up a special time each week to do something alone with your teen that is mutually pleasurable. This provides opportunities for parent–teen interactions that are not work oriented, school related, or fraught with the tensions that work-oriented activities can often bring with ADHD teens. These outings can contribute to keeping your relationship with your teen positive. They can also counterbalance the conflicts that school performance demands frequently bring to families. You'll find more on making sure you don't stress schoolwork at the expense of your relationship with your child in the next chapter.

CHAPTER 17

Keeping School Performance in Perspective

Y ou may recall the story of Steve's mother (in the Introduction), who had come to our clinic because she was having trouble with her eight-year-old son. When I asked her (as I usually do) what had brought her to us, she threw me for a loop when she said, simply, "Help me, I'm losing my child." It was a plea, and an interview, that I have never forgotten, for it summed up in a few words the excruciating pain felt by so many parents of children with ADHD.

In the rest of my interview with her I learned that the problem with her son had begun, innocently enough, with a teacher conference about her son's poor classwork, lack of attentiveness, and erratically completed homework early in first grade. It was further nurtured by her natural desire to help her son do better in school. And her mission at that level had been accomplished very well indeed. But there was no celebrating of this achievement by her. To her the schoolwork that had seemed so important and was now being done well seemed a hollow victory. Something more primal was being lost in the process here that made academic success rather paltry by comparison.

As a result of that first conference, Steve's mother began to set aside virtually all of her other activities and responsibilities after school and in the early evening to spend with Steve on schoolwork. Initially Steve enjoyed the time with his mother, and initially she thought that helping her son complete his unfinished classwork and do his homework would take only about an hour a day. But of course his carelessness and inattention complicated matters, and soon it was not

Portions of this chapter are adapted from the speech "Help Me, I'm Losing My Child" that I gave as keynote speaker at the national convention of Children with ADD (CHADD) in Chicago on October 15, 1992. The complete transcript is available on tape from CHADD, 305-587-3700.

uncommon for them to be spending several fitful hours on this work every day.

Despite some teaching experience she had to support her efforts, Steve's mother quickly became frustrated, angry, and bitter in the face of her son's failure to respond to her "help." From being upbeat, cajoling, prodding, and joking she moved to threatening to withdraw privileges. He might work then, sometimes with tears faintly visible in his eyes; other times angry and resentful at having to do so much schoolwork. Later in the year he also began to challenge her about the nature of assignments, even though the goal was clear.

In time, sporadically at first, Steve began to avoid his mother after school, sometimes lying to her about what work he had to do. When the work was finished, he would retreat from her quickly to his room or the family room. Gradually the arguments and conflicts began to permeate other daily activities that involved the two of them, like bedtime and mealtimes.

Over the year Steve's grades improved, and he finished first grade with an above average grade, to the delight of his mother. The sarcasm and withdrawal that had grown over the school year abated during the summer, though Steve went to great lengths to avoid the weekly tutoring sessions his mother imposed. When second grade began, bringing a return to the rigors of the first-grade after-school schedule, Steve began to dig in his heels in earnest. Now it was his father, who had only nominal responsibility for schoolwork, he sought out for company at home. When Steve's mother tried to hug or kiss him good night, he merely stiffened at her embrace, turned his cheek, and replied in a monotone, " 'Night, Mom," with little feeling. She was devastated. She would retreat to her bedroom to cry quietly or complain bitterly to her husband that while he still had a son she did not seem to have one anymore.

Once again Steve finished the school year with excellent grades. She set about tutoring him again that summer, but it was the worst summer of their life together.

Why was she losing Steve, she asked herself? Couldn't he see how hard she was working on his behalf? Didn't he realize how important school was to his future? Where was his sense of priorities?

This crisis ultimately led her to call me for an appointment at the beginning of third grade. She did not think she could go through another academic year following the same course. She was growing increasingly depressed. She envied her husband's closeness with Steve and resented his limited involvement with schoolwork, though she knew she had volunteered for this role. She tried to assuage her sadness with the consolation that Steve was succeeding at school. It didn't work. She now realized that something very precious was being taken from her, probably in part by her own doing. She was no longer sure she wanted to pay the price she was being asked to pay for creating her son's academic success.

My interview with Steve only affirmed what his mother had already sensed: He was consciously avoiding her, in a sense really letting go of her. All his mother thought of, he said in essence, was school and how well he was doing and so forth. When asked if he was pleased by his report cards, he shrugged his shoulders. "So what?" he seemed to be saying, as if they were his mother's grades, not his. The bitterness and anger were almost palpable, but I also detected a forlorn-ness like his mother's. He, too, appeared to realize at some, not fully conscious, level that something precious was being taken from him.

Steve's mother and I both knew, and his father agreed once we brought him into our meetings, that the job before us was difficult. What textbook tells you how to repair a damaged parent–child bond? What trite little management technique or trapper notebook system could reorganize this situation? What medicine corrects that underlying substrate so absolutely crucial to a parent's and a child's life with each other?

From here these parents and I proceeded not as doctor and patient but as a team searching for possible solutions to a problem for which none of us were well prepared. What we learned to do is explained later in this chapter. Along the way, however, we all learned several major lessons in family life:

Lesson 1

A parent's relationship with a child is a sacred bond and trust and ultimately must be appreciated by both parents and teachers as having a higher priority to and serving as a fundamental underpinning of any academic priority. Consciously acknowledge its existence. Give it full respect. And don't trample it with unnecessary or excessive stress such as the pressures of unfinished schoolwork.

Lesson 2

The failure to cultivate and sustain this relationship can have devastating emotional consequences for both parties.

Lesson 3

School staff often may be too quick to let parents take over academically related responsibilities to the detriment of family life and the parent–child relationship. When homework is assigned to an elementary-age child, in all honesty, it is assigned to that child's family, particularly to a parent working with that child, not to the child alone. Thus assigning homework should be viewed as a delicate balance to be negotiated between the need to further the child's education and the need of that child to have a well-rounded and fulfilling relationship with parents apart from schoolwork.

Furthermore, most of us as parents are lousy tutors and are mediocre in simply supervising homework. Late in the day we, like our children, are tired, sometimes irritable and impatient—we simply want to get the homework done at all costs. Few of us even think of the impact of unfinished classwork and excessive homework on family life. Fewer still choose to raise it with a teacher as a reason for limiting such assignments.

Lesson 4

Even without confrontations over schoolwork you may not be nurturing a relationship with your child or preventing harm being done to it. Your child may be filling this time with TV, Nintendo, or time away from home, and you may be permitting this to happen. Your relationship with your child does not sustain itself by its own momentum; it must be actively encouraged and fueled by the ongoing investment of love, intimacy, contact, attention, respect, and acceptance by a parent toward a child.

Lesson 5

The natural, gradual individuation of our children from us need not be accompanied by a loss of our emotional bond to them. We can, however, lose this bond or relationship prematurely by overemphasizing one priority of parenting to the near exclusion of all others. Schoolwork, while it is critical among the developmental tasks a child must master, is not singularly so.

Lesson 6

As this case will show, if damage to a parent–child relationship has begun to occur because of an excessive emphasis on schoolwork, it is not irreparable, at least not if resuscitated within the first few years of the discovery of this destructive process. Probably such damage can be partially reversed even years later. But it will not happen on its own.

Our first step in trying to repair the bond between Steve and his mother was to identify what parents' priorities should be in raising a healthy, well-rounded, well-adjusted child so we could see which areas were being sacrificed to the priority of academic achievement. This is the list we came up with:

1. The active promotion of the physical survival and well-being of the family unit and its members through the provision of adequate food and shelter to sustain life and the provision of safety to its members.
2. The instilling of a sense of family and membership within it as a needed, loved, valued, respected, and responsible participant in its successful functioning. As Craig Knippenberg said so well in a column for the *ADD Vance* newsletter several years ago, there are two things we as parents give our children: one is roots and the other wings.
3. Providing the foundation for the child's moral development. This means making a commitment to the preparation of children to be socialized to enter society and benefit from the wisdom of its members.
4. The instruction in and development of interpersonal skills that lead to adaptive and successful social transactions and acceptance. Learning to wait, take turns, share, listen to, praise, forgive, problem-solve, and cooperate with their

peers are just a few of the skills that parents must take time to teach their children apart from the daily demands of school homework. This area can be a major problem for families of many ADHD children given the social interaction problems such children are likely to have. Evidence for the importance of this domain of children's development can be found just by looking at the pain many parents experience vicariously for their ADHD children when they have no friends and have never received an invitation to a birthday party.

5. The instruction of our children in a sense of community and our obligations to it as a member of a larger society. Whether we depend on formal organizations like scouting or schools to assist us, we as parents carry the major responsibility for introducing our children to and eventually sponsoring our children into this larger community.

6. The proper development of our children's physical and mental health and well-being—not just diet, exercise, hygiene, and the like but also the acquisition of self-help and adaptive skills to permit the children to assume self-sufficiency. Moreover, this means seeing that there is adequate time for and attention to the pursuit of happiness and self-satisfaction for the child through leisure, recreation, hobbies, and informal sports. Sometimes we forget that children need a break too.

7. Instilling a sense of belonging to a larger humanity, of our obligations to it, and of being a member of a finite planet of progressively diminishing resources. How we introduce our children to the multitude of ethnic, religious, and cultural groups in our world affects how well they will be integrated into a larger society.

Do you still think doing unfinished classwork is a high priority? Then think about the pictures in your family photo album or your collection of home videos of your children. Are any of them of you and your child doing schoolwork together? Probably not. Why not? Think about it.

Once Steve and his family—remarkably, without effort—articulated these priorities, the importance of academic work began to shrink in relative significance. Ultimately Steve's parents agreed that excellent grades, while laudable, were not to be mandatory; average ones would do just fine.

But that left the problem of the extensive unfinished schoolwork and homework. In a meeting with the teacher, we came to agreement that Steve's inability to finish classwork was itself a symptom of a larger problem *in that classroom*, not a problem in the home. If the problem was to be truly solved, the solution would have to occur *in that classroom*. This led us to the types of modifications of classwork typically made for ADHD children and discussed in Chapters 15 and 16. Similar compromises were made on homework.

The next step was to divest Steve's mother of much of the burden of schoolwork by having his father take equal turns at this task and to shift her relationship with her son away from the solely academic. We began scheduling recreational outings at which discussing schoolwork was forbidden and encouraged her to give nondirective attention to Steve with positive feedback but never feigned, excessive praise.

Things did not change quickly. Steve seemed naturally suspicious of the changes we were attempting to make. Even so, as the changes became the routine, the edginess, sarcasm, and oppositionality toward his mother began to subside. He even began asking to go places with her again and seemed faintly pleased by her presence at his scouting and sports events. Within a few months his mother reported that she sensed a reestablishment of her old relationship but that its closeness was not yet where it had once been. Still, she was hopeful, as was I. Steve's grades dropped somewhat, to Cs with occasional Bs, but his mother felt this was acceptable while they worked on their home relationship. When last I met this family, Steve and his mother were getting along well, and she felt their relationship was pretty much back to normal. The affection they naturally had felt for each other returned, and they were striving to keep academic work in perspective relative to the other areas of family life and parent–child relations of equal importance. They seemed to have accepted Steve's ADHD as a disability and adjusted their expectations of academic success accordingly, realizing that average ADHD students can, nevertheless, be well-rounded, morally upright, and just plain terrific apart from their class standing.

And so, as you pursue the academic achievement that your child can aspire to, do not lose sight of the other, equally compelling priorities of raising children. Do not sacrifice your parent-child relationships and emotional bonds on the altar of academic performance. If the academic wolf comes calling at your door, which it most certainly will, greet it and accord it its just due, but by all means do not relinquish your children to it.

PART IV

Medications for ADHD

CHAPTER 18

The Stimulants

with George J. DuPaul, Ph.D., and Anthony Costello, M.D.

Medication is probably the most widely publicized, most hotly debated treatment for ADHD. As a whole, the hundreds of studies conducted indicate that stimulants, antidepressants, and clonidine (a drug used to treat high blood pressure in many adults) can be of great help to those with ADHD. The stimulants, the drugs most commonly used, have been shown to be effective in improving behavior, academic work, and social adjustment in anywhere from 50 to 95% of children with ADHD. How well your child responds may, however, depend on the presence of other problems, and the truth is that medication does not help everyone. For that reason—and because medication is no exception to the rule that misinformation about ADHD abounds—you should gather as much background knowledge as you can before agreeing to a trial of medication for your ADHD child. This chapter gives the most up-to-date information available on the stimulant medications; the antidepressants and clonidine are discussed in Chapter 19.

As a supplement to this chapter, one source you can turn to is the *Physicians' Desk Reference* (*PDR*) available at most public libraries. This reference book includes information on all commercially available drugs—what the drugs are most useful for treating (indications), when they should not be used (contraindications), and the unwanted reactions (side effects) of the medications. Although the *PDR* is updated annually, it does not usually keep pace with the latest findings from drug research, especially with respect to the main effects and side effects of the drugs. It also will not tell you how likely it is that your child will experience side effects; it merely lists all side effects that have been reported. This can mislead you to think that all these negative effects are common, which is not the case.

The best way to use the *PDR* is as an introductory reference. Don't believe that everything it tells you may be a problem will be so with your child.

A better source of information is your family doctor or pediatrician—as long as he or she has kept up to date by reading the medical journals reporting on such research. Ask your doctor how familiar he or she is with this class of medicines and how often the doctor prescribes them for children with ADHD. (Also ask the questions in the sidebar before agreeing to a trial of medication for your child.) Request a copy of any fact sheets the doctor may dispense to parents.

Two other sources may also help you learn what you want to know about medications: *Practitioners Guide to Psychoactive Drugs for Children and Adolescents* by Drs. John Werry and Michael Aman, though written for professionals and therefore sometimes a difficult read for laypeople, is worth tackling because it is very current on the use of psychiatric drugs for children. The first issue (spring 1990) of the *Journal of Child and Adolescent Psychopharmacology* (New York: Mary Ann Liebert Publishers) contains brief reviews of each type of psychiatric medication used with children and how it should be used, and the summer 1992 issue contains more readable fact sheets for parents on the same medications. Most medical school libraries will probably have this journal.

What to Ask Your Physician about Medication

If your doctor recommends a trial on any medication for treatment of your child's ADHD, ask at least the following questions, many of which are answered in this chapter:

1. What are the effects and side effects, both short-term and long-term, of this particular medication?
2. What doses will be used, and by what schedule should they be given?
3. How often should you see my child for reevaluation while he or she is taking this medication?
4. When should the medicine be stopped briefly to see if it is still required for treatment of ADHD?
5. Are there foods, beverages, or other substances my child should not consume while taking this medication because they will interfere with its effects in the body?
6. Will you be in contact with the school periodically to determine how my child is responding to the medication in that environment, or am I expected to do that?
7. If the child accidentally takes an overdose of the medication, what procedures should I follow?
8. Do you have a fact sheet about the medication that I can have to read?

What *Not* to Believe

*"Isn't Ritalin a dangerous drug? I've heard a lot
of bad stories about this drug. Isn't it addictive?
Won't it make my son more likely to take drugs later?"*

Before you read on about how the stimulants work and what they may be able to do for your child, let's clear up a few misconceptions about these drugs:

Myth 1: Stimulant Drugs Are Dangerous and Should Not Be Taken by Any Child. During the 1980s an inaccurate and, regrettably, successful media propaganda campaign against the use of stimulants, particularly Ritalin (methylphenidate), with children was waged by a fringe religious group, causing a dramatic decline in the prescribing of this medication in 1987–1989. Although the trend seems to have reversed since 1990, the use of stimulants with ADHD children continues to be controversial in the public's mind. Unfounded fear of these drugs is unfortunately perpetuated by some physicians' requirement that parents sign a consent form indicating that they have been informed about the medicines and their side effects and have agreed to have their child placed on one of them for treatment of the child's ADHD. *If your doctor asks you to sign such a form, don't assume it means the drugs are dangerous.* These forms arose only in response to the highly publicized threats of malpractice suits by the religious sect mentioned above, and some doctors still feel the need to protect themselves this way. Up-to-date information on possible side effects is given later in this chapter. If you are asked to sign a consent form, read it carefully since it will contain information about the medicine, but do not let it make you afraid of the stimulant medicines or of signing the form.

Myth 2: Stimulants Just Cover Up ''the Real Problem'' and Do Not Deal Directly with the Root Causes of the Child's ADHD. Many parents come to us with this concern, but it is simply untrue. The stimulants deal directly with the part of the brain that is underactive and gives rise to the outward symptoms of ADHD, as explained later in this chapter. In this sense, the stimulants are no different from using insulin for a child with diabetes. Unfortunately, like insulin, stimulants have only a temporary effect, which leads some people to believe they're masking the problem rather than helping it. Like a diabetic who needs insulin, your child may have to take stimulant medicine daily for a long time, but these drugs *are* a way of tackling the problem directly. *Stimulants are the only treatment to date that normalizes the inattentive, impulsive, and restless behavior in ADHD children.*

Myth 3: Stimulants Make Children ''High'' as Other Drugs Do and Are Addictive. You may have heard that adults who take stimulants often have a sense of elevated mood, euphoria, or excessive well-being. While this does happen, it is not common, and in children it is rare. Some children do describe feeling "funny," "different," or dizzy. Others actually become a little bland in their mood, and a few even report feelings of sadness. These mood changes occur a few hours after the medicine is taken and occur more often among children treated with higher doses. In most children these changes are very minor.

Parents are often also quite concerned about the risk of addiction to stimulants and about an increased risk of abusing other drugs when the children become teenagers. There are no reported cases of addiction or serious drug dependence to date with these medications, and the several studies that have examined whether children on these drugs are more likely to abuse other substances as teenagers than those not taking them suggest that they are not.

Myth 4: Stimulant Medications Stunt Children's Growth, and Their Use Is Strictly Limited by Age. Some studies in the early 1970s seemed to suggest that children taking these medicines might be stunted in their height and weight gain. More recent and better studies have shown that this is not as much of a problem as was once thought. Your child's eventual adult height or skeletal size is not going to be affected by taking the medicine, and the effects on your child's weight are also likely to be minimal, resulting in a loss of one or two pounds during the initial year of treatment. Any weight lost should return by the second or later years of treatment. Keep in mind that children respond very differently to these medicines, some experiencing no weight change and others losing more than just a few pounds. Your child should be followed by your physician to make sure that this weight loss is not serious.

Myth 5: Stimulants Can Be Used Only by Young Children. Contrary to what you may have heard, stimulant medicines can be used throughout the life of the person with ADHD, not just during childhood. There was widespread concern in earlier decades that the stimulant medications could not be used once puberty started because they would no longer be effective. This was a fallacy, and we are now seeing a dramatic increase in the prescribing of these medications for teenagers having ADHD. We are also witnessing an increase in the use of these drugs with adults who have ADHD.

How the Stimulants Work

The stimulants are so named because of their ability to increase the level of activity or arousal of the brain. Then why don't they make people more hyperactive? Because it seems that the area of the brain they activate is responsible for inhibiting behavior and maintaining effort or attention to things. In a way, they increase the braking power of the brain over behavior. That seems to be why they are so helpful for those with ADHD.

The three most commonly recommended stimulants for ADHD are the drugs d-amphetamine (Dexedrine), methylphenidate (Ritalin), and pemoline (Cylert).

Because caffeine (found in coffee, tea, soft drinks, and other foods) is a stimulant, some parents ask whether this drug or the beverages containing it will help their children with ADHD. Although there were some early reports in the popular press in the 1970s that caffeine might be useful, the scientific studies done on this subject have not borne this out. Therefore, we recommend that you consider only the three stimulant drugs just listed.

The stimulants work primarily by increasing the action of certain chemicals that occur naturally in the brain. The way the brain handles information is based on how these chemicals are produced in the brain cells (neurons). Although we don't know exactly which chemicals are influenced by the stimulants, we do know that two of them are dopamine and norepinephrine, both of which occur naturally throughout the brain but are concentrated very heavily in the frontal region, which we believe may be the site of the problem in ADHD (see Chapter 3). By increasing how much of these chemicals is available in the brain, the stimulants increase the action of these brain cells, which seem to be those most responsible for inhibiting our behavior and helping us stick to something we are doing.

Therefore it's not surprising that the hundreds of studies conducted on how these drugs change the behavior and learning of ADHD children show that between 70 and 90% of children treated with one of the stimulants improve in their behavior. Still, that leaves as many as 10 to 30% who show no positive response, some whose behavior is even made worse. So you can't assume that your child will necessarily benefit from medication, and we all must recognize that medication is no panacea for the problems that come with ADHD. There are some cases in which medication alone is enough or is the only practical way to address the concerns you and the teachers have about your child's ADHD. For most cases, though, the greatest benefit of stimulant therapy seems to be its ability to increase the effectiveness of psychological and educational treatments. Consequently, we normally recommend that when medication is indicated it be used as part of a combination of treatments, not as the sole form of therapy.

What Do the Drugs Do for Behavior and Emotions?

Unquestionably the stimulants produce positive effects on sustained attention and persistence of effort to work. The medicines also reduce restlessness and gross motor activity. In many cases the child's attention to assigned classwork is so greatly improved that his or her behavior appears normal. Most children taking the medicine are far less impulsive and have fewer problems with aggression, noisiness, noncompliance, and disruptiveness—you can see why these medicines are so often recommended for children with ADHD.

How Do the Drugs Change Learning and Academic Performance?

Numerous studies have been conducted on the effects of stimulants on children's intellect, memory, attention, and learning. They show that the stimulant medicines are very likely to improve a child's attention, impulse control, fine-motor coordination, and reaction time. Some children even show improvements in their short-term memory. When ADHD children have to do learning tasks, the medicine seems to help them perform more efficiently and in a more organized manner. No medicine can actually improve intelligence, but the stimulants increase your child's ability to show what he or she has already learned. In general, the drugs produce their greatest influence in situations that require children to restrict their behavior and concentrate on assigned tasks—situations like school.

You may have heard that once children stop taking the stimulants they will not be able to remember as easily what they learned while on it. Scientific studies of this problem have found it uncommon and too minor to be noticeable when it does occur.

Stimulant medications are not likely to improve your child's scores on school achievement tests, which measure the grade level or difficulty of the material children have learned. The medicines do, however, result in substantial increases in the amount of work a child is able to produce and in some cases increase the accuracy of the work as well.

Do the Medicines Change Social Behavior?

Yes. Treatment with stimulant medication has been found to reduce the intensity and improve the quality of social interactions between children with ADHD and their parents, teachers, and peers. Stimulants increase the children's ability to comply with a parent's commands and to maintain that compliance over time. The medicines also reduce behavior that competes with getting work done, such as inattention, distraction, and restlessness. In turn, parents and teachers respond by reducing their level of commands and the degree of supervision over the children.

They may also increase their praise and positive reactions to the children. There has been some concern among professionals that these medicines may reduce a child's interest in socializing with others. Recent studies have not shown this to be a problem, but it may be possible if the child is taking a very high dose.

The degree of improvement differs among children, and each should be expected to have a unique response. We've seen no overall difference between boys and girls. We do expect to see greater improvement with higher doses, but your child's physician will have to try your child on several different doses before he or she discovers which one is best and may also have to try more than one drug.

How Long Do the Effects of the Drugs Last?

Stimulants are almost always given orally when used for ADHD. They are swiftly absorbed into the bloodstream and cross into the brain quickly and easily. They are also eliminated from the body within 24 hours. This means you can rest assured that if your child has an undesirable reaction it will usually last only a few hours to a day. But it also means your child must take this medication several times a day, every day.

The medicines reach their peak in improving behavior within one to three hours and may control behavior for three to six hours, but each child reacts somewhat differently, and each drug acts differently. Some changes in behavior are noticeable within 30 to 60 minutes after taking the medicine, again depending on which drug is being taken.

Both Ritalin and Dexedrine come in sustained-release preparations that usually begin to take effect after one to two hours, reach their peak influence after three to five hours, and may still have an effect after eight or more hours. However, these sustained-release forms may not be as powerful in their control over behavior, and again, all children react differently.

Cylert, or pemoline, works a little differently. It may start to have an effect after one to two hours, reach its peak in about two to four hours, and last for seven to nine hours or longer, but it does seem to build up in the body and may take a few days to a week before exerting its full effect.

Parents often ask whether children develop a tolerance to stimulants and whether they will need to have regular blood tests to monitor the amount of the drug in their bloodstream. Though some physicians have reported that a few children in their practice seemed to develop some tolerance (loss of effect) over a long period of use, research studies have not been able to document such an effect. Nor should the blood tests be of concern. The amount of drug in the bloodstream does not seem to be related to how well it works to control behavior, so there is no need for such tests.

The Side Effects

There are many side effects that children can experience when taking these medicines, but the vast majority are minor. Again, keep in mind that if any of these are bothersome enough to warrant stopping the medication, they will likely go away once the medicine "washes out" of the child's body—within 24 hours. Most of these side effects are clearly related to the dose of medicine the child is taking: Higher doses produce more side effects. It has been estimated, however, that 1 to 3% of children with ADHD cannot tolerate *any* dose of *any* stimulant medication.

It's impossible to predict whether your child will have any of the side effects discussed here, but we do have some revealing test findings: Over half of ADHD children we tested in our clinic showed decreased appetite, insomnia, anxiousness, irritability, or proneness to crying. *However, many of these side effects (especially those associated with mood) were present when the children took a fake pill (called a placebo). This means that these side effects may represent problems that are associated with ADHD rather than with the medicine.* In most cases the actual side effects are quite mild. Stomachaches and headaches were reported in about a third of the children, but these were also mild.

Decreased Appetite

All of the stimulants seem to reduce a child's appetite to some degree—temporarily and mainly in the late morning or early afternoon, which explains why over half of all children on these drugs may eat little of their lunch while on the medicine. For many children their appetite comes back (sometimes with a vengeance!) by evening. That is why you should make sure that a child who is on this medicine has a chance to eat an adequate amount of calories each day to grow well.

Increased Heart Rate and Blood Pressure

Your physician may find that your child's heart rate and blood pressure increase a little while taking these medicines. These changes are minor and do not place most ADHD children at any risk. However, if your child is one of the rare children who has high blood pressure already, you should make sure your doctor takes this into consideration. Cylert may be less likely to produce these effects on heart rate and blood pressure.

Increased Brain Electrical Activity

You wouldn't know about this directly unless your child were to take an EEG (electroencephalogram) for some reason, but many studies have found that brain electrical activity increases while a child is on these medicines. You will notice this indirectly because your child's behavior will be improving in conjunction with these changes in brain activity, as discussed earlier.

Insomnia

Nearly half of all children placed on medication may notice that it is harder to fall asleep at bedtime after taking these medicines during the day. Most children fall asleep within an hour or so after their typical bedtime. If not, and this is a problem for your child, tell your physician so that he or she can lower the dose.

Nervous Tics

One side effect that you should be concerned about is the possibility of nervous tics—abrupt twitches of small muscle groups around the face or, less likely, in other parts of the body. Blinking, squinting, or making faces are just some of the tics that can be seen. Other tics are vocal—abrupt noises such as repeated sniffing, throat clearing, or sharp, loud utterances. In its extreme form the combination of multiple body tics with these vocal noises is called *Tourette syndrome*. You should know that over 10% of normal children will show some sort of tic or nervous mannerism during childhood, so simple or occasional tics are nothing to worry about. Such tics in ADHD children are likely to be made worse by the medicine in over half of the cases, though the tics return to their normal level within a week or so after stopping the medicine. In other cases the tics may actually get better on medication.

We have noticed that up to 15% of children placed on stimulants may develop such simple tics or nervous mannerisms even if they did not have them previously. Again, withdrawing the medicine usually corrects the problem in a week or so. A few children have developed the full Tourette's syndrome, though it is not clear that the medicine actually caused the disorder. It may have worsened it or hastened its appearance in a child who was prone to get the disorder in the first place.

Physicians should ask whether a child with ADHD has a personal or family history of tics or Tourette's syndrome before trying a stimulant drug with that child. If so, we recommend that the child start out on a very low dose of medicine or not take the medicine at all until more is known about how such children may react to these drugs. When these medications are used and tics develop, the treatment should be stopped immediately. The tics will usually subside within 7 to 10 days. Treatment can then be resumed at a lower dose if the child's behavioral adjustment has deteriorated dramatically. If the tics return even at the lower dose, trying an alternative medication, such as an antidepressant, may be successful. Failing this, parents should be warned not to have their children treated with stimulants in the future without alerting the treating physician to this history of tic reactions to the stimulant medicines.

Side Effects of Particular Drugs

Each stimulant medication may produce unique side effects. A few children may develop allergic skin rashes after a few weeks or more of treatment with Cylert. Stopping the drug seems to eliminate the rash. The child may be able to return to the medication with no recurrence of the rash. Pemoline may produce a liver ailment called *chemical hepatitis* in rare cases (about 3%), and it may not always be reversible. This is why any child taking Cylert should have blood tests of liver functioning every three to six months.

Temporary Psychosis

All of the medications can produce temporary symptoms of psychosis (thought disorganization, rapid speech, skin hallucinations, extreme anxiety, supersensitivity to noises, etc.) at very high doses. In very rare cases this can happen at low doses. Such reactions occur in fewer than 1% of the cases and last only until the dose wears off.

Should Your Child Receive Stimulants?

You and your doctor will have to consider many factors in making this decision. You'll also have to remain alert to your child's reactions so you recognize quickly when a trial of medication has failed and should be ended. The stimulant medications are the most commonly used psychiatric drugs employed with children, especially where inattentive, hyperactive, or impulsive behavior is sufficiently severe to create problems with school or social adjustment. It has been estimated that between 600,000 and 1 million children annually, or between 1 and 2% of the school-age population, may be using stimulants for behavior management. Traditionally most of these children were between 5 and 12 years of age, but as we've mentioned, many of them are now older. So you can enter this decision-making process confident that we know more about this form of treatment for ADHD than any other.

Unfortunately, there is no foolproof way to predict who will do well on stimulant medication. So far the most helpful criterion we have is the degree of inattention and impulsiveness in the child. The more severe these symptoms are, the better a child is likely to respond to the medicine. We have also learned that the more anxious a child is, the less likely he or she will have a positive reaction to the medicine. Some studies have also found that the quality of the relationship between a parent and the child may predict the child's drug response: The better the mother–child relationship, the greater the response to medication. It may be that mothers who are more appreciative and rewarding of the behavior changes brought by the stimulants produce further gains in their children from the medicine.

Your doctor will also take into account the following factors:

1. The percentage of ADD children (those without hyperactivity) who respond well to the medication may be somewhat lower—55 to 65%—than that seen in ADHD children, and the magnitude of the response may not be as impressive, though on the plus side the necessary dose may be lower.

2. Stimulants may help ADHD children who are also mentally retarded only if the retardation is not too severe. In one study, children with mental ages greater than 4.5 years or IQs above 45 often had positive responses, whereas those with lower mental ages or IQs generally responded poorly.

3. ADHD children who have seizures may have more side effects (behavior problems) while on the stimulants than is seen in ADHD children who do not have epilepsy.

4. Children with pervasive developmental disorders (otherwise known as autism) usually do not respond well to the stimulant medicines. Some children with brain injuries from trauma may develop symptoms of ADHD to a degree that warrants a possible trial on stimulant drugs. These children may also respond well, but it is our experience that the probability of a good response is somewhat lower in this group of ADHD children.

As you have undoubtedly discerned by now, *a diagnosis of ADHD should not constitute a recommendation for automatic drug treatment.* If your doctor seems to be taking this approach, we suggest you find a new doctor. The following rules might help you in making a decision about trying medication, but remember—

this applies to both parents and physicians—to remain flexible to the unique needs and circumstances of each case.

1. *Has the child had adequate physical and psychological evaluations?* Medications should never be prescribed if the child has not been directly examined in a thorough manner.

2. *How old is the child?* Drug treatment is often less effective or leads to more severe side effects among children below the age of four years. It is therefore not usually recommended for them.

3. *Have other therapies been used?* If this is your family's initial contact with the professional, the prescription of medication might be postponed until other interventions (e.g., parent training in child management skills) have been attempted. Alternatively, when the child's behavior presents a severe problem and your family cannot participate in child management training, medication may be the most viable initial treatment.

4. *How severe is the child's current misbehavior?* In some cases the child's behavior is so unmanageable or distressing that medication may prove the fastest and most effective manner of dealing with the crisis until other forms of treatment can begin. Once progress is made with other therapies, some effort can be made to reduce or terminate the medication, but it's not always possible.

5. *Can you afford the medication and associated costs (e.g., follow-up visits)?*

6. *Can you adequately supervise the use of the medications and guard against their abuse?*

7. *What is your attitude toward medication?* If you are simply "antidrug," don't let your doctor pressure you into agreeing to this treatment because you probably won't be able to comply wholeheartedly with the regimen.

8. *Is there a delinquent or drug-abusing family member in the household?* In this case, stimulant medication should not be prescribed since there is a high risk for its illegal use or sale.

9. *Does the child have any history of tics, psychosis, or thought disorder?* If so, the stimulants are not indicated because they may worsen such difficulties.

10. *Is the child highly anxious, fearful, or more likely to complain of bodily symptoms?* Such children are less likely to respond positively to stimulant medications and may show a better response to antidepressant medications.

11. *Does the physician have the time to monitor medication properly?* In addition to an initial evaluation of the drug's effectiveness with a child for establishing the optimal dosage, the physician needs to see the child periodically to monitor for side effects. We recommend that a child taking stimulants be seen by the physician every three to six months for this monitoring.

12. *How does the child feel about medication and its alternatives?* With older children and adolescents it is important that the use of medication be discussed and the reasons for its use fully explained. In cases where children are "antidrug" or oppositional, they may resist efforts to use it, such as refusing to swallow the pill.

How Stimulants Are Prescribed

The following procedure is that typically followed in our own clinic by our physician colleagues and is also used by many physicians elsewhere. Even so, your own physician may follow a somewhat different procedure based on the unique needs of your child as well as the doctor's own training and preferences.

The first choice of medication is usually Ritalin because it has proven effective with individuals over a wide age range, and more information is available on the best doses to use. A child's failure to respond to one stimulant may not rule out a positive response to another stimulant, however, so we recommend a trial of Dexedrine or Cylert if a poor response (without side effects) to Ritalin occurs. If this trial fails, we suggest switching to an antidepressant. If this, too, fails, then drug treatment may need to be stopped for at least one year. It may have to be eliminated altogether in some cases. Children under age six who show a poor response to stimulants may well respond positively in later years.

With Ritalin, the usual practice is to start a child at a low dose such as 5 milligrams (mg) (2.5 mg for children under age five) in the morning and at noon, though some physicians recommend starting with just one dose in the morning. The dose is then increased by 5 mg (or 2.5 mg) every week until a good response is found or a dose of 1 mg/kg (1 mg for every 2.2 pounds [1 kilogram] of the child's weight) is reached. Children who wake up early in the morning or who have a more rapid elimination of the drug from their body may require doses three times per day. The dose used rarely exceeds 20 mg per dose, two to three times daily, because of the risk of more severe side effects at higher doses. Some professionals use daily doses of as high as 60 to 70 mg, although we rarely go beyond 30 to 40 mg/day in our clinic. Nevertheless, because every child responds differently, some children may need higher doses. If yours does, don't be alarmed. So long as no serious side effects are occurring, your child is in no harm. Giving the doses with or after meals may lessen the appetite problems or stomachaches sometimes associated with these drugs. Where such side effects are not a problem, the medications can be given 30 minutes before mealtimes.

Dexedrine is typically given in doses about half the size of those of Ritalin because of its greater potency. Because Cylert works differently, it is generally given only once a day, in the morning. The initial dose is usually 37.5 mg and is adjusted upward in 18.75-mg increments every three to five days until a positive response is achieved up to a maximum of 112.5 mg or 2.2 mg/kg for adolescents. On occasion a second dose, often half that of the morning dose, may be given in midafternoon if the morning dose is not effective during the afternoon. This, however, will likely increase the chances of insomnia occurring. The effects of Cylert may last for two to three days following stopping the drug.

As discussed earlier, the sustained-release forms of Ritalin and Dexedrine may be less effective than the shorter-acting forms, but they may negate the need for a noontime dose and thus enhance confidentiality for the child.

Generic forms are also available. Although no research has studied whether they differ from the brand-name drugs in effectiveness, some physicians have told us that the generic form does not work as well.

These drugs can be given according to various schedules depending on the severity of the child's ADHD and the associated difficulties. Many children find that the side effects they initially experience decrease over the first few weeks as they become adjusted to its presence in their body. For this reason (if the medicine is stopped over the weekend, side effects may reappear on Mondays) and because weight loss is not a problem for many children, at our clinic we no longer recommend that a child stop the medicine on weekends during the school year. We are also less likely to stop the medicine during the summer months, unless the child's ADHD has been affecting mainly his or her school performance. We have found that many children benefit from staying on their medicine throughout the summer, especially if they're going to be busy with sports, camps, scouts, summer school, tutoring, or other structured activities.

It is frequently necessary to use the medicines twice a day or even three times a day if the effects disappear quickly. This problem is often noticed by the child's teachers, who may observe that the morning dose has essentially worn off by mid-morning. In such cases a breakfast dose can be given at 7:00 to 8:00 A.M., a second dose at 10:30 to 11:00 A.M., and a final dose at 2:00 to 3:00 P.M. Only when the child's behavior problems are *exceptionally severe* is a dose closer to the dinner hour recommended, because a late dose increases the odds of decreased appetite at dinnertime and insomnia at bedtime. Closer attention to behavior management programs is a better alternative. However, adolescents may need this third dose late in the afternoon to help them concentrate during their homework. Your physician can try your teen on this third dose to see whether or not it can be tolerated well.

In general, the dose should always be the lowest possible and should be given only as many times per day as necessary to achieve adequate management of the child's behavior. Parents should never assume they have the physician's permission to adjust the dosage of medication without consultation with the physician.

When Should the Medicines Be Stopped?

There are no firm guidelines for stopping treatment. The medicine can be used until it no longer seems necessary. Up to 20% of children may be able to stop taking medication after a year or so, for several reasons. Some children have only mild cases of ADHD and may well mature to a point where the medication is not needed. Other children with ADHD may improve to the extent that they also do not need medication even though some symptoms of their ADHD remain. Still other children may continue to have significant symptoms of ADHD, but they have a better teacher for the new academic year, and their symptoms do not handicap them as much as they did with previous teachers. However, some children with ADHD may need to return to medication later that year or in subsequent years, depending on the demands for sustained attention and behavioral inhibition made on them at school or elsewhere. Most children with ADHD, however, will need to remain on their medication for years.

Treatment can be stopped annually for a week or two, usually a month or so after the beginning of the new academic year to give the child time to get used to the new school year and the teacher to get to know the child before stopping the medicine. When a doctor waits to see if a child who has been off medication for the summer has trouble in school without it, the child is put in the position of developing a bad reputation with the teacher and classmates—an image he or she must then overcome after going back on the stimulants. We believe it's better to get the school year off to a good start with the medication and then stop the medication briefly during October. If there is a brief decline in school performance, the child can be kept on medication during that school year.

CHAPTER 19

Other Medicines
for ADHD

Although they are not as effective as the stimulants, both the class of drugs called *antidepressants* and *clonidine*, used to treat high blood pressure, can be of some benefit to those with ADHD. If your doctor recommends either of these medications, or any other for that matter, be sure to ask the questions listed in the sidebar in Chapter 18.

Antidepressant Medicines

The brand names (generic names in parentheses) of the antidepressant medicines most frequently used with ADHD are Norpramin or Pertofrane (desipramine), Tofranil (imipramine), Elavil (amitriptyline), and Prozac (fluoxetine). There are other antidepressants as well, such as Pamelor or Aventyl (nortriptyline) and Anafranil (clomipramine), but clinical scientists have not studied their effects on ADHD very well, so they will not be discussed here. Because Prozac is very different from these other antidepressant drugs, I will discuss it separately.

These drugs were all developed primarily to treat depression, but they have also been used to treat some children with ADHD as well as children with anxiety or panic reactions, some with bed-wetting problems, and others with sleep problems such as night terrors. They are useful when the ADHD child has not shown a good response to the stimulants, cannot tolerate taking a stimulant, or has depression or anxiety in addition to ADHD. Like all other drugs that modify behavior, these drugs change behavior by altering the brain's chemistry in certain locations. We believe that in ADHD they increase the amount of the chemicals norepinephrine and dopamine available for work within the brain, especially the frontal area, as do the stimulants. The drug most frequently studied for treating ADHD is Norpramin (desipramine), but it is likely that the other antidepressant drugs would produce similar benefits.

Sometimes the changes in behavior related to ADHD can be seen within a few days of starting the medicines, while in other cases it may take several weeks. If the medicines are being used to treat depression in an ADHD child, it is likely that several weeks will be needed to judge how well a dose of medicine is working. The dose will be increased or decreased depending on the results of the first trial, and then a few more weeks will have to pass before the benefits of the new dose are noticed.

Studies have found that ADHD children given this type of drug are likely to show mild to moderate improvements in their ability to pay attention and control their impulses. They may also be somewhat less restless or hyperactive. Often the most obvious result is an improvement in mood. The children may seem less irritable or quick to anger, somewhat happier or in better spirits, and less anxious or worried. Because these drugs are not as effective at changing the symptoms of ADHD as the stimulants, they may have to be combined with one of the stimulants to achieve the best results. However, this combination of medicines is necessary in only a small minority of children who are both depressed and have ADHD.

Like the stimulants, the antidepressants are taken by mouth once or twice a day (mornings and evenings). Unlike the stimulants, they do not wash out of the body very quickly and must build up in the bloodstream over longer periods of time. This means that once a useful level of the drug is reached its effects last throughout the day, but it also means that it can take several weeks to gradually withdraw the child from the medication if necessary. Missing a dose or stopping the medicine abruptly may not be dangerous, but it could cause a headache, stomachache, nausea, or aching muscles. The child could also show some emotional or behavioral reactions, such as crying, sadness, nervousness, and problems with sleeping.

The best doses of these medicines are 1 to 5 mg for each kilogram (about 2.2 pounds) of body weight per day. For instance, if your child weighs 80 pounds (38 kg), the lowest probable dose for this child would be 38 mg and the highest 190 mg. Some children may respond well between 1 and 3 mg/kg (between 38 and 117 mg in the example), whereas others will need more medicine to receive any benefit from the drugs. Sometimes, when a child is taking these medicines for the treatment of depression, blood tests may be necessary to see if enough medicine is getting into the bloodstream to benefit the child. This is usually done when the dose seems adequate, but the child either is not responding or is showing signs of having too much medication. Even then, however, it is not clear from current research that knowing the blood level of the medicine is of much help in determining the best dose.

Unlike with the stimulants, children can build up a tolerance to the antidepressants, so typically they cannot take these medicines for more than a year or two. Sometimes the antidepressants begin to lose their effectiveness after only four to six months. In these cases the medicine may have to be stopped for a few months before it can be tried again.

The Side Effects

Slower Heart Rate

One of the problems with these medicines is that they can slow down the transmission of the electrical signal in the heart, causing problems in the heartbeat or heart rhythm. For this reason every child who is to be tried on a tricyclic antidepressant, such as Norpramin, Tofranil, or Elavil, should first be given an electrocardiogram (EKG), an easy test that measures how well the heart is beating. If the test gives any abnormal findings, the child should not be placed on any of these medicines. Also, any family history of sudden cardiac (heart) arrest should be a warning to avoid these medicines in most cases.

In fact, because these medicines can have serious effects on the heart, *they must be kept out of reach of children or anyone else who might accidentally take too much of the medicine; an overdose could be fatal.*

Seizures

Another problem with these medicines is that they may increase the risk of seizures, or convulsions, particularly if the child has a history of seizures, has had a serious head injury, or has had some other serious neurological problem. In such cases it is probably best not to use these medicines.

Minor Physical Effects

The most common side effects seem to be a feeling of dry mouth, which can be handled by giving the child some sugar-free gum to chew, and constipation, which can be dealt with by using stool softeners or adjusting the diet so it contains more fiber or bulk. Some children may also experience blurred vision or even near-sightedness. Occasionally children have had difficulty getting their flow of urine started when they try to urinate. None of these is a serious problem, and they can all be handled by lowering the dose of medicine.

Rare Side Effects

Some of the side effects are rare but can be very serious. Besides the slowed heart rate and increased risk of seizures already mentioned, some children may have a psychotic reaction in which they have disturbed thinking, highly excessive speech, seriously increased activity level, and even hallucinations. Also at high doses, some children experience mental confusion. Where any of these side effects occur, the child's physician should be informed immediately and the medication discontinued under a physician's guidance. Increases in blood pressure can occur, although they are mild, and can be of concern if the child already has a history of high blood pressure.

Also rare but not as serious are the occasional cases of rash that have been reported. These are probably the result of an allergic reaction to the food coloring used in making the pills and not to the medicine itself. Changing to a different form of the medicine that does not contain the food coloring (tartrazine) can solve this problem. Very rarely children may show some nervous tics from these medicines. If this occurs to a significant or frequent degree, the medicine can be stopped, and the tic reactions will usually go away. The drugs can also increase the sensitivity of the skin to sunlight, requiring that the child wear strong sunscreen more often or better protective clothing than normal when active outdoors.

Drug Interactions

Because these medicines can interact with a number of other medicines in undesirable ways, it is best to ask your physician which medicines should be avoided while a child is taking any of these antidepressants.

Prozac (Fluoxetine)

Prozac is a new type of antidepressant that is very different in its chemistry from the other antidepressants. This drug is used extensively in the treatment of adults with depression and has been reasonably well studied for that purpose. Less is known of its effects on children. However, several recent studies with ADHD children have shown that it can be of some benefit to them, either by itself or combined with a stimulant medicine such as one of those discussed in the last chapter. Like the other antidepressants discussed, Prozac may be most useful for those ADHD children who also have some mood disorder, such as problems with depression, anxiety, or irritability. It also may offer some benefit to ADHD children who are highly aggressive because the drug is known to increase a chemical in the brain (serotonin) related to the inhibition of aggressive behavior. In general, this drug seems to improve the mood of depressed or anxious children, reduce their aggressiveness, and improve their impulse control. Although it may result in improvements in attention span, these improvements are not as dramatic as those produced by the stimulant medications discussed in Chapter 18.

What Are the Side Effects?

Why would Prozac be a better drug to use than the other antidepressants described? Mainly because it is safer for children. Prozac does not seem to cause slowing of heart activity and therefore does not pose a serious risk for children who may have abnormal heartbeat or heart rhythm. Also, recent studies suggest that the effects of Prozac on ADHD and aggression may be noticed sooner in the trial of the medicine than is seen with the other antidepressants, but this is still debatable. Prozac may produce side effects such as nausea, mild weight loss (or gain in some children), anxiety or nervousness, headaches, excessive sweating, or insomnia (trouble falling asleep or staying asleep). There is a small possibility that children may actually develop increased restlessness on this medicine or even become agitated or irritable. Their speech may also be increased or rapid, and they may report subjective feelings of tenseness or feeling "speeded up." Experts suggest that lowering the dose may help reduce these symptoms. Some reports in the popular media have claimed that Prozac might increase thoughts of suicide in some adults taking the medicine. This has not been corroborated in research studies of the drug. If it occurs at all, it is likely to be very rare and probably related to the person's depression before starting the medicine. *Parents whose children express thoughts of suicide, whether on or off this medicine, should always contact their treating physician or a local emergency room immediately.* As with any medicine, the use of this medicine must be prescribed and monitored regularly by a physician who is well informed on its clinical management.

How Is the Drug Used with Children?

Children with ADHD who are recommended for a trial of Prozac should be started on a dose of 2.5 to 5 mg given once a day. After a week or so, the dose can be increased by 2.5 mg and kept at that level for another week. Each week the dose can be raised another 2.5 mg until a good response is noticed or until side effects begin to occur at an undesirable level. Most ADHD children should show a positive response to this medicine between doses of 2.5 and 20 mg per day. During the initial trial of the medicine, you should be in contact with the treating physician weekly as the dose is being adjusted. Once the proper dose has been determined, be in contact with your physician monthly for a while. The physician may then advise you that less contact is needed as your child is maintained on this medication. Your child should also be taken off the medication at least once a year to determine whether any medicine is still needed.

As with all medicines, Prozac should be kept at home in a safe place out of the reach of children. It should not be used within six weeks of your child's having taken another form of antidepressant medicine known as an MAO inhibitor (for instance, drugs such as Nardil, Parnate, or Marplan). Prozac *does interact* with other medicines, so you should be sure to tell your treating physician all of the medicines that your child has been taking recently. Also, do not start using any new medicines while your child is taking Prozac without first discussing these with your physician.

Clonidine (Catapres)

Another type of medicine recently shown to have some benefit for children with ADHD is clonidine, a drug frequently used to treat high blood pressure in adults. The fact that it also can produce changes in behavior and mood makes it of some benefit to ADHD children who have problems with or get no beneficial effects from the stimulants. Other disorders for which clonidine has been used include migraine headaches, schizophrenia, manic–depression, obsessive–compulsive disorder, panic disorder, and serious eating disorders like anorexia nervosa. Clonidine has also been used in treating the tics, vocal noises, and other involuntary movements seen in Tourette's syndrome.

When used with ADHD children, clonidine may reduce the motor hyperactivity and impulsiveness seen with the disorder. It may also increase a child's cooperativeness with tasks and directions and increase the child's tolerance for frustration. Dr. Robert Hunt of Vanderbilt University, a nationally recognized expert on the use of this drug with ADHD children, reports that clonidine may not be as effective as the stimulants in improving an ADHD child's sustained attention or reducing distractibility. However, it may be as effective as the stimulants in reducing aggressive and impulsive behavior or the tendency to become overaroused very quickly. Dr. Hunt believes that this medication may be best suited for those ADHD children who are very oppositional or defiant or who have a conduct disorder.

When taken by mouth, clonidine may produce changes in behavior that can be noted within 30 to 60 minutes and may last for 3 to 6 hours. Clonidine also comes in an adhesive patch that can be worn on the skin. Where this skin patch is used, changes in behavior may not be noticed for several days. However, it usually takes several months before one can tell just how much benefit the drug is producing in the management of a child's behavioral or emotional problems.

What Are the Side Effects?

The most common problem children have with this medicine is sedation or a feeling of tiredness or sleepiness. This can last as long as the first two to four weeks after the child begins the medicine. During this period the child may take frequent catnaps, especially during boring activities. In some children, perhaps 15%, this sleepiness or fatigue may last longer and be troublesome enough to warrant stopping the medicine.

There may be a mild drop in your child's blood pressure after starting this medication, but this is rarely significant. There may also be a slight decrease in heart rate, but again this is rarely serious. Headaches or dizziness may be noted in some children, again typically within the first four weeks of starting the medicine. Some children have complained of nausea, stomachaches, and even vomiting, but these are also usually limited to the first few weeks of starting the medicine. Constipation and dryness of the mouth may also be seen in some children. Much less likely to occur are depression, erratic changes in heartbeat or rhythm, nightmares or disrupted sleep, increased appetite, or increases or decreases in weight. Rarely, problems with increased anxiety, a sensation of coldness in the fingers or toes (known as *Raynaud syndrome*), or water retention may be seen.

The medicine should never be stopped abruptly. If it is, a child may experience a rapid rise in blood pressure, show agitation, become anxious, complain of chest pain or fast and irregular heartbeat, and develop headaches, stomachaches, nausea, or sleep problems.

Clonidine can also interact with other drugs to create problems for a child, so you should advise your physician of any medication a child is on before he or she is given clonidine or of any new medications being considered for the child while he or she is on clonidine.

How Is Clonidine Used with Children?

Before starting this medicine, your physician may want to conduct a complete physical examination of your child, including an EKG and some blood work. Dr. Hunt recommends that ADHD children be placed on doses of 0.15 to 0.30 mg/day. The drug is usually begun at much lower doses (0.05 mg given at night). The dose is then gradually increased every few days or less often by adding additional doses of 0.05 mg given at different times of the day until the child is taking this dose 4 times a day. At this time it may be necessary to increase the dose from 0.5 to 1.0 mg for 1 of the 4 doses each day. These increases can continue until some benefit has been noticed from the medicine or the side effects become a problem for the child. The drug is usually taken orally three to four times a day (commonly at mealtimes and bedtime). Although some improvement in behavior may be seen in the first two to four weeks, it can usually take two to four months before the full benefit of the medicine is noticed.

A skin patch of clonidine, named Catapres-TTS, is available. It is worn like a bandage and should be placed on a clean, relatively hairless patch of skin out of easy reach of the child's hands (usually the lower back or over the back of the hips). Each patch can be worn for about five days. Children can take baths or showers with the patch on, but after swimming or heavy sweating, the patch may need to be replaced. Dr. Hunt recommends that children be started on the oral clonidine until the proper dose is determined. They can then be switched to the skin patch, which avoids the problems of taking oral medication at school, if desired.

Any child taking clonidine should be followed by the physician weekly while the different doses are being tried and then every four to six weeks once a stable dose has been reached. Blood pressure, heart rate, and growth should be monitored at these regular visits.

If your physician is not familiar with clonidine or you would like to read more about it yourself, you may wish to consult two excellent sources:

"Clonidine in child and adolescent psychiatry" by Robert Hunt, Lisa Capper, and Patricia O'Connell (1990). *Journal of Child and Adolescent Psychopharmacology*, Volume 1, Number 1, pages 87–102. New York: Mary Ann Liebert Publishers.

"Anxiolytics, sedatives, and miscellaneous drugs" by John Werry and Michael Aman (1993) in their book *Practitioners Guide to Psychoactive Drugs for Children and Adolescents*, pages 403–404. New York: Plenum Press.

Support Services for Parents

A large number of parent support associations for ADHD now exist throughout the United States and Canada. In addition, there are a number of smaller, local or regional groups. Since the contacts for these groups change so frequently, we suggest that you start by calling one of the national organizations, which maintain current records of all the various support groups. They will be glad to refer you to the group closest to your home. The largest national association is Children with Attention Deficit Disorders (CHADD), which now has more than 500 such support associations affiliated with it from almost every state. To find the support group nearest you, contact the national headquarters of CHADD at:

CHADD
National Headquarters
499 Northwest 70th Ave.
Suite 109
Plantation, FL 33317
(305) 587-3700 or (800) 233-4050

Another parent support association is the National Attention Deficit Disorder Association (ADDA):

ADDA
P.O. Box 972
Mentor, OH 44061
(800) 487-2282

A support association for adults with ADD or ADHD is:

Adult Attention Deficit Foundation
132 North Woodward Avenue
Birmingham, MI 48009
(810) 540-6335

The Association for Children and Adults with Learning Disabilities also provides support groups for parents of all children with learning problems, not just with ADHD. They have at least one chapter in every state. Information on the chapter nearest you can be found by contacting the national organization at:

Learning Disabilities Association of America (LDAA)
4156 Library Rd.
Pittsburgh, PA 15234
(412) 341-1515

National newsletters on ADHD can be obtained from:

CHADD (see address above)—publishes a newsletter and the quarterly full-color magazine, *Attention!*

ADDA (see address above)—publishes a newsletter

The ADHD Report
(edited by Russell A. Barkley, Ph.D.)
The Guilford Press
72 Spring St.
New York, NY 10012
(800) 365-7006

Challenge: A Newsletter on Attention Deficit Hyperactivity Disorder
P.O. Box 2001
West Newbury, MA 01985
(508) 462-0495

ADDendum
(for Adults with ADD)
c/o C.P.S.
5041-A Backlick Road
Annandale, VA 22003
(540) 986-1953

ADDult News
c/o Mary Jane Johnson
ADDult Support Network
2620 Ivy Place
Toledo, OH 43613
(419) 866-9183

An on-line computer bulletin board has recently been created for those wishing to discuss ADHD issues, and a web site for CHADD's chapter listings can be found on the Internet. Here are the addresses:

alt.support.attn-deficit
www.chadd.org

Suggested Reading and Videotapes

Professional Textbooks

American Psychiatric Association. (1994). *Diagnostic and statistical manual of mental disorders* (4th ed.). Washington, DC: Author.

> This is a manual for professionals that sets forth the criteria to be used for diagnosing mental disorders (within the United States). It includes the most recent criteria for ADHD and related disorders.

Barkley, R. A. (1987). *Defiant children: A clinician's manual for parent training.* New York: Guilford Press.

> A manual intended to instruct professionals step by step in conducting a 10-session training program for parents of children (between 2 and 12 years old) with ADHD and/or oppositional defiant disorder.

Barkley, R. A. (1990). *Attention-deficit hyperactivity disorder: A handbook for diagnosis and treatment.* New York: Guilford Press.

> A highly detailed professional textbook intended to serve as a handbook for clinicians who provide diagnosis, assessment, and treatment services for children and adults with ADHD, including parent training, classroom management, family therapy, and medications for ADHD.

Mash, E. J., & Barkley, R. A. (Eds.). (1989). *Treatment of childhood disorders.* New York: Guilford Press.

> A textbook intended for use by professionals and graduate students that covers the major childhood psychological disorders, reviewing and critically evaluating the treatments frequently provided for each disorder. Each disorder is reviewed by a recognized expert in that disorder. A chapter on ADHD is included.

Mash, E. J., & Barkley, R. A. (Eds.). (in press). *Child psychopathology.* New York: Guilford Press.

> Also intended for graduate students and professionals, this forthcoming text has chapters from numerous nationally recognized experts, each providing a thorough review of the disorder in which they are expert. Each chapter deals with the nature, major symp-

toms, prevalence, etiologies, and developmental courses of the relevant childhood disorder. It contains a chapter on ADHD.

Mash, E. J., & Terdal, L. G. (Eds.). (1988). *Behavioral assessment of childhood disorders* (2nd ed.). New York: Guilford Press.

A thorough review of the assessment methods often employed with each of a variety of childhood disorders. Each chapter is prepared by an expert on that disorder.

Nadeau, K. G. (Ed.). (1995). *A comprehensive guide to attention deficit disorders in adults: Research, diagnosis, treatment.* New York: Brunner/Mazel.

One of the best professional textbooks currently available on the subject; provides coverage of a number of topics ranging from history and diagnosis to assessment and treatment.

Robin, A. L., & Foster, S. L. (1989). *Negotiating parent–adolescent conflict: A behavioral–family systems approach.* New York: Guilford Press.

An excellent text intended to train professionals in one approach to behavioral family therapy with families who have frequent conflicts with their teenagers.

Ross, D., & Ross, S. (1982). *Hyperactivity* (2nd ed.). New York: Wiley.

One of the most thorough reviews of the scientific literature for its time. It continues to be a richly detailed resource concerning the historical development of the concept of hyperactivity in children, and documents the significant research issues up to the early 1980s.

Sleator, E. K., & Pelham, W. E. (1986). *Attention deficit disorder.* Norwalk, CT: Appleton-Century-Crofts.

A brief but clinically useful textbook on ADHD, its diagnosis, and management prepared by two nationally recognized experts on the disorder.

Taylor, E. (1986). *The overactive child.* Philadelphia: J. P. Lippincott.

A textbook for scientists and clinical professionals providing the British perspective on ADHD and summarizing much of the significant research done by the author and his colleagues in Great Britain and elsewhere.

Weiss, G., & Hechtman, L. T. (1993). *Hyperactive children grown up (2nd ed.):* ADHD in children, adolescents, and adults. New York: Guilford Press.

The best single source for a review of the scientific literature on the developmental course and outcome of hyperactive children, written by two clinical scientists who have spent much of their careers following a sample of Canadian children for over 25 years.

Wender, P. H. (1995). *Attention-deficit hyperactivity disorder in adults.* New York: Oxford University Press.

A recent textbook for professionals concerning the nature of ADHD in adults, its prevalence within the population, evidence for the neurobiological nature of the disorder, and its assessment and treatment. Written by a well-respected authority on ADHD who has been contributing to the scientific and clinical literature for over 30 years, and who was one of the first to conduct medication studies with adults with ADHD and develop clinical criteria for its diagnosis.

Werry, J., & Aman, M. (1993). *Practitioners guide to psychoactive drugs for children and adolescents.* New York: Plenum Press.

Intended for a professional audience, this text provides state-of-the-art information concerning each class of behavior-modifying medications used with childhood and adolescent mental disorders, their effects and side effects, and their proper prescription. The authors are internationally recognized authorities on psychiatric drugs for children, and the first author has been one of the leading researchers on ADHD for nearly 30 years.

Whalen, C., & Henker, B. (1980). *Hyperactive children: The social ecology of identification and treatment.* New York: Academic Press.

Although somewhat dated, this is one of the few textbooks for professionals that stresses the importance of understanding the social ecology in which hyperactive children exist and the manner in which this influences referral, diagnosis, assessment, and treatment.

Videotapes for Parents, Teachers, and Kids

ADHD—What do we know?, ADHD—What can we do?, ADHD in the classroom, and *ADHD in adults* by R. A. Barkley. The Guilford Press, 72 Spring St., New York, NY 10012; telephone: (800) 365-7006.

Four award-winning videotapes on ADHD spanning a variety of topics and using children and adults with ADHD who tell their own stories about living with ADHD.

Jumping Johnny get back to work!: The video by M. Gordon. Gordon Systems, Inc., P.O. Box 746, DeWitt, NY 13214; telephone: (315) 446-4849.

An excellent animated video for children with ADHD that discusses the disorder and its treatment from a child's perspective.

It's just an attention disorder, Why won't my child pay attention?, and *Educating inattentive children* by S. Goldstein & M. Goldstein. Neurology, Learning and Behavior Center, 230 South 500 East, Suite 100, Salt Lake City, UT 84102; telephone: (801) 532-1484.

The first video is an excellent introduction to ADHD intended for older children and teens with ADHD. It has a fast-paced format and uses comments from teens with ADHD about coping with their disorder. The second and third videotapes are intended for viewing by parents and teachers, respectively, and provide a fine overview of the disorder and its management at home and school.

All about attention deficit disorder by T. Phelan. ADD Warehouse, 300 N.W. 70th Ave., Suite 102, Plantation, FL 33317; telephone: (800) 233-9273.

A good review of the disorder for parents and teachers, from a popular clinical professional whose videotape *3-2-1 Magic* has been widely acclaimed for its help in managing noncompliant child behavior.

Books for Parents and Teachers

Bain, L. (1991). *A parent's guide to attention deficit disorders.* New York: Delta/Dell.

An informative book for parents on ADHD and its management.

Forgatch, M., & Patterson, G. R. (1989) *Parents and adolescents living together.* Eugene, OR: Castalia.

A superb set of books for parents on strategies for managing conflicts with adolescents. Good not only for teens with ADHD but also for families experiencing the normal stresses and conflicts that often arise in adolescence. The authors are widely recognized clinical-research experts on defiant and aggressive child and adolescent behavior.

Fowler, M. C. (1992). *CHADD educators manual.* Plantation, FL: CASET Associates; telephone: (800) 545-5583.

A terrific review of important information for teachers on ADHD and its management from one of the founding parents of the CHADD organization, who has become an expert on educational advocacy for children with ADHD.

Fowler, M. C. (1990). *Maybe you know my kid: A parents guide to identifying, understanding, and helping your child with attention-deficit hyperactivity disorder.* New York: Birch Lane Press.

One of the few books for parents on the subject of ADHD written by a parent, and one of the best. The author has become a lay expert on the subject of ADHD through her extensive work on the national level with CHADD.

Goldstein, S., & Goldstein, M. (1992). *Hyperactivity: Why won't my child pay attention?* Salt Lake City, UT: Neurology, Learning and Behavior Center.

A well-written, informative book for parents on hyperactivity (ADHD) and its management by two clinical experts in the subject.

Gordon, M. (1991). *ADHD/hyperactivity: A consumer's guide.* DeWitt, NY: GSI.

A witty, often humorous review of ADHD and its management written by a recognized clinical expert on ADHD. Covers many of the most-often asked questions by parents (to professionals) and provides informative answers.

Ingersoll, B. (1988). *Your hyperactive child.* New York: Doubleday.

One of the first books for parents on ADHD and its management prepared by a skilled clinical professional; still quite informative despite its date of publication.

Ingersoll, B., & Goldstein, M. (1993). *Attention deficit disorder and learning disabilities: Realities, myths, and controversial treatments.* New York: Doubleday.

The best book for parents reviewing the unproven and disproven remedies offered to parents for treatment of children with ADHD; very helpful in sorting out the shams, fakeries, and other quack remedies for ADHD. Also provides a short review of the most useful and scientifically substantiated treatments for ADHD.

Johnson, D. (1992). *I can't sit still: Educating and affirming inattentive and hyperactive children.* Santa Cruz, CA: ETR Associates.

A fine book for parents and teachers about ADHD and its management, with lots of good ideas for taking positive approaches to often difficult children.

Kennedy, P., Terdal, L., & Fusetti, L. (1993). *The hyperactive child book.* New York: St. Martin's Press.

A very helpful book for parents prepared by a parent, psychologist, and pediatrician (respectively) that instructs parents not only about ADHD, but also about how best to deal with professionals in seeking treatment.

Latham, P., & Latham, P. (1993). *ADD and the Law.* Washington, DC: JKL.

The only book that summarizes the rights of those with ADHD, as well as legal rulings pertaining to these rights, by two of the best disability-rights attorneys in the business.

Parker, H. (1988). *The ADD hyperactivity workbook for parents, teachers, and kids* (2nd. ed.). Plantation, FL: Specialty Press; telephone (ADD Warehouse): (800) 233-9273.

The founding professional of CHADD and one of the strongest and most vigorous advocates for those with ADHD has prepared this highly useful workbook containing numerous strategies for working with children with ADHD at home and in school.

Parker, H. (1991). *The ADD hyperactivity handbook for schools*. Plantation, FL: Specialty Press; telephone (ADD Warehouse): (800) 233-9273.

Dr. Parker provides a richly detailed book for school psychologists, administrators, and educators on useful approaches to the recognition, evaluation, and management of ADHD within the school setting.

Parker, H. (1992). *ADAPT: Attention deficit accomodation plan for teaching*. Plantation, FL: Specialty Press; telephone (ADD Warehouse): (800) 233-9273.

A veritable cookbook of techniques for helping children with ADHD succeed within school settings from one of the most knowledgeable clinicians specializing in ADHD in the business today.

Silver, L. (1993). *Dr. Larry Silver's advice to parents on attention-deficit hyperactivity disorder*. Washington, DC: American Psychiatric Press.

A nicely written book for parents covering most of the major issues related to ADHD on which parents need information. It provides accurate, timely, sensitive, and practical information on ADHD.

Wender, P. H. (1987). *The hyperactive child, adolescent, and adult*. New York: Oxford Press.

Somewhat dated now, this was one of the first books for parents on hyperactivity in children and the first containing a chapter on ADHD in adults. Still informative despite its date of publication.

Wodrich, D. (1994). *What every parent wants to know: Attention deficit hyperactivity disorder*. Baltimore: Brookes.

A fine overview of current information on ADHD and its treatment for parents.

Books for Kids about ADHD

Corman, C., & Trevino, E. (1995). *Eulcee the jumpy jumpy elephant*. Plantation, FL: Specialty Press; telephone (ADD Warehouse): (800) 233-9273.

Galvin, M. (1995). *Otto learns about his medicine: A story about medication for children* (rev. ed.). New York: Magination Press.

Still a great illustrated book for kids with ADHD on the subject of taking medication for the management of hyperactivity.

Gordon, M. (1992). *I would if I could*. DeWitt, NY: GSI.

A fine, brief book about ADHD written from a child's perspective, showing both humor and sensitivity.

Gordon, M. (1992). *My brother's a world class pain*. DeWitt, NY: GSI.

The only book of which I am aware that addresses the issues of being a sibling to a child with ADHD. A fine contribution to the children's literature on ADHD.

Moss, D. (1989). *Shelly the hyperactive turtle*. Rockville, MD: Woodbine House.

This short, illustrated story was one of the first to explain ADHD (hyperactivity) to children and remains useful in this regard despite the change in terminology from Hyperactivity to ADHD.

Nadeau, K. G. (1994). *Survival guide for college students with ADD or LD.* New York: Magination Press.

A highly useful manual for young adults with ADHD or LD who are heading off to college. Filled with lots of tips for success in the college setting, which can often prove daunting to those with ADHD.

Parker, R. (1992). *Making the grade.* Plantation, FL: Specialty Press; telephone (ADD Warehouse): (800) 233-9273.

A brief, warm, sensitive story about the impact of ADHD on school success and self-esteem told from an older child's perspective.

Quinn, P., & Stern, J. (1991). *Putting on the brakes: Young people's guide to understanding attention deficit hyperactivity disorder.* New York: Magination Press.

Written expressly for children entering adolescence (or older), renders the information about ADHD in a thoughtful, caring, and upbeat manner.

Quinn, P. (1994). *ADD and the college student.* New York: Magination Press.

A most informative text for parents of ADHD college students and the students themselves on surviving in the university environment with ADHD.

Books for Adults with ADHD

Hallowell, E., & Ratey, J. (1994). *Driven to distraction.* New York: Pantheon.

A bestseller on ADHD in adults written by two psychiatrists who profess to be ADHD adults themselves. Well-written, thoughtful, and filled with numerous informative case vignettes from their adult clients with ADHD as well as many useful tips on coping with the disorder.

Kelly, K., & Ramundo, P. (1993). *You mean I'm not lazy, stupid, or crazy?!* Cincinnati, OH: Tyrell & Jerem Press.

A nice addition to the literature on adult ADHD providing numerous helpful suggestions for recognizing and dealing with the disorder.

Murphy, K., & Levert, S. (1995). *Out of the fog.* New York: Hyperion.

The most recent book for adults with ADHD by the Chief of the Adult ADHD Clinic at the University of Massachusetts Medical Center (my own employer) and a respected journalist. One of the most up-to-date and detailed books on the subject of ADHD in adults.

Weiss, L. (1992). *ADD in adults.* Dallas, TX: Taylor.

This is an informative, compassionate, and supportive text for adults with ADHD written by a skilled therapist who treats many such adults and loaded with tips for coping with ADHD in daily life.

Wender, P. H. (1987). *The hyperactive child, adolescent, and adult.* New York: Oxford University Press.

Although somewhat dated, this remains an informative book for parents of children with ADHD as well as for adults with ADHD.

Periodicals

ADDendum: Newsletter for Adults with ADHD, edited by P. Jaffee. Box 296, Scarborough, NY 10510; telephone: (540) 986-1953.

A newsletter for adults with ADHD prepared by adults with ADHD and containing personal perspectives, useful advice, reviews of available materials and resources, and discussions of controversial topics related to ADHD in adults.

The ADHD Report, edited by R. A. Barkley, The Guilford Press, 72 Spring St., New York, NY 10012; telephone: (800) 365-7006.

The only newsletter specifically dedicated to practicing clinicians who want to remain current in the extensive and rapidly changing scientific and clinical literature on ADHD. Parents of children with ADHD and adults with ADHD may also find the contents useful for staying current on controversial issues and research reports as well.

Attention!, CHADD, 499 N.W. 70th Ave., Suite 101, Plantation, FL 33317; telephone: (954) 587-3700.

A flashy, entertaining, and informative magazine on ADHD created by the largest national support organization for ADHD (CHADD) dedicated to keeping parents and adults with ADHD informed about the numerous issues related to ADHD.

Brakes: The Interactive Newsletter for Kids with ADD, edited by J. Stern & P. Quinn. Magination Press, 19 Union Square West, New York, NY 10003, telephone (800) 825-3089.

The only newsletter (of which I am aware) dedicated specifically to children and early adolescents with ADHD. Each issue is filled with lots of information and entertaining activities for children to do prepared by two very compassionate writers on the subject.

CHADD Newsletter, CHADD, 499 N.W. 70th Ave., Suite 101, Plantation, FL 33317; telephone: (954) 587-3700.

A newsletter for parents of children with ADHD and adults with ADHD for members of CHADD.

Challenge: A Newsletter on ADHD, edited by J. Conner. P.O. Box 2001, West Newbury, MA 01985; telephone: (508) 462-0495

References

A number of published studies were referenced throughout this book and are listed here for the interested reader. Many other references to research can be found in my earlier text (1990) and the bibliography on ADHD compiled by R. J. Resnick and K. McEvoy (1994), both listed below.

American Psychiatric Association (1994). *Diagnostic and statistical manual of mental disorders* (4th ed.). Washington, DC: Author.

Anastopoulos, A. D., Guevremont, D. C., Shelton, T. L., & DuPaul, G. J. (1992). Parenting stress among families of children with attention deficit hyperactivity disorder. *Journal of Abnormal Child Psychology, 20,* 503–520.

Barkley, R. A. (1990). *Attention-deficit hyperactivity disorder: A handbook for diagnosis and treatment.* New York: Guilford Press.

Biederman, J., Faraone, S. V., Keenan, K., Knee, D., et al. (1990). Family–genetic and psychosocial risk factors in DSM-III attention deficit disorder. *Journal of the American Academy of Child and Adolescent Psychiatry, 29,* 526–533.

Bremer, D. A., & Stern, J. A. (1976). Attention and distractibility during reading in hyperactive boys. *Journal of Abnormal Child Psychology, 4,* 381–387.

Bronowski, J. (1977). Human and animal languages. In *A sense of the future* (pp. 104–131). Cambridge, MA: MIT Press.

Burd, L., Kerbeshian, J., & Fisher, W. (1987). Does the use of phenobarbital as an anticonvulsant permanently exacerbate hyperactivity? *Canadian Journal of Psychiatry, 32,* 10–13.

Campbell, S. B., Szumowski, E. K., Ewing, L. J., Gluck, D. S., & Breaux, A. M. (1982). A multidimensional assessment of parent-identified behavior problem toddlers. *Journal of Abnormal Child Psychology, 10,* 569–592.

Cook, E. H., Stein, M. A., Krasowski, M. D., Cox, N. J., Olkon, D. M., Kieffer, J. E., & Leventhal, B. L. (in press). Association of attention deficit disorder and the dopamine transporter gene. *American Journal of Human Genetics, 56.*

Covey, S. R. (1989). *The seven habits of highly effective people: Restoring the character ethic.* New York: Simon & Schuster.

Damasio, A. R. (1994). *Descartes' error.* New York: G. P. Putnam's Sons.

Denson, R., Nanson, J. L., & McWatters, M. A. (1975). Hyperkinesis and maternal smoking. *Canadian Psychiatric Association Journal, 20,* 183–187.

Edelbrock, C., Rende, R., Plomin, R., & Thompson, L. A. (1995). A twin study of competence and problem behavior in childhood and early adolescence. *Journal of Child Psychology and Psychiatry, 36,* 755–786.

Fuster, J. M. (1989). *The prefrontal cortex.* New York: Raven Press.

Gilger, J. W., Pennington, B. F., & DeFries, J. C. (1992). A twin study of the etiology of comorbidity: Attention deficit hyperactivity disorder and dyslexia. *Journal of the American Academy of Child and Adolescent Psychiatry, 31,* 343–348.

Gillis, J. J., Gilger, J. W., Pennington, B. F., & Defries, J. C. (1992). Attention deficit disorder in reading-disabled twins: Evidence for a genetic etiology. *Journal of Abnormal Child Psychology, 20,* 303–315.

Gordon, M. (1979). The assessment of impulsivity and mediating behaviors in hyperactive and non-hyperactive children. *Journal of Abnormal Child Psychology, 7,* 317–326.

Hartsough, C. S., & Lambert, N. M. (1985). Medical factors in hyperactive and normal children: Prenatal, developmental, and health history findings. *American Journal of Orthopsychiatry, 55,* 190–210.

Hauser, P., Zametkin, A. J., Martinex, P., Vitiello, B., Matochik, J. A., Mixson, A. J., & Weintraub, B. D. (1993). Attention deficit-hyperactivity disorder in people with generalized resistance to thyroid hormone. *New England Journal of Medicine, 328,* 997–1001.

Hoover, D. W., & Milich, R. (1994). Effects of sugar ingestion expectancies on mother–child interactions. *Journal of Abnormal Child Psychology, 22,* 501–515.

Hynd, G. W., Semrud-Clikeman, M., Lorys, A. R., Novey, E. S., & Eliopulos, D. (1990). Brain morphology in developmental dyslexia and attention deficit disorder/hyperactivity. *Archives of Neurology, 47,* 919–926.

Hynd, G. W., Semrud-Clikeman, M., Lorys, A. R., Novey, E. S., Eliopulos, D., & Lyytinen, H. (1991). Corpus callosum morphology in attention deficit-hyperactivity disorder: morphometric analysis of MRI. *Journal of Learning Disabilities, 24,* 141–146.

Jacob, R. G., O'Leary, K. D., & Rosenblad, C. (1978). Formal and informal classroom settings: Effects on hyperactivity. *Journal of Abnormal Child Psychology, 6,* 47–59.

Jensen, P. S., Shervette, R. E., Xenakis, S. N., & Bain, M. W. (1988). Psychosocial and medical histories of stimulant-treated children. *Journal of the American Academy of Child and Adolescent Psychiatry, 27,* 798–801.

Kavale, K. A., & Forness, S. R. (1983). Hyperactivity and diet treatment: A meta-analysis of the Feingold Hypothesis. *Journal of Learning Disabilities, 16,* 324–330.

Lambert, N. M., Sandoval, J., & Sassone, D. (1978). Prevalence of hyperactivity in elementary school children as a function of social system definers. *American Journal of Orthopsychiatry, 48,* 446–463.

Milich, R., & Pelham, W. E. (1986). Effects of sugar ingestion on the classroom and playground behavior of attention deficit disordered boys. *Journal of Consulting and Clinical Psychology, 54,* 714–718.

Milich, R., Wolraich, M., & Lindgren, S. (1986). Sugar and hyperactivity: A critical review of empirical findings. *Clinical Psychology Review, 6,* 493–513.

Porrino, L. J., Rapoport, J. L., Behar, D., Sceery, W., Ismond, D. R., & Bunney, W. E., Jr. (1983). A naturalistic assessment of the motor activity of hyperactive boys. *Archives of General Psychiatry, 40,* 681–687.

Rapport, M. D., Tucker, S. B., DuPaul, G. J., Merlo, M., & Stoner, G. (1986). Hyperactivity and frustration: The influence of control over and size of rewards in delaying gratification. *Journal of Abnormal Child Psychology, 14,* 181–204.

Resnick, R. J., & McEvoy, K. (1994). *Attention-deficit/hyperactivity disorder: Abstracts of the psychological and behavioral literature, 1971–1994.* Washington, DC: American Psychological Association.

Rosen, L. A., Booth, S. R., Bender, M. E., McGrath, M. L., Sorrell, S., & Drabman, R. S. (1988). Effects of sugar (sucrose) on children's behavior. *Journal of Consulting and Clinical Psychology, 56,* 583–589.

Rosenthal, R. H., & Allen, T. W. (1980). Intratask distractibility in hyperkinetic and non-hyperkinetic children. *Journal of Abnormal Child Psychology, 8,* 175–187.

Shaw, G. A., & Giambra, L. M. (1993). Task-unrelated thoughts of college students diagnosed as hyperactive in childhood. *Developmental Neuropsychology, 9,* 17–30.

Szatmari, P., Offord, D. R., & Boyle, M. H. (1989). Ontario Child Health Study: Prevalence of attention deficit disorder with hyperactivity. *Journal of Child Psychology and Psychiatry, 30,* 219–230.

Tallmadge, J., & Barkley, R. A. (1983). The interactions of hyperactive and normal boys with their mothers and fathers. *Journal of Abnormal Child Psychology, 11,* 565–579.

Weitzman, M., Gortmaker, S., & Sobol, A. (1992). Maternal smoking and behavior problems of children. *Pediatrics, 90,* 342–349.

Wolraich, M., Millich, R., Stumbo, P. & Schultz, F. (1985). The effects of sucrose ingestion on the behavior of hyperactive boys. *Pediatrics, 106,* 657–682.

Index